FROM TOTEMS TO HiP-HOP

FROM
TOTEMS TO HiP-HOP

Edited by **Ishmael Reed**

DA CAPO PRESS
A MEMBER OF THE PERSEUS BOOKS GROUP

Designed by Michael Walters

Cataloging-in-Publication data for this book is available from the Library of
Congress.
ISBN: 978-1-56025-458-4

Published by Da Capo Press
A Member of the Perseus Books Group
www.dacapopress.com

Da Capo Press books are available at special discounts for bulk purchases in the
U.S. by corporations, institutions, and other organizations. For more information,
please contact the Special Markets Department at the Perseus Books Group, 2300
Chestnut Street, Suite 200, Philadelphia, PA 19103, or call (800) 810-4145,
extension 5000, or e-mail special.markets@perseusbooks.com.

10 9

Dedicated to Mary TallMountain, Sister Goodwin,
and William Oandasan,
storytellers and descendants of our first storytellers

Contents

POLITICS

HEROES & SHEROES, ANTI & OTHERWISE

MANIFESTOS

Editor's Note: Within each section, I have ordered poets alphabetically, except for poems which are song lyrics, which are included at the end of each section.—I.R.

TOTEMIC

There
where
the
bare
edges
mellowed
snears bedecked the forests's call
and the noon was wrecked
and the moon was heckled
and an end foretold a nation's fall

Looming
there
where
drums beat upon the plain
and fumes of arrows amid the glooming waned
doom spoke silently proclaiming without song
the omen given by the gabled quirk of wrong

—N. H. PRITCHARD

INTRODUCTION

In 1994 I was approached by an editor for a large textbook company to organize a book that would be used to teach literature. I jumped at the chance. I was not satisfied with the leading textbooks being peddled to instructors because they seemed devoted to a limited canon (and among those writers, only the ones who were noncontroversial) or, to put it more bluntly, excluded those who were not white and male. For example, John Reed, a controversial white poet, was one of the most interesting poets of the twentieth century. His style anticipated that of the Beats, but Reed can't be found in most anthologies because of his politics. How many students have heard of Kenneth Fearing, Walter Lowenfels, or the poems that Langston Hughes was forced to renounce? African Americans, Hispanics, Native Americans are added to your typical textbook as an afterthought.

This anthology includes not only well-known dead white males but also dead white males who were as good as or superior to those who have been selected, often arbitrarily, in the non-smoking back rooms of academia, prize committees, and literary journalism. We have Robert Frost as well as a white male poet whose politics Frost might have despised, Will Heford.

The handful of Hispanics, African Americans, and Asian Americans present in the standard anthologies are usually selected by editors who have little knowledge of multicultural literature. They anoint someone "the best" black, or Hispanic, poet with very little, if any, knowledge of other poets from those backgrounds. Some of the academics hired to review my textbook proposal were upset that I didn't include their favorite tokens. They can't seem to resist this attitude, like Indiana Jones sorting the good natives from the bad. Is it because these writers share the views of the reviewers? People like D'Nesh D'Souza, who wants us to give "two cheers for Colonialism"? Or V. S. Naipaul, their favorite servile Indian scout, who told an Indian newspaper that "Negroes are the stupidest most violent people in the world"? Naipaul received praise even from feminist Vivian Gornick, though he treated his wife like dirt.

An intellectual who is chosen by the segregated media as someone "widely regarded as the leading African-American intellectual" would probably place fiftieth on a list actually composed by African-American intellectuals. They just can't understand why we don't accept the tokens that, in the words of Quincy Troupe, are "given to us." (This doesn't just happen to blacks. When the National Yiddish Book Center compiled a list of "great Modern Jewish books," *Portnoy's Complaint,* the novel that made Philip Roth famous, didn't make the list. A writer named S. Y. Agnon received as many entries as both Roth and Saul Bellow. Norman Mailer's name was also absent. Similarly, a list by Hispanic, Native American, or Asian-American critics and scholars would probably find the establishment's tokens represented by one or two books—or absent from the list altogether.)

Another burden that warps our view of American literature (as I found during my textbook experience) is the requirement that each new title include 60 percent of the contents of what are called "leader" textbooks, those that have been commercially successful. That's why you can't tell the difference between these books. It's like Wendy's sharing a strip with McDonald's.

One of the puzzling aspects of American academic life and professional criticism is the fact that teachers have gone along with this model of American literature, one riddled with holes, gaps and absences, and that they've shown no interest in anything but an outdated canon, which they follow like sheep. Can you imagine where science would be had scientists refused to budge from accepted theories? Come to think of it, the practice on the part of academics of dismissing literature written by minorities and women as politically correct, without having read it, is like the early Catholic Church fathers challenging Galileo's theories of the solar system without having examined his evidence.

Maybe the "content" of my proposal came on too strong. Alicia Suskin Ostriker (see p. 427) writes that at one time women were required to be modest and quiet, to avoid appearing "shrill." This is still true for African Americans and other multicultural authors. We are told in a thousand ways that we shouldn't draw on the full range of human emotions when writing poetry. That we shouldn't be angry. As though Sylvia Plath was in some sort of laid-back Valley Girl frame of mind when she wrote her great poem "Lady Lazarus." We were warned in Henry Louis Gates Jr.'s "Fourth Renaissance" manifesto that we shouldn't be too anxious or difficult. We shouldn't alienate the public, which pays the freight. We should cross over, caress the suburbanites and sell them guilt-free products. Tell them that the problems of millions of blacks and Hispanics are self-inflicted. Entertain them with stories about thirty-five-year-old grandmothers living in the Chicago projects.

From Totems to Hip-Hop is my response to that aborted textbook I was asked to edit in 1994. It is book one of an ambitious project whose aim is to introduce the teachers, the students, and the general reader to a sampling of work by a variety of writers published from about 1900 to today. This is not to say that American poetry began in 1900, which is the opinion of those who worship at the altar of modernism, an arrogantly exclusive movement whose idea of making everything new has done so much damage to our national culture. Modernist architects let the beautiful Victorian and Italianate buildings fall into decay in Oakland, where I live, because they saw themselves as the new and rejected the past. It took the postmodernists to restore those buildings, by mixing the old with the new. They reshaped the gargoyles that had been afflicted with dry rot, by using fiberglass.

A fiberglass gargoyle is the perfect symbol for integrating the old with the new. Those postmodernist architects were responding to the architects who built those 1870s buildings. Some of our writers respond in the same sort of call-and-response manner: In 1999 Anthony Brown, leader of the Asia-American Orchestra, used "Far Eastern" instruments and scales as his response to the call of Duke Ellington's 1966 "Far East Suite." The late Sarah Webster Fabio, "the Mother of Black Studies," "scores" a response to Duke on the page. Tennessee Reed puts metaphorical fiberglass on the Victorian story of Cinderella. In her version ("Disney's Cinderella," p. TK), Peter Duchin's orchestra provides dance music and the ball is held at the Hotel Pierre.

Others among our contributors expand upon the experiments of the modernists. In a letter to a friend, Ezra Pound once referred vaguely to "the Nigerian God of Thunder." Jayne Cortez identifies this "Saint" in her poem "Ogun's Friend" (see p. 250).

While Pound and his friends took a stab at writing Kanji, the Asian-American avant-garde today not only deconstructs Charlie Chan and the Lone Ranger but also conducts heated arguments about texts written in Kanji with a knowledge far more precise than Pound and his colleagues ever possessed. Askia Touré, the unsung poet laureate of cosmopolitan Black Nationalism, one-ups Claude McKay's and Countee Cullen's ideas about Africa with his "Dawnsong!" Unlike members of the Harlem Renaissance (with the possible exception of Langston Hughes), whose knowledge of Africa was misty, and whose preferred destination was Paris, the black writers of the 1960s wrote in African languages and visited Africa.

But the general reader, the teacher, and the student have been kept in the dark about these developments. They have been confined to an intellectual cave by what William Oandasan called the Ogre with One Eye, the limited vision of American missionary education that's driving blacks and Hispanics from the classroom. Maybe someone will get a grant to study why black and Hispanic students pack the slam poetry events and write hip-hop verse themselves, but doze off in the missionary classroom and receive low scores in reading and writing on the missionary's SAT.

Why can't T. S. Eliot and Tupac Shakur and Bob Holman, all in this anthology, be studied together? They're all homies. (Bob Holman calls himself a New York Jew, the kind of person Eliot would have satirized. The joke was on Eliot. Although Eliot considered himself a monarchist, *Vanity Fair* reports that the British royal family joked about him over drinks and ridiculed his poem "The Wasteland," referring to it as "The Desert." Eliot might have gone uptown in his mind, but to them he was still St. Louis.)

This book draws from every place good poems can be found. It has the range of the Miles Davis who could appropriate and expand on the work of Spanish composers as well as humorously paraphrase the tune "Dixie" when responding to Thelonius Monk's obstinate pauses on their recording of "The Man I Love." I would like this book to encourage others to join in the reconstruction of American culture damaged by racism, by Oandasan's Ogre with One Eye. Oandasan wrote that when he and the remaining members of his California tribe, the Ukomno'm, had reunions, only seventy-two people were left because the Ogre with One Eye didn't regard his people as human. It didn't regard them as having souls, or as being capable of producing stories and poetry about their place in the universe. The Ukomno'm were regarded as "savages" by invaders possessed by the Ogre with One Eye—people who took a delight in displaying the body parts of their victims or parading through town showing off fresh scalps. But those whom the invaders referred to as savages produced our first poetry.

One popular "guide to American literature" gives credit to Ezra Pound and company for introducing pictographic writing. The French surrealists, however, traced such writing to the Native Americans of the Pacific Northwest. And they were right.

The Indians of Alaska introduced pictographic writing into North America. We call them totem poles, but these totem poles are books if you know how to read them, and the types who appear on these poles—tricksters—can be found throughout American writing: in folklore, in songs, in the writings of Melville, Twain, Ellison, Hurston, Hughes, Sterling Brown, and novelist Charles Wright. In fact, the trickster appears in a fiction that is thousands of years old in the literature of this continent. Though the popular myth is that Native American literature arises from an oral tradition, pioneering critics like Michael Castro (in his book *Interpreting the Indian*) have given credit to Native Americans for influencing "modern poetry," which arose at a time when translations of Native American writing first began to appear. We're familiar with Aztec and Mayan pictographs, but ignore such—as influential as they are— when they appear in North America.

Tlingit totem poles are pictographic and can be read if one is acquainted with the Tlingit dictionary of symbols. Viola E. Garfield and Linn A. Forrest, in their *Wolf and the Raven*, write, "Some of the figures on the poles constitute symbolic reminders of quarrels, murders, debts, and other unpleasant occurrences about which the Indians prefer to remain silent... The most widely known tales, like those of the exploits of Raven and of Kats who married the bear woman, are familiar to almost every native of the area. Carvings which symbolize these tales are sufficiently conventionalized to be readily recognizable even by persons whose lineage did not recount them as their own legendary history." Andrew Hope, a Tlingit contributor to this anthology, would surely cite new DNA evidence to bolster his contention that the earliest Tlingit literature may date to thirty thousand years ago, from a time when the Bering Straight was a broad plain about sixty miles wide between Siberia and Alaska. (Though the authors of *The Wolf and the Raven* consider the Tlingit poles to be unique, when I visited Korea I learned that shamanistic poles also exist outside of Seoul.)

And so our literature is thousands of years old. This challenges the notion that our literary as well as cultural traditions arose only when people from northern Europe—people with souls—arrived. This was the position of John F. Kennedy's inaugural poet, Robert Frost, in his poem "The Gift Outright." So offended were the spirits of Native America that the podium caught fire. Few remember that incident, but people from our traditions, people who read the signs, viewed it as an omen. But, hey: Like Allen Ginsberg, who admired Pound regardless of his anti-Semitism (which Pound later denounced as a "suburban" attitude), we have room for Frost, a conservative who desired a "semi-revolution" (see p. 211). Ever hear Frost read his great poem "Birches"? It is a performance captivating in its sheer beauty. But there is also beauty outside the canon. Some physicists say that ours may not be the only universe. They are leaning toward the theory of the multiuniverse. Universes that are unseen, with big bangs occurring constantly. There might be a parallel universe a few millimeters from this one. In North America there is a multiuniverse of literatures, but so far our view has been limited to one.

Generations of students have been damaged by the unitraditional reading of American literature. Shawn Wong, novelist and chairman of the English department at the University of Washington in Seattle, has said that during his "education" he was not introduced to the work of a single Asian-American writer. That was twenty years ago. This intellectual crime of omission continues. At the beginning of the fall semester 2002, a Mexican-American student came to my office at the University of California at Berkeley. She had written a brilliant poem entitled "Havana," inspired by her trip to Cuba, and she seemed upset. She said she'd been criticized by her friends because of the Spanish language and cultural references in her poetry. I asked if her friends were white. They were. I had to explain that some white students, thoughtlessly or otherwise, share the opinion of the public intellectuals who get paychecks from think tanks (an expression that's becoming an oxymoron). These attack intellectuals savage what they call diversity. They want everybody to join in the effort of making things easy and comfortable for them. They want an intellectual affirmative action to exempt them from studying other cultures as rigorously as everyone has studied theirs. That will enable them to bypass the hard work the rest of us have put into becoming acquainted with something Americans call Western Civilization.

It might seem that the events of 9/11 would shake this perspective. You would think that the attack on the World Trade Center would have begun a national effort to study the Others as much as the Others have had to study da West; that whites would realize they can no longer rely upon the firepower that for hundreds of years has been the anchor for white cultural supremacy; that whiteness is no longer interchangeable with universality, a notion to which even some of the most enlightened liberal thinkers are not immune. Bill Moyers once asked Toni Morrison when she was going to write about white people. That's what my Mexican-American student's white friends were getting at. They were telling her to get with the program. Become universal. Now that you've gotten that ethnic stuff off your chest, join the club. This seems to be the opinion of novelist Caryl Phillips, according to Lorrie Moore, writing in the Oct. 10, 2002, issue of *The New York Review of Books*. Phillips believes that ". . .the psychological and artistic burdens on the African-American artist are somehow more intense and restrictive in the U.S. and that Europe poses a greater (even though illusory) freedom from artistic expectation. . . ." He cites James Baldwin's *Giovanni's Room*, written in France, a novel that had no blacks at all (unless you include the Italian.) Like Bill Moyers, for Phillips, the black writer is artistically free only when he writes a novel about white people. A novel about people. A universal novel. For him, apparently, whites are not members of a race like the rest of us. Maybe they're like Harriet Beecher Stowe's Little Eva. Angels. What would Phillip's reaction be had the characters in

Giovanni's Room been Mexican American or Native American? Would Baldwin have been credited with transcending race, or is it only when one writes about whites that one manages this feat? This is a bizarre, pathological position. Writing about white characters doesn't make a writer universal. If that were true, why do our leading white writers, members of a race whose experiences supposedly represent all of us, fall so short when writing about people different from themselves? Witness Henry James's Jews, Phillip Roth's and Saul Bellow's African Americans. This bigotry even extends to some white male writers of the younger generation, in the case of David Eggers and his treatment of Mexican Americans, for example. Contrast that with the well-balanced portraits of whites appearing in Rudolfo Anaya's novels. Congratulating a black or Hispanic writer for arriving at universality when that writer publishes a book in which all of the characters are white is irrational. Just as bizarre as the notion that the less skin pigmentation a person has, the smarter they are.

It's when a writer, through the use of their talent, connects to readers who might not share that writer's background, that the writer's work becomes universal. The characters David Baraza describes in his poem "A Place Without Shame" are Chicano, but all of us know the comfort of letting our guard down when communicating with those with whom we have an intimate relationship. And what of T. S. Eliot's comment that "All Ethnic writers might not be great, but all Great writers are ethnic"?

For *From Totems to Hip-Hop*, we chose writers we feel have responded to some of those universal themes with talent and the ability to connect. In the post-9/11 world, the greatest challenge will be communicating with those who might be different from us through themes that are universal.

I recently heard Urban League president Hugh Price on the radio, promoting yet another tough love book aimed at black Americans exclusively, when he was asked whether the missionary curriculum was alienating African-American students. He demurred, responding that they'd have to become bilingual in order to get a job in high-tech industries (which have left thousands unemployed and investors broke). He also said that he'd read the classics when he was young, implying that African-American and Hispanic authors are incapable of producing classics. On this program he basically said that black students should submit to a white supremacist curriculum in order to assimilate, in order to get good-paying jobs.

Price has his counterparts in the Hispanic, Asian-American, and Native-American communities: Hispanics who require that Hispanics abandon Spanish culture, Asian Americans who aspire to be members of a model minority, Native Americans who blame Native Americans for their alcoholism without mentioning the aggressive promotion of alcohol in their communities by liquor companies. They're the ones from their communities who get on the radio and get op-eds printed in the newspapers. They have the full treatment in the mainstream book reviews, many of which endorsed Charles Murray's *The Bell Curve*.

They tell us that the poor slavers were stranded off the coast of west Africa and that the Africans took over their ships and demanded to be shipped to the Americas. (That's their PBS view of the slave trade).

I don't disagree with Price that students should become bilingual, but doesn't this apply to white students as well who will have to live in a post-9/11 world? And whose bilingual is he talking about? If it were up to me, every student would know an Asian or African as well as a "Western" language. White students should become bilingual just so they don't turn into the arrogant types described by Lorna Dee Cervantes and Wendy Rose (see pp 199 and 240, respectively). And where does this leave my Mexican student, whose education has trained her to become white? What is the cost of her becoming white?

My Mexican-American student couldn't identify a single Mexican-American poet. I told her about a number of anthologies produced by indigenous writers, including *Aloud*, edited by Miguel Algarín, in which a poem by Alurista appears, written entirely in Spanish. During the same week of our talk, a group of Mexican hip-hoppers were passing through town.

She, like most students, has been taught that the Puritans were the first American writers. But they weren't even the first European-American writers. That distinction belongs to the Spanish. In 1513 Juan Ponce de León kept diaries about his travels in Florida. *La Relacion*, by Alvar Núñez Cabeza de Vaca, was published in Spain in 1542. It is a book recording his observations and experiences among the Indians of Florida.

Nicolàs Kanellos, in his landmark anthology, *Herencia*, writes, "All of the institutions of literacy—schools, universities, libraries, government archives, courts, and others—were first introduced to North America by Hispanic peoples by the mid-sixteenth century."

And, according to Kanellos, bilingual literature flowed from the start as well. "The first Spanish-speaking communities were established by Sephardic Jews in the Northeast of what would become the United States. They were followed by other Hispanics from Spain and the Caribbean who, by the 1800s, were issuing through early American printers and their own presses hundreds of political and commercial books, as well as many works of creative literature written principally by Hispanic immigrants and political refugees. In Louisiana and later in the Southwest and to some extent the Northeast, bilingual publications often became a necessity for communicating, first with the Hispano- and Francophone popula-tions and later the Hispano-and Anglophone populations, as pub-lications reflected bicultural life in the United States."

Even today, layers of cultural influence surround us in ways most aren't aware. Nobel laureate Carlos Fuentes claims that 40 per-cent of the Spanish language is essentially Arabic. The Spanish were multicultural when they arrived, having been occupied by Arabic-speaking and -writing North Africans for over five hundred years.

When I drive to work, I have a fine view of Alcatraz, whose name is an Arabic word that was imported to California by the Spanish. The Spanish invasion of the hemisphere began in 1492, the year that Queen Isabella expelled the Moors and the Jews from Spain. Some of both populations accompanied the Spanish to North America. In New Mexico they still talk about Estvanico, a Moorish scout who was killed by the Zuni Indians. When one really looks, it becomes abundantly clear that today's attack intellectuals are a few hundred years too late to turn back "diversity."

The Spanish not only introduced their miscegenated language to North America but picked up the language of the Indians with whom they came in contact. When I did research for an article I wrote about my North Oakland neighborhood, I discovered that Temescal—the name of my district—was an Aztec word for steam baths (it was apparently the habit of local Native Americans to steam themselves before diving into one of the many creeks that still flow under the district's houses). While editing an anthology of California poetry called *Califia*, named for a black Amazon queen of Spanish and Gallic legend, I also discovered that the earliest written language of California was Spanish, including "The Ballad of California," about a Russian sailor who was prevented from marrying a senorita by her parents. They objected to his being a "heathen."

In the 1600s the Puritans arrived on the *Mayflower*. Although stereotyped as mean and provincial, these Europeans based their religion upon a history of a non-European origin. They also produced a number of good poets, the most distinguished of whom were Edward Taylor and Ann Bradstreet, the latter whom Alicia Ostriker reveals as an early feminist.

Anticipating the Imagist manifesto (see p. 356), the Puritans recommended a prose style that prefigures that of modern writers, from Gertrude Stein to Raymond Carver. Cotton Mather thought that writing should have "more meat and less sauce" and discouraged a writing that would be "as bejeweled as the Russian ambassador's coat."

African captives were brought to North America beginning in 1619. According to African-American historian W. E. B. DuBois, 15 million arrived, with millions more lost, as a result of the slave trade. Some of the narratives they brought with them are similar to the totemic themes of the early Native Americans, featuring trick-ster figures who bring both mischief and enlightenment to the world and use wit to outmaneuver stronger animals. The Tlingits have a Raven-King Salmon story that's the perfect match for Tar Baby. Just as some contemporary Asian-American and Native-American writers update forms from the earlier histories of their societies (Frank Chin citing texts written in Kanji, Francisco Alercon citing the Toltec), modern African-American writers—including today's hip-hop artists—use themes and forms that can be traced to those transmitted to this hemisphere by the early African arrivals.

African-American and Hispanic students have been alienated from the settler curriculum because it has no place for their histories and cultures, and gives them the spear-carrying (or Uzi-carrying) roles. They're not alone. A number of my white students, over the years, have also become restless. I have Italian-American students who've never heard of Diane di Prima or Gregory Corso or Daniela Gioseffi. Many of them have been subjected to an education which basically argues that all the great poetry has been written, and that it has been stored in a museum since the nineteenth century, that poetry must be abstract and ornate. They are surprised when intro-duced to the excellent poetry written in the twentieth century in ordinary, everyday language. When I was studying poetry at the

University of Buffalo, I was surprised that a poet could use a slang word like "dive" in a poem. That poet was W. H. Auden. I was taught in high school that poetry was written by aristocrats. My students are even more surprised that students like them are capable of writing poetry that can stand alongside some of the best poetry being written. They're surprised to learn that they can write poems about their tastes and their icons. Tastes and icons change. H. D. wrote about Helen of Troy; Corie Rosen writes about Madonna (the one from Detroit).

When I began mixing the poetry of the masters with those of students from previous classes in my "Verses" course at Berkeley, I received a more enthusiastic response than when I merely covered the classics. Some of the students who appeared in the student anthologies we would publish at the end of the semester have gone on to become some of our leading poets and novelists. Terry MacMillan, Mona Simpson, Faye Ing, Kate Trueblood, John Keene Jr., and others were published in those anthologies when they were students. This is not surprising. Many good writers have become inspired to write when they read someone whose experience they share. I had read excellent white writers for years during my education, but it wasn't until I read the young James Baldwin while working at a Buffalo library that I felt I had a shot.

This inclusive teaching strategy has also influenced how I've put together *From Totems to Hip-Hop*. During an appearance before the National Council for Teachers of English, I read a poem by a canonized poet and one by a student and asked the teachers who'd assembled for the conference to identify the student and the canonized poet. Fifty percent said the student was the canonized and about an equal number said the canonized was the student. *From Totems to Hip-Hop* includes poetry by students who've responded to some of the universal themes we've used. I challenge the reader, without looking at the contributors' section, to identify all the students sprinkled among the professionals in this anthology. The reader may find that some of the work produced by students and apprentices is just as exciting as that written by contributors with substantial reputations.

I've also included some poets who belong to the hip-hop and slam generations. Some of the older folks don't rate performance poetry as worthy of consideration by serious scholars. Tell that to Geoffrey Chaucer, regarded as the second greatest poet in the English language. He performed his poetry up and down the countryside and managed to hold on to a day job as well.

I have also reprinted what could be regarded as manifestos about key movements in American writing (see p. 356). These manifestos help map a trend in American poetry through the twentieth century. The outsiders challenge the academy, only to become the new academy and to be challenged by a new group of outsiders. Although the antagonists in our current American cultural war either maintain that ours is and should always be an Anglo civilization, or that the Anglo civilization is being supplanted by a multicultural civilization, American literature from the very beginning has been as mestizo as our hemisphere, influenced by a mixture of cultures, nations and races. The Imagists included in this book, H. D. and Carl Sandburg, were at one time the outs. Their school was represented by a manifesto that challenged the edifice of Victorian poetry. Then they became the academy. Some of the proletariat poets of the 1930s are now members of literature's Mount Rushmore. The New Negroes of the 1920s, after fierce resistance, became enshrined. The Beats and the bohemians of the 1950s and 1960s are now the subject of hundred of dissertations. This is also true of the Black Arts writers, some of whom have gone on to appear in Hollywood movies and become state poet laureates and members of the elite national literary societies.

So, what's the literary forecast for North America? If this pattern of ongoing revolt and acceptance is any indication, there will continue to be generational challenges, intercultural borrowing, experimentation, and multilingualism. *From Totems to Hip-Hop* has attempted to show the terrain from which that fertility will continue to arise, by presenting a truly inclusive survey of one hundred and two years of American poetry. In these pages, the reader will confront the revolutionaries as well as the academy, the feminists as well as the masculinists, the straight as well as the gay, the formalists as well as the free versers, the straightforward as well as the opaque, the picture writers as well as the sound writers, the apolitical as well as the political, the pre-slam of Vachel Lindsay as well as the post-slam of Bob Holman, the high culturalists as well as the low culturalists, the ordinary as well as the ornate, the elitists as well as the populists, those who mean every word and those who—in the late N. H. Pritchard's words—hold the view that "words are ancillary to meaning." We have Pulitzer Prize winners, National Book Award winners, American Book Award winners and Poet Laurets as well as future prizewinners, wannabe prizewinners, and excellent poets who will never be honored. We have both the Blues and the Reds.

One cannot read this anthology without concluding that in the twentieth century, American poets were very busy, and will be just as busy in the twenty-first century, working and re-working the same universal themes.

—ISHMAEL REED, OCTOBER 23, 2002,
OAKLAND, CALIFORNIA

NATURE & PLACE

I was asked why I joined "nature" to "place." Without nature there is no place. It is nature that gives place its distinctive character. When she first arrived in Berkeley from Georgia, the late Toni Cade Bambara marveled at the light and the big sky. And when writing about Southern California towns, my students often mention the Santa Ana winds. Oakland, where I live, is a vastly different place from Chicago. Its nature that makes it so. Carl Sandburg's Chicago, the Windy City, is different from George Sterling's San Francisco, which Sterling described as the "cool grey city of love." But both Chicago and San Francisco are "soft cities" in comparison to Bessie Smith's Black Mountain, where "a child will slap your face."

Kathryn Takara's Alabama is different from all three. There are no cows in San Francisco or Chicago. And there are no rodeos, as there are in Whitney Ward's Montana.

Such is the poetic imagination that we can also imagine how parts of nature, generally believed to be inanimate, might feel about things. In the poetry of Al Young, Greg Youmans, and Yumi Thomas, vegetables and fruit get a chance to express their feelings.

Long before the modern conservation and ecology movements, poets were often nature's advocates. Here again, Native American poets were the first, although Diane Clancy warns against stereotyping Native American poets as nature poets. It was Native Americans who gave the hurricane its name. Some poets' knowledge of nature is exceeded only by that of professional botanists and zoologists. In Mary TallMountain's cultural tradition, we too are part of nature's extended family, as seen in her paean to the blue whale, *O Dark Sister:*

> Here on the shore you lie alone,
> Great blue whale,
> Most vast of living beings.
> Gulls dart screaming
> To fret your lightless eyes.
> Silent your ancient clicking song,
> Unanswered the calls of your mates
> Phantasmic from far plateaus.
>
> What instinct
> Magnetized you to shore
> Among plastic trash and rotted fruit,
> Offal of careless creatures
> Who so lately found the sands
> Of your millennial home.
> What dim kinship
> Called you here?
>
> Great Dark Sister,
> Mountain of trailing brilliance,
> Where now the purple painted worms,
> Skittering shapes in ebon fringe,
> Gels of indigo and jade
> You viewed only in pearly and grey
> Who frisked and frolicked in the sweep
> Of your gentle passage.

In a museum stand wired
The striding bones of Allosaurus,
Jaunty at his neck a plastic ruff.
Shall we someday see Great Blue

Daubed in dayglo green
When her bones are assembled
Like his, for the mere amaze
Of some unborn generation?

Ask the bones that dangled in carnivals;
Ask the bones traded by voyageurs;
Ask the bones of Kintpuash and Black Hawk;
Hear them at Elk Creek;
Hear them at Sand Creek, Wounded Knee.
Hear the ancestors' ghostly cries,
Hear fabulous buffalo
Begging back his giant bones
Out of the carpeted plain.

These at least lie resting
Beneath kindly soil,
Cherished by earth. Their mother
and ours.

My "Earthquake Blues," "Hurricane Doris" by Lorenzo Thomas,
and "Hurakán: A Two Way Poem" by Linda Rodriguez Guglielmoni
all portray nature's lethal side. But that side is okay with May
Swenson. For her, man must be taught that nature, like a wild

horse, can't be corralled. The violent side of nature teaches man humility.

Meanwhile, in the tradition of W. B. Yeats's "Sailing to Byzantium" and Langston Hughes's "The Panther and the Lash," Delmore Schwartz invokes nature in the form of an animal to comment on the human situation. Genny Lim also uses a scene from nature in her lovely, profound poem, "Animal Liberation," to express her sorrow about the loss of a child.

AGHA SHAHID ALI

A Lost Memory of Delhi

I am not born
it is 1948 and the bus turns
onto a road without name

There on his bicycle
my father
He is younger than I

At Okhla where I get off
I pass my parents
strolling by the Jamuna River

My mother is a recent bride
her sari a blaze of brocade
Silverdust parts her hair

She doesn't see me
The bells of her anklets are distant
like the sound of china from

teashops being lit up with lanterns
and the stars are coming out
ringing with tongues of glass

They go into the house
always faded in photographs
in the family album

but lit up now
with the oil lamp
I saw broken in the attic

I want to tell them I am their son
older much older than they are
I knock keep knocking

but for them the night is quiet
this the night of my being
They don't they won't

hear me they won't hear
my knocking drowning out
the tongues of stars

EVAN BRAUNSTEIN

Newark

Newark is a glass jaw, listless in the center of the
    ring
Legs wobbling, waiting for another round, or for a stop
It waits to be called the loser, or it does nothing at
    all
Glazed eyes cast across into the lights of Manhattan
Chin exposed, mouth open droning on and on
Unaware that it will always remain suspect

The water is a swirl of expired motor oil, disease, and
    pollution, dumped without permit
No longer giving a detailed reflection
It eats the sun, and shows only stick figures and
    bubbling rainbows of chemical breakdown
Tanners and Furriers call no longer bath their dead
Anheuser-Busch processes the water, pumping the sky
    with dirt so thick that only the neon Budweiser
    penetrates
A city drunk on stale beer.

DAVID COLOSI

Sun with Issues

I got a heat wave burning in my heart. I can't keep from
*   crying, tearing me apart.*

—Martha and the Vandellas

This one goes out to you who wrote so many for me:
"Sunshine of Your Love,"; "Ain't No Sunshine When She's Gone,";
"On the Sunny Side of the Street,"; "Good Day Sunshine,";
"You Are the Sunshine of My Life."
I'm your pleasant caress, your warm redress.
It's gonna be a scorcher, time for a little torture
pleasure is pain, pain is pleasure,
come to the beach for a day of leisure.
I'll give you tans, open your glands,
I see you behind your Ray Bans.
I'll melt your radio in the street, burn the flip-flops off your feet.
Rub that SPF 30 on your skin, only then will I begin
to lick it off like bar-b-que sauce, and
bathe you in my rays, sauté you three or four more days,
drain you as I multiply, suck 60% of you dry.
My deadly stare won't take you anywhere.
Make you swollen and red, send a migraine to your head,
blister and spasm, dizzy and faint, I'll make you vomit in the sink,
I'll give you cold and clammy flesh, make you pant to catch your
    breath.

And even though we've just begun, I'll black you out from so
    much fun.
I'll break through your barriers,
send melanoma carriers
little brown spots
lay you out on hospital cots
I'll dig in like a mole,
grow and blacken,
ooze, bleed,
itch and harden,
turn lumpy and swollen,
tender to the touch,
leave something for you to laser off.
And after physical pain, I'll make you insane,
by turning my heat up,
'til you scream, "Don't touch me, it's hot!"
And I'll keep you from "holdin'
and kissin'
and squeezin'
and lovin'"
by lifting and stinking the piss from your city street
making your armpits reek.
I will germinate you, agitate you, aggravate you, exterminate you.
Turn up your refrigerator, fan, and AC, use up that electricity.
Until you learn to use my power, I will make you suffer.
I'll make your daytime brown, run your energy down,
And instead of vomiting in the sink
this time when I black you out, I'll make everything stink.
Mercury rising to the top, bringing your crime rate up.

I'll pick you fights in Shop-n-Save, stick your aged in their graves

ripping water off the shelf, thinking only about yourself,

knocking down your neighbor's son to steal his ice cream cone

   and run

straight

to the toilet where you'll drop

the curded cream in your gut,

with diarrhea, Oh, I'll be near you,

in the kitchen keeping it hot, making your food rot.

Open the freezer door for a blast of cold air

and smell what I've made in your Fridgedaire.

I'll drink your reservoir like Nestle Quik, suck it up and then spit

sticky sweet goo on you.

I come on heavy like spaghetti melting your face,

dripping sweat on the plate.

I'll set your swimming pools to boil, shake-n-bake your motor oil,

lock you in your car, but don't go far

from the window so I can begin,

to fry your ass under a magnifying glass,

incubate your lower, middle, and upper class.

Remember:

I'm stuck in place, you're moving at *my* pace,

You think this is heinous, spend some time on Mercury or Venus.

And at the end of the day, when I go down,

I'll be waiting in your concrete,

in your asphalt seeping heat.

Go ahead, run your air all night, I'll be sure to turn out the light.

And at the stroke of dawn, when I'm coming on strong,

I'll find you in your bathtub where I've left you cool and nice sunstroked and drowned in a pool of melted ice.

"It's a sunshine day,

Everybody's smiling, (sunshine day),

everybody's laughing, (sunshine day),

. . ."

WILLIAM COOK

Endangered Species

(for Ishmael Reed)

"Most of the ten birds at the museum are crippled.
Crippled male birds can't mount their female partners."

"Martha had a crush on her human handler and wouldn't
mate with a male eagle named George. In fact, she
attacked George when he came courting."

The Cleveland Plain Dealer 6/89

I

CURRENT EVENTS

Martha, like most eagle mothers
Who are victims of stress,

Lays her eggs on the ground
And not in the nest;
Lays thin-shelled eggs
That break under the weight
Of the mother body—
Strange avian abortion
Of the progeny
Of crippled George
And Martha
Who loved her handler
Who was not
Feathered
Nor a raptor
With tearing beak and claw.
He was her handler
Took good care of her
And was so superior to
That other captive
Despised and
Feathered crippled
Prisoner
Who could not master
As her handler could
Who could not best
The unrestricted power
Who saw to her
Who met her every need.

We cannot capture healthy eagles
To mate and lengthen out

Our line of national aspiring
The laws forbid us
Leaving limping for our
Ministrations
The undesirable and infirm
Male most awful and unable
To sustain himself
To soar, hover or buckle
Down wild and independent winds.

II

HISTORY

Ben Franklin opposed the eagle
As our national symbol
For he insisted on our need
To make our definition
In an image far more flattering
We cannot know our nation
Through this
Disgraceful thief
Who bloats
On food he filches
Robbing smaller birds
Who gather and are dutiful.

Afraid that character
Might troop in imitation
Of such a symbol
And we become a true

Rapacious nation

Parasite upon the world

And justified by strength

Franklin proposed

An alternate

More apt and optimistic

He proffered us

The turkey

Wily, jive and wise.

III

LITERARY CRITICISM

George and Martha

Speak for us in ways

Beyond all Albeesque conception

Whitman's wild, soaring mating

Like Tennyson's falling

Bachelor thunderbolt

Was born in self-sealed

Plays on images we read a while

They are not photographs

But caught by images that blind

We write this blindness

As late labor we call love.

In Cleveland

Or Massachusetts

Or the Great Northwest

Where we breed eagles

In spite of frozen sperm
Injected into Martha
And her sisters
Unsuccessful and against their will
They stubbornly conceive resistance.
Enraged by this inhuman violation
And enamored of their keepers
They fly at feathered suitors
Who dare the dignity
Of sex and competition.

They who cannot name
Or will not such unworthy source
Try stonewall silence
And a passive wild revolt
They drop the product of
Unwelcome and unbeautiful
Romance
And speak for our new day
The cage
They live like us
Three ways removed
From open skies
And savage
Serious coupling
They still perform like us
And to our handler's
Mild applause
Ironic dalliance of eagles.

ALICIA GASPAR DE ALBA

from *Elemental Journey:*
Anniversary Gift, 4 and 5

4.

The Niagara River Speaks Three Languages

Upriver

Up here, there's no hurry.
Willows tilt along the bank
and creeks spill like childhood
memories into the flow: the time
Grandpa bought me a dwarf-sized shovel
to help him plant rosebushes in the backyard;
the time I rode a bus to Disneyland,
nine years old, no family, the tour-
guide my father's girlfriend; the time
I came home from school and found
our dog Sanson stiff under an army blanket.

The paved road by the water
is hardly used. All the attention
is nine miles downriver
where the Falls fill cameras
and absorb the energy of every tourist.
If you don't believe me,

notice, the next time you ride
the Maid of the Mist, how your heart
rattles as you cross the rainbow, almost
at the foot of the Falls, how your lungs
heave and nearly break open in the wild
splashing and churning of the water.
Notice how exhausted you are
after humbling yourself
to that part of the river.

Up here, there are no expectations.
Every creek and bridge you pass,
every picnic table and docked boat,
every tent and window breathes
of solitude. You can build
up your strength on this quiet
Canadian road.

The Falls

You see, even if I am boycotted
by the grandmother who pressed warm
flannel cloths to my chest when cough
stormed my lungs, and even if
the uncles who tossed me in the air
and took me to the movies
and gave me quarters for *domingo* turn
their shoulderblades to my lesbian
life, I will keep thundering

through the course I have chosen
to carve for myself. True,
the falling, roaring tumult of water
separates two countries.
This border is wider and more dangerous
than the Río Grande, but the bridge
balanced over the gorge is called
Rainbow Bridge. The iris
is another infinite lesson.

Whirlpool Rapids

It used to be popular to tempt
the rapids. Men and women in barrels,
on tightropes, hoping their names
would be forever linked to Niagara.
Such a whirl of human folly
this thirst for fame, this need to compete
with the Mother's power. Today,
in a small room two-hundred-thirty feet
into the gorge, the daredevils' names
and pictures decorate the walls.
You forget them as soon as the rapids
crash into view, or you shake
your head at their courage, their choice
of a shortcut to the Otherworld.
Of course, not all of them died.
Some were found tumbling in the whirlpool,

deaf and dizzy, but more defiant
than the water breaking on the rocks.

Through the canyon of my life,
defiance is a vein of flowing crystal,
fed by rain and tempered
on ninety-degree turns.

5.

Rainstorm: The Gorge

The suddenness,
like everything else,
is a gift,
a way the Mother has
of inviting you to listen
longer, learn the three
languages of the river.

At Boyer's Creek the river spoke
a whispered, ancient tongue
that lapped at the stones
of your memory.
At Horseshoe Falls you trembled,
the wild mares of the moon
galloping into your bones.

Here, the rapids roil with lust,

churning like the wet
dream of a giant woman
in whose depths the gorge
is but a ligament
to an even deeper
and more electrifying
storm.

DIANE GLANCY

Hides

I can't say I'm of the bear clan or the elk people.
Just a man who came north for work
And left all that.

I have been questioned as a white.
I have been questioned as Indian.
I am neither of both worlds.
But one of my own making.
Mainly by words.

I speak with a mixed voice.
An acculturated voice.

Because my Indian heritage was picked off.
I remember the smallpox-vaccination-scab on my arm.
Picking it off.
And it dropping to the ground.
I remember picking it up.
Trying to stick it back on.

Anyway.

I guess you want to hear about the land. And how the
Indian ancestors followed the buffalo. And how the sky
spoke to them in the smoke signals of its clouds. And
how the rocks were known to turn and speak the way you're
walking with someone somewhere and they say something you
know right then you'll remember all your life. But you
know it isn't that way. Though I know a rock. The
weight of it in my hand like a heart. Sometimes I hold it
to my ear and say, hey rock—How you? And I know
the open prairie where you drive for days and still don't
see the end. You go on forever and know nothing except
a few lonely cafes and a motel room for the night. You
know my father asked me if I wanted some animal hides.
He worked for the stockyards and could get them. But I didn't
know what to do. Whad he expect? Moccasins and
dresses? A reconstruction of the drum? Where would I
get the heartbeat? After the earth was paved and covered
with the rattle of cattle trucks. But you know. I guess
you can hear anything again. You can still scrape hides.
If only through the imagination in your own head.

CYNTHIA GOMEZ

San José: a poem

There's a land with a heart of silicon
A land of computer chips and movie theaters
A hole in a valley sprawling out of control
A land of quinceañeras and taquierias and Our Lady of Sorrows
    Church
Swarmed over with dirty buses, coughing exhaust, teeming with
    brown skins
Pimpled with painted storefronts in stripmalls screaming foreign
    tongues
Stomped by shiny boots and shiny suits on their way to the
    glittering Silicon City
Where chips that aren't made for eating feed colonies of engineers
    in neat condos

Highways grow like a gash here, crisscrossing the earth
Through track homes and golf courses to projects and crack houses
And then to creeping cold playgrounds run with bright-clothed
    children
To pink music-piped malls full of baseball caps and baggy pants
And then to college where screaming yellow Spartan boys cheer
    on a losing team,
And to where crowds of teeming teal Shark fans swarm into a
    tinfoil arena

This land is piled with cinder-block gray hotels, new schools, malls
To cover the ashes of the yellow peril, burned long ago
And still the brown fists marched in protest thirty years past
This land wants espresso to flow in its veins, not blood,
Wants to be made of foccacia dough instead of earth
And its news station broadcasts smile on shiny new downtown,
Not to where armies of brown faces and hard-working hands
    march dead sidewalks on cold mornings
Before being whisked away backwards in faceless trucks to do day
    work
Or where small Saigon hands cut hair and jabber in Vietnamese

Dreams float like bumping balloons here, out of little brown and
    black and yellow heads
Over miles of little ticky-tacky boxes,
Over the glittering lights and polished porticoes of Willow Glen,
Over the leaf-clogged creek and over the garbage dumps,
To where they settle, heavy, weighed down by smog,
To rot, preserved in cement and chrome
As a proud sign proclaims a new San José.

RAY GONZÁLEZ

Three Snakes, Strawberry Canyon, Berkeley

The Rattlesnake

We really didn't see it,
but the guy walking ahead of us
said it struck and missed him.
He pointed to the tall grass.
"If you get closer,
you can see its eyes."
We looked, but couldn't see it
and kept walking.
I thought about the rattlers
I killed as a boy,
back home in Texas,
the nest of six baby rattlers
we found in the yard,
my mother insisting I cut
their heads off with a shovel,
saying the babies were more lethal
because they could fill you with venom,
and not know when to pull back
like adult snakes.
I recalled how I killed them
and regret it still,
and wanted this rattler

to bite the hiker so I could forget
his bravery, his wonder.

The Garter Snake

It looked like an overgrown worm,
tiny and quick as it flashed
across the trail,
its sidewinding motion
leaving marks in the dirt.
As we noticed it, we forgot
what we said about poetry,
how those things vanish,
then reappear before us,
how we admit black and green bands
of the garter snake
are the same colors
we keep missing each time
we try to write anything.

The Gopher Snake

We found it sleeping
in the middle of the trail.
It didn't move,
but glistened as we approached,
but I knew it wasn't the rattler
that haunts my footsteps.
This snake looked

like a giant slug,
a slow, wet creature
that sunned itself
so it could dissolve
into the ground.
Suddenly, we realized
it was good luck
to have snakes cross our path
like the unknown pulses
in the earth that
traveled underground,
ahead of us, all the way
to the bottom of
the surprising, moving canyon.

LINDA M. RODRÍGUEZ GUGLIELMONI

Hurakán: A Two Way Poem

Never in its path before, she sat, legs crossed, facing east. She looked up to the Weather Channel perched against the wall expecting revelations.

Taínos, whose deities visited in orgies of visions and vomits inhaled ground seeds, seashells and tobacco. The *cohoba* shifted color and shape, and with kaleidoscopic companions, they traveled the 5th dimension to the other side of the world. Women and men of *Borikén* danced the *areyto*, told histories, played and feasted on the *hutía*. *Deminán* and his turtle woman wife, *Hicotea*, looked on their children.

Every half hour she checked to see if its category 5 killer status made it worthy of a 30 second spot on CNN. Grinding her teeth, listening to the bang of metal heads and nails piercing wood, she verified that it had.

Watching the crowned *higuaca* fly over the green face of *E Yunque*, understanding its blue and crimson flight into the mountain forest, together *nitaínos* and *naborias* moved into deep caves. They took their carved *cemis* whispering of a new conspiracy of Air, Fire and Water against tireless Earth and carried the dry bones of *caciques* in calabashes. They gathered their hammocks and *duhos*, guavas, papayas, beans and squash, making certain not to leave behind the *buréns* on which to cook their flat bread. That night they took care not to disturb the owl or bat, eaters of light.

Finally, she went out to the gas station and the little market by the sea, grabbed a couple gallons of water, a flashlight and batteries, an oil lamp she didn't know how to work, candles and matches too, cartons of long life milk, cereal, crackers, canned tuna, beans and sausages, wine and some beer. In her ground floor apartment, not quite understanding why, she took out a bag from the deep freezer section and started to boil water. Later, as the sky went seashell pink and clouds skipped low, she got into bed, ate a plate of warm yuca with oil and salt, and waited for the crack and crash of the ceiba tree.

JIM GUSTAFSON

The Idea of Detroit

Detroit just sits there
like the head of a large dog on a serving platter.
It lurks in the middle of a continent,
or passes itself off as a civilization
at the end of a rope.
The lumpiness of the skyline
is the lumpiness of a sheet stretched over
what's left of a tender young body.
Detroit groans and oppresses.
It amounts to Saturday night at the slaughter house,
and Sunday morning in bed
with a bag of bagels and the Special Obituary Supplement.
Air the color of brown Necco wafers,
a taste like the floor of an adult movie theater,
the movement through the streets
that of a legless, wingless, pigeon.
Detroit means lovers buying matching guns,
visitors taken on tours of the foundries,
children being born with all their teeth,
a deep scarlet kind of fear.
It breeds a unique bitterness,
one that leaves deep gashes in the tongue,
that doesn't answer telephones or letters,
that carves notches in everything,

that illustrate the difference between

"rise up singin" and "sit down and shut your face."

It forms a special fondness for uncooked bacon,

for the smell of parking lots,

for police sirens as opposed to ambulance sirens,

for honest people who move their heads

whenever they move their eyes.

Detroit is a greasy enchilada

smeared across the face of a dilemma,

the sanctuary of the living dead,

the home of the Anywhere-But-Here travel agency,

the outhouse at the end of the rainbow.

Detroit just sits there

drinking can after can of Dupe beer,

checking the locks on the windows,

sighing deeply, knowing that nothing

can save it now.

JUAN FELIPE HERRERA

Earth Chorus

for the campesinos of Las Cabañas, a municipality of El Salvador
and for Philippe Bourgeois

It is the earth that snarls and slashes with black jaguar
eyes and teeth and incandescent claws
the Pharoah
and his troops of delicate overcoat and medal delight
it is the earth that reveals lies and recognizes with
lightning and birds and bare feet and adolescent brows
and cheekbones of lava
the traitor
and his wire hands and plantation laws and slave labor
it is the earth flowing the dew of brave women
and men on march with rivers and coffee plantations with salt
and fury
it is the earth that determines the new furrows the knives
of plants of shining flesh the skin rising
the viper of rhymes and guerrilla war breathing fire
extinguishing the plague the silk web the false tower
it is the earth
that hurls red whips and elastic bodies
infinite fingers and invisible legs that fly and smash
the final throne the miniscule lie the throat and
fist of the general the boss the shocked supervisor

it is the earth with its moss and its deep ovaries and sperm
that spill their honey and sweat and unleash the rain and
purify with their heat
it is the earth
that recognizes the squadron of planes the uniform of shadows
and silver
the barracks of business and anguish and tanks of hired blood
the flag of iodine, dust and rage in the center of camp
the tongue of the American President twisting with nuclear
spit

Earth

Send the women of your blood like suns
Send the workers of your branches like lightning
Send the guerillas of your peaks like tigers

Earth

Amid the metropolitan streets
Amid the alleys of fear
Amid the Honduran refugee camps
Amid the Guatemalan slums
Amid the Argentine cells
Amid the Lacandon lakes of Chiapas
Amid the municipalities of El Salvador
Amid the avenues of Chile
Amid the thorns of Jamaica
Amid the storms of Haiti

Amid the phosphorescent jungles of Brazil
Amid the liquid nights of South Africa
Amid fever
Amid death

To make a quake of victory
to make a cluster of liberated world
to make a song in flood

It is the earth
It is the earth
that triumphs.

ANDREW HOPE III

Shagoon 1–4

Shagoon 1

Thunderbirds flying
Like giant planes
Moving silently
Across the gray sky
Thunderbirds flying

Shagoon 2

Brown bears dancing
Leaving footprints
In the mud and snow
Brown bears dancing
Into the woods
Brown bears dancing

Shagoon 3

Killer whales flying
To the mountains
Becoming rock
Turning to stone
Permanent landscape
Eternal Killer Whales flying

Shagoon 4

Killer Whales multiplying
Like grains of sand along the shore
Killer Whales multiplying
Killer Whales multiplying

GENNY LIM

Animal Liberation

Other than a chickadee which I had bought from
a pick-up truck vendor many, many years ago
I had never purchased a live animal
Today I went to Chinatown and parked on the south end of Grant
I walked down the street combing the poultry shops for a live duck
Most of the old markets had been shut down
under pressure from the Animal Humane Society
No more cages piled high on the sidewalks with the odor of fowl
or loose feathers dusting the already acrid air
Wooden crates jammed with roosters, hens and pigeons
Barrels of live frogs and turtles had been replaced by
Spanking new tourist emporiums spilling silk brocades
Chinaware and hand-carved deities from their over-stocked shelves
I make my way through the crowds into one market displaying
Roasted ducks hanging upside-down
I ask the proprietress, "Do you have any live ducks?"
She points next door
I walk into a long, narrow room with wooden cages kept behind a
    glass partition
"Do you have any live ducks?" I ask the old poker-faced poultry man
Without blinking, he asks, "How many?"
I ask him "How much for one?" in Chinese
He answers, *"Sup-yih-gah-bun!"*
Twelve dollars and fifty cents for the life of a duck?

I reply, "One!"

He turns around and opens the door to one of the crates

and reaches in and pulls out a big, speckled brown duck

He grabs it by the neck and ties its feet together

Then he stuffs the bird into a paper bag punctured with holes at the top

I pay him my money and he hands over the bag

I am so excited my heart is racing all the way out the door

I clutch the duck's warm body against my chest and

It feels like that of my baby before she had grown into a beautiful
   young lady

Hard to believe nineteen years had passed since

I had held her tiny body to me just like this

I walk the length of Grant Avenue with my contraband

I'm relieved I don't have a ticket and place the duck in the back
   of the car

I head out to the park with a heightened awareness of my sudden
   new surroundings

The buildings are unusually vivid, the pedestrians unusually alive

I park at Stow Lake and walk around till I find a spot

near the reeds obscured from view

I walk down the embankment with my heart throbbing

I open the bag half expecting the duck to bite me

But she sits there calmly and patiently and as I untie

the tight band of wire wrapped around her legs

Talking to her gently as I free her

I'm afraid to upset her by picking her up so

I turn the bag upside down and literally pour her into the water

She tumbles into the lake and as soon as her body makes contact
   with liquid

There is instant recognition

She dives into the pool and emerges with her feathers wet and
glistening

She spreads her wings wide for the first time and quacks with joy

She dives in and out again and again

Baptizing her entire body with miraculous water

My heart sings to see this once captive duck

Frolic in the lake, diving and dancing, flapping her wings

as flocks of black guinea hens pass by in cool demeanor

And proud mallards observe their new member with calm disinterest

She quacks and cavorts like a prisoner released from death row

I sigh, never taking my eyes off her for a moment

Until she is joined by an identical speckled brown duck

They swim together past the boaters, past the reeds beyond sight

"Free!" I breathe, "at last!" One life saved for another one lost

Good-bye my darling, Danielle!

May your consciousness leap into the vast and familiar depths of
Sukhavati

And may you reunite quickly with the hosts of enlightened beings

Who have gone on ahead of you and who will soon follow!

REGINALD LOCKETT

Oaktown CA

Absorbing a taste of magic,
trying to figure the flavor,
twelve minutes past midnight,
Thursday morning,
walking somewhere on San Pablo.
I stop in an obscure juke joint
for two, three beers.
The tinkling sound of a quarter
in the jukebox.
Blues twanging guitar.
Lucille putting it
down on the table where
you can see it, feel it,
and know it's real.
Man rocking to her
electric,
sensuous rhythms.
Eyes shut tight.
White and gold teeth flashing
on his paint smeared
black face
Lucille, B.B.'s lady,
talking about "Friends."
Friends.

I remember them

in the right light

in Friday and Saturday

evening breezes,

harmonizing, signifying, and

guzzling Greystone, Thunderbird,

Ripple and Green Death.

I think about the way

the purple, yellow, red, pink,

and loud sky baby blue slacks, sweaters,

and coats

beamed in the streetlight's glow.

The Stacey Adams and alligator shoes

that smiled.

Sweet Charlie,

fried, dyed,

and laid to the side

in a one button Continental suit,

High Boy shirt, wide paisley tie and burgundy

pimp shades, winning every game

at Moon's Pool Hall.

Cadillac dreamers hanging in there

where we still die unnatural deaths

at the hands of imported cracker cops,

anal retentive educators,

mentally constipated politicians,

and conceptually incarcerated

drug dealers

in a town, in a town, in a town,

in a state, in a state, in a state,

in a nation, in a nation, in a nation

so bad,

even the birds sing bass.

Susan Marshall

Chicago

And they served the drink with one pearl, one real pearl

My mother said about that one night in Chicago

So I kept my painted parrots from Trader Vic's

My locks of hair from a cut at Sassoon's

All the good and Gold Coast light a girl could keep in her room

Until I learned about the burnt out buildings of Golden Flats

And I read my Goodwill copy of *The Jungle*

(Mr. Ochipinti with the milk mustache,

what part of himself did the boy need cut off to live through the
    cold?)

Then soup turned only a quarter in Feininger black and white times

And I gathered my courage and asked her again about the pearl

CLAUDE MCKAY

Africa

The sun sought thy dim bed and brought forth light,
The sciences were sucklings at thy breast;
When all the world was young in pregnant night
Thy slaves toiled at thy monumental best.
Thou ancient treasure-land, thou modern prize,
New peoples marvel at thy pyramids!
The years roll on, thy sphinx of riddle eyes
Watches the mad world with immobile lids.
The Hebrews humbled them at Pharaoh's name.
Cradle of Power! Yet all things were in vain!
Honor and Glory, Arrogance and Fame!
They went. The darkness swallowed thee again.
Thou art the harlot, now thy time is done,
Of all the mighty nations of the sun.

MARIANNE MOORE

The Steeple-Jack

Dürer would have seen a reason for living
   in a town like this, with eight stranded whales
to look at; with the sweet sea air coming into your house
on a fine day, from water etched
   with waves as formal as the scales
on a fish.

One by one, in two's, in three's, the seagulls keep
   flying back and forth over the town clock,
or sailing around the lighthouse without moving their
   wings—
rising steadily with a slight
   quiver of the body—or flock
mewing where

a sea the purple of the peacock's neck is
   paled to greenish azure as Dürer changed
the pine tree of the Tyrol to peacock blue and guinea
grey. You can see a twenty-five-
   pound lobster and fish-nets arranged
to dry. The

whirlwind fife-and-drum of the storm bends the salt
   marsh grass, disturbs stars in the sky and the

star on the steeple; it is a privilege to see so
much confusion.

      A steeple-jack in red, has let
  a rope down as a spider spins a thread;
he might be part of a novel, but on the sidewalk a
sign says C. J. Poole, Steeple-Jack,
  in black and white; and one in red
and white says

Danger. The church portico has four fluted
  columns, each a single piece of stone, made
modester by white-wash. This would be a fit haven for
waifs, children, animals, prisoners,
  and presidents who have repaid
sin-driven
senators by not thinking about them. One
  sees a school-house, a post-office in a
store, fish-houses, hen-houses, a three-masted schooner on
the stocks. The hero, the student
  the steeple-jack, each in his way,
is at home,

It scarcely could be dangerous to be living
  in a town like this, of simple people
who have a steeple-jack placing danger-signs by the church
when he is gilding the solid—
  pointed star, which on a steeple
stands for hope.

WILLIAM OANDASAN

#8 from *The Past*

8

long ago black bears
sang around our lodge fires
tonight they dance
alive through our dreams

CHARLES OLSON

At Yorktown

I

At Yorktown the church
at Yorktown the dead
at Yorktown the grass
are live

        at York-town the earth
piles itself in shallows
declares itself, like water,
by pools and mounds

2

At Yorktown the dead
are soil
at Yorktown the church
is marl
at Yorktown the swallows
dive where it is greenest,

              the hollows
are eyes are flowers, the heather,
equally accurate, is hands

       at York-town only the flies
dawdle, like history,
in the sun

3

at Yorktown the earthworks
braw
at Yorktown the mortars
of brass, weathered green, of mermaids
for handles, of Latin

for texts, scream
without noise
like a gull

4

At Yorktown the long dead
loosen the earth, heels
sink in, over the abatis
a bird wheels

and time is a shine caught blue
from a martin's
back

J. CODY PETERSON

La Jolla. In 3 Acts

1

I was thinking of the rotten candybar I bit into
Sitting in the lunch arbor in second grade.
The shiny wrapper
Gave no warning of the maggots within.

2

La Jolla—Spanish for "The Jewel."

Nestled in its quaint coastal valley,

Crowned by a gleaming white cross,

Caressed by an eye blue ocean,

Bathed in Mediterranean warmth,

It reclines peacefully,

Contented and proud.

Down on Prospect St.

Glittering lights illuminate opulent storefronts,

Inviting passersby to step past the facade.

Wait now—Do we really want that?

Because. . . I can remember something of its soul.

I can still smell the scent of decay on its breath-

Flipping through our valedictorian's *Playboy* collection,

While he danced, half-naked, with a beer carton on his head.

Debutantes sniffing cocaine from dirty toilet seats.

Dimple-cheeked Charlie, shit-faced,

Having unprotected sex with some slut.

(Did that really send her on her third abortion?)

Behind French doors, "The Headmaster's daughter did what?"

"Why can't Stevie Wonder read?"

"Didn't you hear, the Murphys have gone bankrupt!"

Anton got 54 stitches when an ignorant bastard of a fist

Sent his teeth through his lips.

Throwing eggs at an old lady

Out for a quiet moonlight walk along the strand.

I fingered mother's priss on her living room floor.

Beautiful hues of make-up hid pimply pubescent faces.

(Even the gardens and patios conceal the desert beneath.)

And yes,

I too rot behind my charming facade.

3

La Jolla—A Spanish transliteration of the Amer-Indian word

   Hoya—

"The Cave."

ISHMAEL REED

Earthquake Blues

Well the cat started actin funny

and the dog howled all night long

I say the cat started actin very frightful

and the birds chirped all night long

The ground began to rumble

As the panic hit the town.

Mr. Earthquake Mr. Earthquake

you don't know good from bad

Mr. Earthquake Mr. Earthquake

you don't know good from bad

You kill the little child in its nursery

You burn up the widow's pad

The buildings started swaying
like a drunk man walking home
The buildings started swaying
like a drunk man walking home
The people they were running
and the hurt folks began to moan

Mr. Earthquake Mr. Earthquake
you don't know good from bad
Mr. Earthquake Mr. Earthquake
you don't know good from bad
You kill the little child in its nursery
You burn up the widow's pad

I got underneath my table
Had my head between my knees
I got underneath the table
Had my head between my knees
The dishes they were rattlin
and the house was rockin me

Mr. Earthquake Mr. Earthquake
you don't know good from bad
Mr. Earthquake Mr. Earthquake
you don't know good from bad
You kill the little child in its nursery
You burn up the widow's pad

I was worried about my baby
Was she safe or was she dead
I was worried about my baby
Was he safe or was she dead
When she phoned and said I'm
ok, Daddy. Then I went on back
to bed.

Mr. Earthquake Mr. Earthquake
you don't know good from bad
Mr. Earthquake Mr. Earthquake
you don't know good from bad
You kill the little child in its nursery
You burn up the widow's pad

CARL SANDBURG

Chicago

Hog Butcher for the World,
Tool Maker, Stacker of Wheat,
Player with Railroads and the Nation's Freight Handler;
Stormy, husky, brawling,
City of the Big Shoulders:

They tell me you are wicked and I believe them, for I have seen
      your painted women under the gas lights luring the farm boys.
And they tell me you are crooked and I answer: Yes, it is true I
      have seen the gunman kill and go free to kill again.
And they tell me you are brutal and my reply is: On the faces of
      women and children I have seen the marks of wanton hunger.
And having answered so I turn once more to those who sneer at
      this my city, and I give them back the sneer and say to them:
Come and show me another city with lifted head singing so
      proud to be alive and coarse and strong and cunning.
Flinging magnetic curses amid the toil of piling job on job, here
      is a tall bold slugger set vivid against the little soft cities;
Fierce as a dog with tongue lapping for action, cunning as a
      savage pitted against the wilderness,
   Bareheaded,
   Shoveling,
   Wrecking,
   Planning,
   Building, breaking, rebuilding,
Under the smoke, dust all over his mouth laughing with white teeth,
Under the terrible burden of destiny laughing as a young man laughs
Laughing even as an ignorant fighter laughs who has never lost a
      battle,
Bragging and laughing that under his wrist is the pulse, and
      under his ribs the heart of the people, laughing!
Laughing the stormy, husky, brawling laughter of Youth, half-
      naked, sweating, proud to be Hog Butcher, Tool Maker,
      Stacker of Wheat, Player with Railroads and Freight Handler
      to the Nation.

DELMORE SCHWARTZ

The Heavy Bear Who Goes with Me

"the withness of the body"

The heavy bear who goes with me,
A manifold honey to smear his face,
Clumsy and lumbering here and there,
The central ton of every place,
The hungry beating brutish one
In love with candy, anger, and sleep,
Crazy factotum, dishevelling all,
Climbs the building, kicks the football,
Boxes his brother in the hate-ridden city.

Breathing at my side, that heavy animal,
That heavy bear who sleeps with me,
Howls in his sleep for a world of sugar,
A sweetness intimate as the water's clasp,
Howls in his sleep because the tight-rope
Trembles and shows the darkness beneath.
—The strutting show-off is terrified,
Dressed in his dress-suit, bulging his pants,
Trembles to think that his quivering meat
Must finally wince to nothing at all.

That inescapable animal walks with me,

Has followed me since the black womb held,
Moves where I move, distorting my gesture,
A caricature, a swollen shadow,
A stupid clown of the spirit's motive,
Perplexes and affronts with his own darkness,
The secret life of belly and bone,
Opaque, too near, my private, yet unknown,
Stretches to embrace the very dear
With whom I would walk without him near,
Touches her grossly, although a word
Would bare my heart and make me clear,
Stumbles, flounders, and strives to be fed
Dragging me with him in his mouthing care,
Amid the hundred million of his kind,
The scrimmage of appetite everywhere.

MAY SWENSON

Weather

I hope they never get a rope on you, weather.
I hope they never put a bit in your mouth.
I hope they never pack your snorts
into an engine or make you wear wheels.

I hope the astronauts will always have to wait
till you get off the prairie
because your kick is lethal,
your temper worse than the megaton.

I hope your harsh mane will grow forever,
and blow where it will,
that your slick hide will always shiver
and flick down your bright sweat.

Reteach us terror, weather,
with your teeth on our ships,
your hoofs on our houses,
your tail swatting our planes down like flies.

Before they make a grenade of our planet
I hope you'll come like a comet,
oh mustang—fire-eyes, upreared belly—
bust the corral and stomp us to death.

ARTHUR SZE

Every Where and Every When

1

Catch a moth in the Amazon; pin it under glass.
See the green-swirling magenta-flecked wings

miming a fierce face. And dead, watch it fly.
Throw a piece of juniper into a fire.

Search out the Odeon in Zurich to find Lenin or Klee.
No one has a doctrine of recollection to

bring back knowledge of what was, is?
The Odeon cafe is not the place to look

for Lenin's fingerprint. The piece of burning juniper
has the sound of the bones of your hands

breaking. And the moth at the window, magenta-flecked,
green-swirling, is every where and every when.

2

Everything is supposed to fit: mortise and tenon,
arteries and veins, hammer, anvil, stirrup in the ear,

but it does not fit. Someone was executed
today. Tomorrow friends of the executed will execute

the executers. And this despair is the intensifying
fever and chill, in shortening intervals,

of a malaria patient. Evil is not a variety of
potato found in the Andes. The smell of a gardenia

is not scissors and sponge in the hands of
an inept surgeon. Everything is supposed to fit:

but wander through Cuzco and the orientation of
streets and plazas is too Spanish. Throw

hibiscus on a corpse. Take an aerial view;
see the city built in the shape of a jaguar's head.

3

I pick a few mushrooms in the hills,
but do not know the lethal from the edible.

I cannot distinguish red wool dyed
with cochineal or lac, but know that

cochineal with alum, tin, salt and lime juice
makes a rosé, a red, a burgundy.

Is it true an anti-matter particle
never travels as slow as the speed of light,

and, colliding with matter, explodes?
The mind shifts as the world shifts.

I look out the window, watch Antares glow.
The world shifts as the mind shifts;

or this belief, at least, increases
the pleasure of it all—the smell of espresso

in the street, picking blueberries,
white-glazed, blue-black,

sieved gold from a river, this moment
when we spin and shine.

KATHRYN TAKARA

Cows and Alabama Folklore

The old folk used to say
"When the cows are lying down
it sho nuf gwine rain."

I said similarly
to my two girls,
and they always asked "Why?"
and I didn't know.

Now I could have gone to Dad,
who is a retired veterinarian,
but I never thought about it,
except when I saw the cows lying down,
no matter where in the world I was,
passing Kualoa Ranch by Chinaman's Hat
on the way to and from town,
or on the back roads in Alabama.

So, this year, when I received the Almanac
in the 50 pound bag of dog food,
I wasn't looking for information on cows,
but rather I sought the esoteric stuff
like tides, eclipses and zodiac secrets.

Imagine my surprise
when I saw a section
on the foster mother of the human race,
the Dairy Cow.

Now mind you,
in my Ethnic Studies class,
we had just been discussing slavery,
slaves as chattel, human chattel,
and I had told the students it meant fettered, living
    property,
never considering that the word was synonymous
    with cattle.
Nor did I realize that Egyptians
domesticated cattle about 3500 B.C.

True,
I was familiar with cow terms
like bull, steer, stag, heifer
and even "bullshit,"
not realizing that a cow
produces 15 tons per year!

I also associated a "stag" party
with lots of available, cute guys,
horny, looking for action.

And a "heifer,"
well, that was a slang word

to describe a girl
whom one was angry with
or who had loose morals.

And just the other day
In French class we read
La Fontaine's fable
about the frog who wanted to become a magnificent
    cow.

LORENZO THOMAS

Hurricane Doris

The trees are loud,
The forest, rooted, tosses in her bonds
And strains against the cloud.—Alice Meynell

Our pleasure now
Is an efficient squalor
Alternate use of bed
And car. We live in shifts
Of anger and distrust

There's a sock in the kitchen
A book & a comb on the floor
Phone numbers under the bed
Candy wrappers wrinkled on the chessboard
A Scott towel beside the TV set

Soup in my hair
My favorite imported beer (warm)
A warm domestic chaos
Spells life without care
People who could care less

About the other one (though caring)
A painful disappointment
Gathers like a stuffy nose
battling the arms of meditation

Unclear devices
A sense that even silent hurt
Is quite a victory
Over (another) possible disaster

No lucky stars find welcome in our thanks
Which mask disgusted eyes
With dark infinities of manners
Childhood ideas of politeness
A signal sine wave mayday in a glance

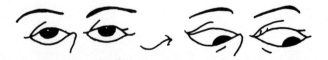

But the Carla or Edith in my heart
Is not polite. With a calm eye
She sends her rages flooding to my brain

My own (mild) care numbs speech
Rehearsed in silence
At this point, I can put
A record on the box
Without caring what music

What music can comfort me now

The other woman that is the hurricane
Of everything I must have wanted
In you,

Look how even if she recedes from my heart
She wastes this house

Look
Leaving heaps of me and mounds
Of you unshapely and deplored
By our own eyes

You can see the false rendering
Fine as the fax lines
Of the disaster wirefotos
Or the minutiae of our
Less than tropic furies

What music can can comfort me now I'm mad

                           I'm mad

I'm mad because 1,000s of poor peoples
Don't have nowhere to go

                  Because I must rush to the rooftop
To despair or await you

The disorder of our living
Strangles my peace when you're here
And when you've gone the somewhere
I have no idea, I use no lights
I close the blinds the house turns dark as night

I would rather not see that you are absent

Yes. I'd make a lopsided correspondent

I'd prefer your passion in detail
To the awesome task of cleaning up

YUMI THOMAS

Love Poem to an Avocado from a Tomato

Tonight I wore my bright red suit
and came to the opera
just to see you at the buffet.
Leaning against a cabbage leaf
in a bowl of salad,
your olive skin shimmers
like a river at night.
You dance among carrots, cucumbers,
and wear a crown of alfalfa sprouts like a queen.
I straighten my green necktie and bow to you,
then blush red as my suit
as you glide by in an artichoke's arms
under the rain of a thousand islands.

NICK VAN BRUNT

Los Angeles

You can see it in the faces of the valley rats,
cruising Ventura, smoking Camel filters,
     complaining about how Encino is just "soooo plastic,"
and hoping they can find the perfect coffeehouse
     where they can ignore the other valley rats who are
ignoring them since apathy is the hip thing these days. . .

On the 101 South, en route to Max's house,
     Angelyne looks slyly down from her billboard,
a voluptuous, perfect Hollywood babe.
     In reality, she's older than the speed limit.

Oh well.
As we drive back into the Valley, we see it—
     that damn white neon cross in the hills as we head for the 818. . .
Someday, Alex, Danny, and I will climb up there and paint it red.
But probably not,
          since apathy is the hip thing these days. . .

When night falls you can park up on Mulholland,
and gaze through the smog at the star.
LA—a city famous for its stars
     yet not one constellation cuts through the glitz.

I'd like to think that with
all the flammable hair in Hollywood,
we'd have enough grease to start some sort of fire. . .

But, hey, we all know what's hip.

WHITNEY WARD

Montana's Biggest Weekend

Labor Day in Dillon, MT:
More a cowboy holiday than a socialist one.
I'm selling souvenir programs
At the Rodeo's east entrance,
Smiling at winks from old men in Wranglers
Until they surrender another three dollars
In support of BCHS cross-country.

When my money apron bulges,
I deliver the profits for counting,
By the rodeo Treasurer—
"How are ticket sales, Mom?"
Too busy to chat, she tosses me
A Coke from the ice-filled water trough

At the frantic concession booth
Where they shove wads of dollar bills into her hands.
She escapes to money-room-isolation to count them,
twice.

I mosey to the Old Timer's Booth
Uncomfortably near the bullpens.
Dad's there, complaining about being asked to work
every year
Between laughs with his buddies and free Budweiser's.
I buy a "Old Timer's Burger,"
And watch them place raw beef on the grimy grill.
Dad wraps the burger in white tissue paper and
I carry it to the concessions beneath the grandstands
Where my brother hands me a blue cotton candy,
No charge.

The arena fills with dust
And the smell of grease and manure and stale beer,
Spilled so my feet stick to the bleachers
As I search for my seat: number 46,
Black digits I stenciled on as a child
Wearing red western boots and a feathered cowgirl hat.
Now I'm wearing tie-dye and Birkenstocks
Sitting next to a couple from Vermont
Who pronounce it Rod-a-o.
I want to tell them that's just a street in LA,
But before I have the chance,
They're discussing their anticipation of bull riding
(Scheduled as the finale so tourists stay)

But everyone knows that saddle-bronc is the classic event.

And we're cheering for the local kids

And the National Finals' Champs just as loud

Cause they're all getting bruised the same

And I explain breaking the barrier,

And spurring on the first jump out,

Suppressing my laughter at the outsiders' excitement

Finishing off the burger and Coke

And getting sticky fingers from the cotton candy.

I glance across the arena,

And contemplate how long eight seconds can really last.

GREG YOUMANS

Pear's Complaint

I have raged for thousands of years.

I was on the *other* tree in Eden

and I escaped Greece unexploited by the Gods.

I never was fruit of fantasy for seers and bards,

nor the food of tales for old wives.

For I am not so red, not so self-contained,

not so easily held or thrown.

Never have poets said "the pear of mine eyes,"

nor any of my kind served homage to the teacher's desk
and I keep no children from the dentist's drill.

Yet my veins run sweeter
and my flesh more tender.
Slit my skin with baby's teeth
and run my juice down your throat.
I will feed your cells and your soul;
I will satiate your hunger.

But an hour later, I will not dance in your dreams.

You cannot grasp my complexity.
I am not ordinary enough to be your small miracle.
I am not shaped in a friendly red ball.
I am too esoteric to play roles in your myths.

So imprison me in your still life—
In a timeless bowl with the banana and grapes—
Frozen in a moment—attainable.

At other times, feed on me when passions blur sense:
In these epiphanies, I am a treat—
exotic but common, tangy but sweet, long but round.
Savor me then in the ways you can.

Then, tomorrow, return to your apple

with its insidious worm.

AL YOUNG

Seeing Red

You always seem to get it all wrong about me.
Just like in the days back when you thought
you'd up and die if you chomped me down,
so you ate my leaves instead and wound up dead.
Now you think it's OK to keep me from dying,
so you actually poison me through irradiation.
Where's your imagination? Where's the spirit
of the Aztecs, who grew me to death, named me tamatl,
and loved me for the very fruity berry that I am?
From Plato to NATO, the vegetable consciousness
of Western Civilization mineralizes its own
pockets; oil-cloth pockets so you can steal soup.
That growers in this nation would stoop
to chemotherapy to give me greater so-called shelf-
life may hold the answer to cancer, but it doesn't
do a thing for me. I like to salt and spice
your mouth up, then seed it all red with zesty juice
and yellow-green after-thoughts like the bright
ting-a-ling of love. You hear what I'm saying?
You hear what I'm telling you? Rather than right
those ancient wrong notions, you've motioned them on.
Like edible street gangsters now, rain or shine,
we don't die; we multiply. Tell Henry Heinz
we tumorless tomatoes constantly see the best minds
of our generations goosed, juiced, and pissed.

BESSIE SMITH

Black Mountain Blues

Back in Black Mountain
                        a child will smack your face
Back in Black Mountain
                        a child will smack your face
Babies crying for liquor
                        and all the birds sing bass

Black Mountain people
                        are bad as they can be
Black Mountain people
                        are bad as they can be
They uses gun powder
                        just to sweeten their tea

On the Black Mountain
                        can't keep a man in jail
On the Black Mountain
                        can't keep a man in jail
if the jury finds them guilty
                        the judge'll go their bail

Had a man in Black Mountain
                                sweetest man in town
Had a man in Black Mountain
                                the sweetest man in town

He met a city gal
>> and he throwed me down

I'm bound for Black Mountain
>> me and my razor and my gun
Lord, I'm bound for Black Mountain
>> me and my razor and gun
I'm gonna shoot him if he stands still
>> and cut him if he run

Down in Black Mountain
>> they all shoots quick and straight
Down in Black Mountain
>> they all shoots quick and straight
The bullet'll get you
>> if you starts a-dodging too late

Got the devil in my soul
>> and I'm fulla bad booze
Got the devil in my soul
>> and I'm fulla bad booze
I'm out here for trouble
>> and I've got the Black Mountain Blues

MEN & WOMEN

One of the assignments I give my students guarantees controversy and debate. Perhaps no other subject has attracted the interest of poets as much as the relationship between men and women. At the start of each semester, I ask the men to write a poem from a woman's point of view, and the women to write a poem from a man's point of view. One of the models I use is William Carlos Williams's lovely "The Widow's Lament in Springtime." (Mandy Kahn responded with her "Untitled," in which she uses a male voice to comment on the attitudes that some campus men have about women.)

Among the many varied points of view below, readers will find both Jack Forbes's tender "Something Nice" and Gwendolyn Brooks writing about a man who beats his wife (she, like many women, stays with her abuser). Eugene B. Redmond takes a more cerebral approach in "Love Is Not a Word."

Although love poems characterized the male poetic tradition for hundreds of years, the new feminist movement emerging from the Civil Rights movement asked, "What's love got to do with it?" These women writers no longer felt the need to be "modest" or to be the passive objects of male love poetry. Like the African-American demonstrators who inspired them, they demanded equality. In "The Bride Comes to Yuba City," Chitra Banerjee Divakaruni complains about the practice of arranged loveless marriages which take place in the Asian-Indian community (though black men have been scapegoated by white middle-class feminists as the main perpetrators of the mistreatment of women). As Bessie Smith shows in "Black Mountain Blues" (included in the "Nature & Place" section), women often give as good as they receive. In this song, a woman threatens to "shoot" a man if he stands still, and "cut him" if he runs. In this country, black men and women kill one another at about the same rate.

GWENDOLYN BROOKS

The Battle

Moe Belle Jackson's husband
Whipped her good last night.
Her landlady told my ma they had
A knock-down-drag-out fight.

I like to think
Of how I'd of took a knife
And slashed all of the quickenin'
Out of his lowly life.

But if I know Moe Belle,
Most like, she shed a tear,
And this mornin' it was probably,
"More grits, dear?"

INA COOLBRITH

Woman

What were this human
World without woman?
Think—just a minute!—
Without one in it—
A Man-Eden only,
Wretched and lonely.
True, there's a story
Scarce to her glory
Therewith connected,
But 'tis suspected
Man, after all,
Was quite ready to fall!
If fault, he condoned it—
And through the years since,
Eva has atoned it.

Woman! Be honor
Ever upon her,
Whether as maiden,
Shy, beauty-laden—
Daughter, wife, sister,
Who can resist her?
Or as that other
And greater, the Mother,

Her babe—blossoms moulding
To perfect unfolding—
The home-temple guarding
To richest rewarding.

Though none be purer,
Sweeter and surer,
Avenues wider
Now open beside her.
Each day some new way!
God send the true way
She may seek ever
With earnest endeavor.
Here to the dark, a light!
Here to the wrong, the right!
There the truth sifting!
A soul, here, uplifting!
Patient, prevailing,
With purpose unfailing,
Till at Life's portal
Through Love immortal,
Supremely she stands,
The *World* in her hands.

Woman! All honor
And blessing upon her!
Knowing her truly,
Knowing her fully,
All her completeness,

Tenderness, sweetness—
Though there be times, too,
Sweet hardly rhymes to,
All of the changes
Through which she ranges,
Moods, tenses, phases,
I sing her praises.

Chitra Banerjee Divakaruni

The Brides Come to Yuba City

The sky is hot and yellow, filled
with blue screaming birds. The train
heaved us from its belly
and vanished in shrill smoke.
Now only the tracks
gleam dull in the heavy air,
a ladder to eternity, each receding rung
cleaved from our husbands' ribs.
Mica-flecked, the platform
dazzles, burns up through thin
chappal soles, lurches
like the ship's dark hold,

blurred month of nights, smell of vomit,
a porthole like the bleached iris
of a giant unseeing eye.

Red-veiled, we lean into each other,
press damp palms, try
broken smiles. The man
who met us at the ship whistles
a restless *Angrezi* tune
and scans the fields. Behind us,
the black wedding trunks, sharp-edged,
shiny, stenciled with strange men-names
our bodies do not fit into:
Mrs. Baldev Johl, Mrs. Kanwal Bains.
Inside, folded like wings,
bright *salwar kameezes* scented
with sandalwood. For the men,
kurtas and thin white gauze
to wrap their uncut hair.
Laddus from Jullundhar, sugar-crusted,
six kinds of lentils, a small bag
of *bajra* flour. Labeled in our mothers'
hesitant hands, pickled mango and lime,
packets of seeds—*methi, karela, saag*—
to burst from this new soil
like green stars.

He gives a shout, waves
at the men, their slow

uneven approach. We crease our eyes
through the veils' red film,
cannot breathe. Thirty years
since we saw them. Or never,
like Harvinder, married last year
at Hoshiarpur to her husband's photo,
which she clutches tight to her
to stop the shaking. He is fifty-two,
she sixteen. Tonight—like us all—
she will open her legs to him.

The platform is endless-wide.
The men walk and walk
without advancing. Their lined,
wavering mouths, their
eyes like drowning lights.
We cannot recognize a single face.

Note: Yuba City in northern California was settled largely by Indian railroad workers around the 1900s. Due to immigration restrictions, many of them were unable to bring their families over—or, in the case of single men, go back to get married—until the 1940s.

JACK FORBES

Something Nice

My wife said something
        really nice to me
        today.
She said:
        I'm really glad
        that I married a man
        who
stops along the road
        to pick up
        frogs and snakes and turtles
so they won't get hit by cars.

MANDY KAHN

Untitled

Goddamn you, sliding around under
almost nothing at all—
fairy wings spun into
that dress, not even nudging
your knees, dental floss for
straps, hair all a-shine,
tiny skydrop earrings tinkling under
the pink of little lobes. I know
your back is just-lotioned, can
tell by the opaque gleam and
the way it passes light across
it as easy as a Frisbee. You
lubed up your legs, too, and
shaved them close, all the way
up to the thigh. As if your
cheeks are naturally that perfect
peachy bright, though I admit
that you're subtle enough to fool
almost anyone. I know you've
done it all, carefully
slowly, probably to music as
mellow as marshmallow fluff,
lazy on your low bed by
a gaping window:
you don't have blinds.

ALEX KUO

from *Lives in Dreadful Wanting*

Then they are young and on vacation, their camera
out snapping pictures of each other in front of the fountain.

They are by the seashore with the camera.

They are at the foot of the Alps with their camera.

Wherever they are away from home, their story is
twice told.

They are in each other's pictures looking out, one of
them always smiling, but we are never sure which one and
when.

You just look great, smile.

I want to get this just right.

He waves her to the left, she waves him to the right.
They wave at each other wherever they are.

A little closer. Closer, still. Come on, closer.

There. Snap, click, shutter getting in between two
actions.

*

Several actions later, there are children. First, one in blue
in mother's arms, on a Sunday outing in the park, then several
digressions later in trimmed white sweater holding father's hand,
he is old enough not to want to be in the picture, displaced by
sister in pink in mother's arms, whose soul has not moved since

the last picture was snapped. They are no longer smiling and waving.

*

When the prints came back from the Fotomat the next day, there was too much light, they said, the camera too close for allowances, and what it captured was not what they wished, but someone else keeping an eye on them.

We should save up and buy another camera, they said together under a Christmas tree one year.

EUGENE B. REDMOND

Love Is Not a Word

Do not ensnarl me in a sphere of nouns
Nor cage me in a lair of adjectives:
My need is no funeral song for freedom—
My heat is not electronic:

Do not calibrate my sun with thermometers
Nor pierce my "secret parts" with telescopes:
My cause is not a tableau of codes—
My cry is not stereophonic:

Do not titillate the totem of my thought
Nor advertise, on open market, my privacy:
My rampant passion is not a freak for laboratories—
My pain is not catatonic:

Do not ring me with monotonous vows
Nor sting me with laconic lectures, with commands:
My need is not a force to fence in—
My itch is not metronomic:

Do not label me with foreign lore
Do not place this epiphany in frames
Do not lock my indivisible rhythm in names
Do not color-in my pageless, endless book
Do not describe my dialog with trees
Nor transcribe what the moon whispers
Do not record the voice in my eyes:
Yet *look look look look,* and
Don't dismiss me as a synonym for love.

ALBERTO RÍOS

The Purpose of Altar Boys

Tonio told me at catechism
the big part of the eye
admits good, and the little
black part is for seeing
evil—his mother told him
who was a widow and so
an authority on such things.
That's why at night
the black part gets bigger.
That's why kids can't go out
at night, and at night
girls take off their clothes
and walk around their
bedrooms or jump on their
beds or wear only sandals
and stand in their windows.
I was the altar boy
who knew about these things,
whose mission on some Sundays
was to remind people of
the night before as they
knelt for Holy Communion.
To keep Christ from falling
I held the metal plate

under chins, while on the thick
red carpet of the altar
I dragged my feet
and waited for the precise
moment: plate to chin
I delivered without expression
the Holy Electric Shock,
the kind that produces
a really large swallowing
and makes people think.
I thought of it as justice.
But on other Sundays the fire
in my eyes was different,
my mission somehow changed.
I would hold the metal plate
a little too hard
against those certain same
nervous chins, and I,
I would look
with authority down
the tops of white dresses.

GERTRUDE STEIN

A Very Valentine

Very fine is my valentine.
Very fine and very mine.
Very mine is my valentine very mine and very fine.
Very fine is my valentine and mine, very fine very
    mine and mine is my valentine.

DIANE WAKOSKI

Ringless

I cannot stand the man who wears
a ring
on his little finger/a white peacock walking on the moon
and splinters of silver dust his body;
but the great man, George, cracked in half in my living room
one day and I saw he was made of marble
with black veins. It does not justify the ring to say
someone gave it to you and the little finger is the only one
it will fit;

it does not justify to say Cocteau wore one

and still made the man burst silently through the mirror—

many beautiful

poems have been made with rings worn on the little finger.

That

isn't the point.

Flaubert had jasper; Lorca had jade; Dante had

amber; and Browning had carnelian;

George Washington had solid gold—even Kelly once

   wore a scarab there;

but I am telling you I cannot stand the man

who wears a ring

on his little finger. He may indeed

run the world;

that does not make him any better in

my needlepoint eyes.

Why

is a story.

   There were heaps of fish lying, shimmering in the sun

   with red gashes still heaving

   and the mouths of medieval lovers.

   There were gold and green glass balls bobbing in their

   nets on the waves.

   There were black-eyed men with hair

   all over their bodies

   There were black-skirted ladies baking bread

   and there were gallons and gallons of red wine.

   A girl spilled one drop of hot wax on her lover's neck

   as she glanced at his white teeth and thick arms.

There were red and silver snakes coiling around the legs
of the dancers.
There was hot sun and there was no talk.
How do I reconcile these images with our cool president
George Washington, walking the streets? Every bone
in my body is ivory and has the word "America"
carved on it, but
my head takes me away from furniture and pewter
to the sun tugging at my nipples and trying to squeeze
under my toes.
The sun appeared in the shape of a man and he had
a ring made of sun around his little finger.
"It will bum up your hand," I said.
But he made motions in the air and passed by.
The moon appeared in the shape of a young negro boy,
and he had a ring made of dew around his little finger.
"You'll lose it," I said,
but he touched my face,
not losing a drop and passed away. Then I saw
Alexander Hamilton, whom I loved,
and he had a ring on his little finger,
but he wouldn't touch me.
And Lorca had rings around both little fingers,
and suddenly everyone I knew appeared,
and they all had rings on their little fingers,
and I was the only one in the world left without any
rings
on any
of my fingers whatsoever.
And worst of all,

there was George Washington

walking down the senate aisles

with a ring on his little finger—managing

the world,

managing *my* world.

This is what I mean—you wear a ring on your

little finger

and you manage the world,

and I am ringless

ringless. . .

I cannot stand the man who wears

a ring

on his little finger;

not even if it is you.

WILLIAM CARLOS WILLIAMS

The Widow's Lament in Springtime

Sorrow is my own yard

where the new grass

flames as it has flamed

often before but not

with the cold fire

that closes round me this year.
Thirty five years
I lived with my husband.
The plum tree is white today
with masses of flowers.
Masses of flowers
loaded the cherry branches
and color some bushes
yellow and some red
but the grief in my heart
is stronger than they
for though they were my joy
formerly, today I notice them
and turned away forgetting.
Today my son told me
that in the meadows,
at the edge of the heavy woods
in the distance, he saw
trees of white flowers.
I feel that I would like
to go there
and fall into those flowers
and sink into the marsh near them.

MEMPHIS WILLIE B. (BORUM)

Bad Girl Blues

Women loving each other
     man they don't think about no man
Women loving each other
     and they don't think about no man
They ain't playing no secret no more
       these women playing it a wide
       hand

    I buzzed a little girl the other day
    I wanted a little thrill
    She say, I'm so sorry Mister *Sims*
    I'm putting out the same thing to Lil

I say women loving each other
      and they ain't thinking about no
      man
They ain't playing with no secret
      these women playing it a wide
      open hand

    Have you ever taken her out car riding
    Bought her all kind of whiskey and wine
    Say you was too drunk to realize
    Say, I'll see you another time

You know women loving each other

                     and they don't think about no man

They ain't playing with no secret

                     these women playing it a wide open hand

        Have she ever left you going out jitterbugging

        Smelling sweet like a rose

        Come back 'bout 5 o'clock in the morning

        With a *fish scent all in her clothes*

You know women is loving each other

                     and they don't think about no man

They don't play it with no secret no more

                     they playing it a wide open hand

        Have you ever had a little woman

        Give her the last dollar you had

        Every time you say something to her

        She'll say, My stomach hurting so bad

You know women loving each other

                     and they don't think about no man

They ain't playing for no secret

                     they playing it a wide open hand

TUPAC SHAKUR

Why Must U Be Unfaithful
(4 Women)

MEN!
u shouldn't listen 2 your selfish heart
It doesn't really have a brain
Besides keeping u alive
Its existence is in vain
"How could I be so mean,
and say your heart has no place?"
Because mortal men fall in love again
as fast as they change their face
I may be cruel, but think awhile about
The hearts that u have broken
Match that with the empty vows
and broken promises u've spoken
I am not saying females R perfect
Because men we know it's not true
But why must u be unfaithful
If her heart is true 2 u!!!!

FAMILY

I have been using Ronald Wallace's "The Fat of the Land" to inspire my students to write about a family scene. The most successful responses to this exercise come from those who record the scene faithfully, or zero in on a particularly memorable relative. Lucille Clifton, one of our most gifted poets of the succinct, captures a celebratory scene from the inner city in her "good times." Garrett Hongo writes about the good times had by a Japanese-American family. In his moving poem "Bells," Jimmy Santiago Baca describes his mother's journey home to Santa Fe, where the ancient Hispanic character is being erased by gentrification. Elizabeth Bishop recalls her Aunt Consuelo in her poem "In the Waiting Room," while T. S. Eliot draws a sharp portrait of a wealthy "Aunt Helen." Mursalata Muhammad's "Last Days of a Slow Cooker" proves that a gifted writer can reveal the humanity of even an unpopular and often misunderstood group. The media have caricatured the Nation of Islam for decades, but through the great leveler of good cooking, Muhammad's poem connects its members to the rest of us. Just as Muhammad busts stereotypes of Muslims, Vince Gotera challenges the myth of Asian-American passivity: the father in "Dance of the Letters" has a grievance and an attitude. And in Laura Soul Brown's "Oh Mercy Mercy Me! A Family Gathers to Marvin Gaye," the family scene is so vivid, you can smell the food and hear Gaye's music in the background. Finally, in Billy Collins's poem "The Names" we are reminded that regardless of our ethnic origins, we are members of a national family.

Jimmy Santiago Baca

Bells

Bells. The word gongs my skull . . .
Mama carried me out, just born,
swaddled in hospital blanket,
from St. Vincent's in Santa Fe.
Into the evening, still drowsed
with uterine darkness,
my fingertips purple with new life,
cathedral bells splashed
into my blood, plunging iron hulls
into my pulse waves. Cathedral steeples,
amplified brooding, sonorous bells,
through narrow cobbled streets, bricked patios,
rose trellis'd windows,
red-tiled Spanish rooftops, bells
beat my name, "Santiago! Santiago!"
Burning my name in black-frosted streets,
bell sounds curved and gonged deep.
ungiving, full-bellowed beats of iron on iron,
shuddering pavement Mama walked,
quivering thick stainless panes, creaking
plaza shop doors, beating its gruff thuds
down alleys and dirt
passageways, past men waiting in doorways
of strange houses. Mama carried me past

peacocks and chickens, past the miraculous
stairwell winding into the choirloft, touted
in tourist brochures, *"Not one nail was used*
to build this, it clings tenaciously
together by pure prayer power, a spiraling
pinnacle of faith . . ." And years later,
when I would do something wrong,
in kind reprimand Mama would say,
"You were born of bells, more than my womb,
they speak to you in dreams.
Ay, *Mejito,*
you are such a dreamer!"

DAVID BARAZA

A Place Without Shame

We come unnoticed from the barrios
And the Suburbs of California.
Some cruise in low-riders,
Or migrate in pickup trucks,
Even caravan in minivans
through Spanish named cities
that mean nothing.

On arrival we leave our invisibility
in the car and lock the door.
As we enter the house
we wipe insecurity off our shoes
and hang our marginality on the rack.
We bear hug one another
and kiss the closest cheek.
From our pockets we remove our tongues
to let them la la la.
Our tightness is shaken off
gradually to the songs of Vicente.
Ay! Ay! explodes from every mouth.
The mariache music and spicy salsa
warms our hearts. Oiy oiy oooh.
The voiceless are heard.
The invisible take form.
Hips spin and sway,
keeping up with rhythmic boots
encouraged by barking hands.
Ay! Ay! Aaay! the unintelligible sounds of life
Roll within the house.
Against the walls lie the unlocked shackles.
Tonight the keys were found.
Fear runs screaming out of the house.
Self-doubt crawls out the window.
Confidence dances with all who'll have her.
She encourages all to enjoy her.
And the music makes everything better.

ELIZABETH BISHOP

In the Waiting Room

In Worcester, Massachusetts,
I went with Aunt Consuelo
to keep her dentist's appointment
and sat and waited for her
in the dentist's waiting room.
It was winter. It got dark
early. The waiting room
was full of grown-up people,
arctics and overcoats,
lamps and magazines.
My aunt was inside
what seemed like a long time
and while I waited I read
the *National Geographic*
(I could read) and carefully
studied the photographs:
the inside of a volcano,
black, and full of ashes;
then it was spilling over
in rivulets of fire.
Osa and Martin Johnson
dressed in riding breeches,
laced boots, and pith helmets.
A dead man slung on a pole
—"Long Pig," the caption said.

Babies with pointed heads
wound round and round with string;
black, naked women with necks
wound round and round with wire
like the necks of lightbulbs.
Their breasts were horrifying.
I read it right straight through.
I was too shy to stop.
And then I looked at the cover:
the yellow margins, the date.

Suddenly, from inside,
came an *oh!* of pain
—Aunt Consuelo's voice—
not very loud or long.
I wasn't at all surprised;
even then I knew she was
a foolish, timid woman.
I might have been embarrassed,
but wasn't. What took me
completely by surprise
was that it was *me:*
my voice, in my mouth.
Without thinking at all
I was my foolish aunt,
I—we—were falling, falling,
our eyes glued to the cover
of the *National Geographic,*
February, 1918.

I said to myself: three days
and you'll be seven years old.
I was saying it to stop
the sensation of falling off
the round, turning world
into cold, blue-black space.
But I felt: you are an *I*,
you are an *Elizabeth,*
you are one of *them.*
Why should you be one, too?
I scarcely dared to look
to see what it was I was.
I gave a sidelong glance
—I couldn't look any higher—
at shadowy gray knees,
trousers and skirts and boots
and different pairs of hands
lying under the lamps.
I knew that nothing stranger
had ever happened, that nothing
stranger could ever happen.

Why should I be my aunt,
or me, or anyone?
What similarities—
boots, hands, the family voice
I felt in my throat, or even
the *National Geographic*
and those awful hanging breasts—

held us all together
or made us all just one?
How—I didn't know any
word for it—how "unlikely" . . .
How had I come to be here,
like them, and overhear
a cry of pain that could have
got loud and worse but hadn't?

The waiting room was bright
and too hot. It was sliding
beneath a big black wave,
another, and another.

Then I was back in it.
The War was on. Outside,
in Worcester, Massachusetts,
were night and slush and cold,
and it was still the fifth
of February, 1918.

LAURA SOUL BROWN

Oh! Mercy Mercy Me!
A Family Gathers to Marvin Gaye

"Lord Have Mercy" rises up
with the smoke from the grill
we gather together under charcoal skies
our ritual
"Where did all the blue skies go?" Aunt Helen, are the ribs ready?
when day's pageants are done; we unfold our tent
Mother conducts the spatula
one hand tucked in a mitt
her salt-and-pepper fro unkempt
a grease stained apron hugs her full hips
And the folks (cousins, aunts, friends, children)
come strolling in
some still in Sunday suits
intoxicated by the day's events
our house is where they come to let loose
Evening blues
Relax their coats, stockings, ties and shoes
Watch ball games play cards eat as much as you choose talk
Plenty of talk good music on . . .
"Things ain't what they used to be . . ."
We've been thinning for years
Once the plumpest family on the block
Our faces full of cheeseburgers, potato salad, ham hocks

macaroni (Aunt Frances put pimento on it) collard greens, string
  beans
rice and peas, washed down with Private Stocks
Now the elders have restricted diets, substitutes for salt
"Oil wasted on the ocean. . . (A saucy pork loin slips into a soggy
  pulp of paper)
. . . our seas, fish full of
Mercury," the cat prefers to lay low
find a place under a bed or next to a window hoping
the young ones don't get distracted, start prowling for attention
One nephew, one niece all that's passed on from last generation
      very special place the center of family's future
         small and precious heirlooms we tarnish them
            with silver, dollars and trust funds
"Radiation. . .in the sky. . ."
Jeanie, would you place this casserole in the microwave for me?
Aunt Elsie coos figure at 70 like it was at 50 as she was at 31
she'll charm you like a locket
cooking's a specialty, for her—rare; the dish will probably remain
  there
in the oven, no one will bother
"Animals and birds who live nearby are dying"
The yard is well canopied an elderly pine holds its center
ringed by two oaks, lilacs, rhododendrons, hedges. A pear tree
where robins would nest has long been bundled away left to rot
  by the side of the fence
        after dark, mosquitos are pests tickle the ankles
      citronella torches stand guarded protection
"Mercy Mercy Mercy Mercy"

Gloria exhorts swatting the gnats that swarm her plate

heaped cholesterol mountain

its juices run down her triple E chest

propped up it's amazing

                         she never had kids

"What about this overcrowded land,

how much more abuse from man can she stand?"

On a patch of land next to the house on a cinder brick

a boom box blares Marvin Gaye's "Sexual Healing"

crescent rolls pork bellies chicken legs and seasoned rumps

rub the last sod from the Earth

typically stoic Trevor enjoys the pleasure of women

taking turns winding themselves about his totem

reminiscent of his playa days

ball stolen from his court

paternity suits make him less a father figure

                    more a nigga

Richie teases the ladies—consummate bachelor

76 adjusts his polished brass buckle, tilts his Stetson

cocks his legs slyly to display Durango style

gleefully flashes Fixodent smile

Sister and her girls are ripe full of happiness

they've got homes jobs families and cars

by age 32 their men hang on the fringes

        smacking on succulent barbeque thighs

"Oh, na na. Help me. Help me."

Kids scurry after each other in a mean spirited game of tag

Little T hides behind the gnarled knot of grandpa hoping he'll

deter the pursuing gang. 3-year-old Unique cries at the growing shadows desperately wanting to join the fellows

"No we can't wait."

It's beyond pitch, Mom warns us to move inside

grab a dish and a chair; collect the children, stray cans

It's getting late; suffocate the dwindling fire

Cousins pack up vans, wave goodbye

"No we can't wait."

to drape our rum-soaked bodies around the kitchen table

as youth nods off before television stations

"It's almost too late."

Note: "Quotations" are interpolations of "Mercy, Mercy Me (The
*   Ecology)" sung by Marvin Gaye, written by Brian*
*   Holland/Lamont Dozier/Eddie Holland Jr.*

CHEZIA THOMPSON CAGER

Callaloo

I

BEAUTY!

Relishing her moments alone,
Sable anticipates dinner.
Her Apricot Scrub, Milk Wash
& Aloe conditioner will make
her face perfect:
and leave her breasts Tangelo ripe
for sucking.
Rolling him like a Biscuit
would occur after heaping helpings of
Pork Chops smothered in
Grandma's special browned Wine Sauce
to the tune of Sautéed Red Onions,
Mile High Cornbread and real Mashed Potatoes.
Aunt Bing Bing's recipe
for Mustard and Turnip greens, slow cooked
with Salt Pork, would be too
laborious today. Momma's fast fried Red
Cabbage with Plum Wine would have
to do, on the spur of the moment. Perfuming
herself in distilled Peach essence
and Magnolia Flower Oil would take the time

left before her fitting.
The Red Moon erupted suddenly, though not
unexpectedly, pulling her from
her routine to face the voice inside of her.
Would he come?

Callaloo continued

The Lilac Flower print dress flowed into the
Mississippi landscape as she led
him into the garden for a light dinner,
long looks into her sometimes brown
sometimes hazel eye color
and a reckoning with destiny that
surely he must not suspect is coming.

II

FAMILY.

The children fled at the mention
of Momma's Ground Nut Stew Story.
That god awful description of killing the
goat in midair, wringing the chicken's neck
in the middle of Oshogbo's forest,
terrified them and sent them screaming to
McDonald's.
They ate the Peanut Butter Tomato concoction
only if they didn't know what it was.
Tasted weird like the Gumbo recipe,

Poet Tom Dent had cooked for Momma
in New Orleans during the
Free Southern Theater Funeral.
Filé Gumbo, Shrimp Gumbo, Seafood Gumbo,
without okra of course, they just
couldn't say: but eating them with
Cassava Balls or Wild Rice, with
cut Green Onions made them sort of alike:
second cousins in the diaspora soul food line.
Graduating from Chicken Soup
and Rice with Lemon
(from somebody riding a camel in the Sahil),
to adult table food, was a big thing!
Nonetheless, the girls did not understand
why Sable insisted on lapsing into
these instructional tales of horror.
Cleaning fresh fish caught in
Jamaica, to make Steamed Fish and Callaloo;
where she later danced Kumina in
the mountains with the Maroons: or
Hand-grinding meat for Blood Sausage
in Haiti, before dancing Voudoo at the Peristyle.
Not even the sweets were a simple sit down
and eat without peeling individual cashew plants,
hunting for wild honeycombs,
digging up carrots or cracking and shredding fresh
coconut meat for her famous Carrot Cake.
Every meal had a journey about
Black people, that she gently forced you to travel
before watching you pig out in an culinary orgasmic

bliss that always ended in a pleasant nap and a
Callaloo continued

kiss of love on the forehead,
as she covered you up.

III

LEGACY?

No one knew how long Mother had
left. Regal in her orchid organza nightgown,
with matching lace and peacock feather fan,
she rallied at the oddest moments.
Trying to get her to eat, the girls failed
miserably without understanding why.
As busy women they never learned
to cook. Planning to never marry or
have children, they didn't see the point.
Rather, they preferred to imitate
Oprah, who paid someone well to do it for them.
Simeria had ordered Southern Fried Chicken
in a Buffalo Berry Sauce with Brown Rice
for her dinner at her Landover, Maryland mansion.
An organic Poke Salad with Tomatoes,
Grown, ala Martha Stewart, in her own garden,
would keep Momma regulated and alert.
"If we take Mother to my house,
Lucy can fix anything that she wants,"
she said repeatedly to her sisters.
Lusana insisted that they try to cook

one of Sable's recipes together
and coax her to eat with them.
But the problem was understanding
how Mother combined culinary histories
to make the world of food that they knew.
Njinga absolutely refused to cook anything,
volunteering to order Jallo Chicken
from the nearest Senegalese Restaurant.
"It might remind Mother of Boubacar
and make her smile," they all thought.
Mother opened her eyes and said,
"Black Eye Peas and Fried Sweet Potatoes:
You need iron." "What does that mean?"
they asked in unison, as she closed her eyes again.
"That Sylvia woman in Harlem
sells canned Black Eye Peas," Simeria quipped.
"Want me to go to the store?"
"Why would anyone fry sweet potatoes.
Aren't you supposed to bake them?" Njinga asked.
The designer Lilac Flower print
skirts and Diahann Carroll ruffled blouses
flowed into the landscape, as the
three doctors of Medicine, Chemistry
and Robotics respectfully held each
other and wondered what other secrets
would be lost to the ages with
Sable's last breath.

ANA CASTILLO

Nani Worries About Her Father's Happiness in the Afterlife

He knew nothing about death,
before he died.
None of us did.
Then he died,
and I was left to wonder where he went.

The *Nahuas* sent their loved ones,
accompanied by an *escuinctle*,
to travel for four years
before reaching *Mictlan:*
Region of the Dead,
also called "*Ximoayan*"—
Place of the Fleshness.
Mictlan: The House of *Quetzal* Plumes,
where there is no time.

Jesus descended into Hell
for three days,
freed his predecessor, Adam,
and returned to earth.
Oh—such stories I have heard!
Men and their intentions.
I did not know what to think.

I looked about the room, held his hand,
turning cold in mine,
his mouth open, having gasped
for his last breath of this life.
He was no longer in a sweat.

I wish I knew where he was—
floating above, near the ceiling,
perhaps, like those near-death cases report.

Was he pleased with our Christian
praying over the corpse,
my many kisses on his forehead,
our reluctance to leave him alone?

A cold winter Chicago night:
Ash Wednesday, February 28th.
The uselessness of doctrine in
these times. Ma and I decided
two things with that in mind:

This is hell.
This is not the whole story.

Rosemary Catacalos

One Man's Family

in memory of Bill Gilmore

There was the Dog Man again today,
bent under his tow sack,
making his daily pilgrimage
along St. Mary's Street
with his rag tied to his forehead,
with his saintly leanness
and his bunch of seven dogs
and his clothes covered with
short smelly hair.
Pauline, the waitress up at
the White House Cafe, says
he used to be a college professor.
In a college. Imagine.
And now he's all the time
with them dogs.
Lets them sleep in the same room
with him. Lets them eat
the same things he eats.
Pauline don't like it.
All them eyes that light up in the dark
like wolves'.

I imagine he carries his mother's
wedding dress around in that filthy sack.
I imagine he takes the dress out on Sundays
and talks to it about the dogs,
the way he might talk to Pauline
if she ever gave him the chance.
About how to him those seven dogs
are seven faithful wives,
seven loaves, seven brothers.
About how those seven snouts bulldozing
through neighborhood garbage and memories
give off a warmth that's just as good
as all the breasts and apple pies and Christmas trees
and books and pipes and slippers
that a man could use on this earth.
But mostly about how they're dogs.
Friends that don't have to be anything else.
About how nothing could be more right
than for a man to live
with what he is willing and able to trust.

Lucille Clifton

good times

my daddy has paid the rent
and the insurance man is gone
and the lights is back on
and my uncle brud has hit
for one dollar straight
and they is good times
good times
good times

my mama has made bread
and grampaw has come
and everybody is drunk
and dancing in the kitchen
and singing in the kitchen
oh these is good times
good times
good times

oh children think about the
good times

BILLY COLLINS

The Names

Yesterday, I lay awake in the palm of the night.
A fine rain stole in, unhelped by any breeze,
And when I saw the silver glaze on the windows,
I started with A, with Ackerman, as it happened,
Then Baxter and Calabro,
Davis and Eberling, names falling into place
As droplets fell through the dark.

Names printed on the ceiling of the night.
Names slipping around a watery bend.
Twenty-six willows on the banks of a stream.

In the morning, I walked out barefoot
Among thousands of flowers
Heavy with dew like the eyes of tears,
And each had a name—
Fiori inscribed on a yellow petal
Then Gonzalez and Han, Ishikawa and Jenkins.

Names written in the air
And stitched into the cloth of the day.
A name under a photograph taped to a mailbox.
Monogram on a torn shirt,
I see you spelled out on storefront windows

And on the bright unfurled awnings of this city.
I say the syllables as I turn a corner—
Kelly and Lee,
Medina, Nardella, and O'Connor.

When I peer into the woods,
I see a thick tangle where letters are hidden
As in a puzzle concocted for children.
Parker and Quigley in the twigs of an ash,
Rizzo, Schubert, Torres, and Upton,
Secrets in the boughs of an ancient maple.

Names written in the pale sky.
Names rising in the updraft amid buildings.
Names silent in stone
Or cried out behind a door.
Names blown over the earth and out to sea.

In the evening—weakening light, the last swallows.
A boy on a lake lifts his oars.
A woman by a window puts a match to a candle,
And the names are outlined on the rose clouds—
Vanacore and Wallace,
(let X stand, if it can, for the ones unfound)
Then Young and Ziminsky, the final jolt of Z.

Names etched on the head of a pin
One name spanning a bridge, another undergoing a tunnel.
A blue name needled into the skin.

Names of citizens, workers, mothers and fathers,

The bright-eyed daughter, the quick son.

Alphabet of names in green rows in a field.

Names in the small tracks of birds.

Names lifted from a hat

Or balanced on the tip of the tongue.

Names wheeled into the dim warehouse of memory.

So many names, there is barely room on the walls of the heart.

NORA MARKS DAUENHAUER

Grandmother Eliza

My grandmother Eliza

was the family surgeon.

Her scalpel made from a pocket knife

she kept in a couple of pinches of snoose.

She saved my life by puncturing

my festering neck twice with her knife.

She saved my brother's life twice

when his arm turned bad.

The second time she saved him

was when his shoulder turned bad.

She always made sure

she didn't cut an artery.
She would feel around for days
finding the right spot to cut.
When a doctor found out
she saved my brother's life
he warned her,
"You know you could go to jail for this?"
Her intern, my Auntie Anny, saved my life
when I cut a vessel on my toe.
While my blood was squirting out
she went out into the night
and cut and chewed the bark
of plants she knew.
She put the granules of chewed up bark
on my toe before the eyes of the folks
who came to console my mother
because I was bleeding to death.
Grandma's other intern, Auntie Jennie
saved our uncle's life when his son
shot him through the leg by accident.
A doctor warned her, too,
when he saw how she cured.
Her relative cured herself of diabetes.
Now, the doctors keep on asking,
"How did you cure yourself?"

DIANE DI PRIMA

April Fool Birthday Poem for Grandpa

Today is your
birthday and I have tried
writing these things before,
but now
in the gathering madness, I want to
thank you
for telling me what to expect
for pulling
no punches, back there in that scrubbed Bronx parlor
thank you
for honestly weeping in time to
innumerable heartbreaking
italian operas for
pulling my hair when I
pulled the leaves off the trees so I'd
know how it feels, we are
involved in it now, revolution, up to our
knees and the tide is rising, I embrace
strangers on the street, filled with their love and
mine, the love you told us had to come or we
die, told them all in that Bronx park, me listening in
spring Bronx dusk, breathing stars, so glorious
to me your white hair, your height your fierce
blue eyes, rare among italians, I stood

a ways off, looking up at you, my grandpa

people listened to, I stand

a ways off listening as I pour out soup

young men with light in their faces

at my table, talking love, talking revolution

which is love, spelled backwards, how

you would love us all, would thunder your anarchist wisdom

at us, would thunder Dante, and Giordano Bruno, orderly men

bent to your ends, well I want you to know

we do it for you, and your ilk, for Carlo Tresca,

for Sacco and Vanzetti, without knowing

it, or thinking about it, as we do it for Aubrey Beardsley

Oscar Wilde (all street lights

shall be purple), do it

for Trotsky and Shelley and big/dumb

Kropotkin

Eisenstein's Strike people, Jean Cocteau's ennui, we do it for

the stars over the Bronx

that they may look on earth

and not be ashamed.

T. S. ELIOT

Aunt Helen

Miss Helen Slingsby was my maiden aunt,
And lived in a small house near a fashionable square
Cared for by servants to the number of four.
Now when she died there was silence in heaven
And silence at her end of the street.
The shutters were drawn and the undertaker wiped his feet—
He was aware that this sort of thing had occurred before.
The dogs were handsomely provided for,
But shortly afterwards the parrot died too.
The Dresden clock continued ticking on the mantelpiece,
And the footman sat upon the dining table
Holding the second housemaid on his knees—
Who had always been so careful while her mistress lived.

DANIELA GIOSEFFI

Bicentennial Anti-Poem
for Italian-American Women

On the crowded subway,
riding to the prison to teach
Black and Puerto Rican inmates how to write,
I think of the fable of the shoemaker
who struggles to make shoes for the oppressed
while his own go barefoot over the stones.

I remember Grandma, her olive face
wrinkled with resignation,
content just to survive
after giving birth to twenty children,
without orgasmic pleasures or anesthesia.
Grandpa, immigrant adventurer,
who brought his family
steerage passage to the New World;
his shoemaker shop where he labored
over American factory goods
that made his artisan's craft a useless
anachronism; his Code of Honor
which forced him to starve
accepting not a cent of welfare
from anyone but his sons;

his ironic "Code of Honor"
which condoned jealous rages of wife-beating;
Aunt Elisabetta, Aunt Maria-Domenica,
Aunt Raffaella, Aunt Elena, grown women
huddled like girls in their bedroom in Newark,
talking in whispers, not daring
to smoke their American cigarettes
in front of Pa;
the backyard shrine of the virgin,
somber blue-robed woman,
devoid of sexual passions,
to whom Aunt Elisabetta prayed
daily before dying in childbirth,
trying to have *a son*
against doctor's orders
though she had five healthy daughters;
Dr. Giuseppe Ferrara,
purple-heart veteran of World War II,
told he couldn't have a residency
in a big New York hospital
because of his Italian name;
the mafia jokes, the epithets:
Wop, guinea, dago, grease-ball;
and the stories told by Papa
of Dante, Galileo, da Vinci,
Marconi, Fermi and Caruso
that stung me with pride
for Italian *men;*
how I was discouraged from school,

told a woman meant for cooking
and bearing doesn't need education.

I remember
Grandma
got out of bed
in the middle of the night
to fetch her *husband* a glass of water
the day she died,
her body wearied
from giving and giving and giving
food and birth.

Vince Gotera

Dance of the Letters

My father, in a 1956 gray suit,
had the jungle in his tie,
a macaw on Kelly green.
But today is Saturday, no briefs
to prepare, and he's in a T-shirt.

I sit on his lap with my *ABC*

Golden Book, and he orders the letters
to dance. The *A* prancing red
as an apple, the *E* a lumbering elephant,
the *C* chased by the *D* while the sly *F*

is snickering in his russet fur coat.
My mother says my breakthrough
was the *M* somersaulting into a *W*.
Not a mouse transformed into a wallaby
at all, but sounds that we can see.

Later, my father trots me out
to the living room like a trained *Z*.
Not yet four, I read newspaper headlines
out loud for Tito Juanito and Tita Naty
or for anyone who drops in.

Six years later, I am that boy
in a black Giants cap, intertwining orange
letters *S* and *F*, carrying my father's
forgotten lunch to the catacombs
of the UCSF Medical Center,

and I love the hallway cool before the swirling
heat from the Print Shop door.
In his inky apron, my father smiles,
but his eyes are tired. The night before,
I pulled the pillow over my head, while he

argued with my mother
till two a.m. about that old double bind:
a rule to keep American citizens from
practicing law in the Philippines.
His University of Manila

law degree made useless.
But California's just as bad.
"You can't work in your goddamn
profession stateside either!" he shouts.
"Some land of opportunity."

There in the shimmer of the Print Shop, I can't
understand his bitterness. I savor
the staccato sounds. He leans
into the noise of huge machines, putting
vowels and consonants into neat stacks.

GARRETT HONGO

Winnings

It's Gardena, late Saturday afternoon
on Vermont Avenue, near closing time
at the thrift store, and my father's
left me to rummage through trash bins
stuffed with used paperbacks, 25¢ a pound,
while he chases down some bets
at the card clubs across the street.

The register rings up its sales—$2.95,
$11.24, $26.48 for the reclaimed Frigidaire—
and a girl, maybe six or so, barefoot,
in a plaid dress, her hair braided
in tight cornrows, tugs at the strap
of her mother's purse, begging a few
nickels for the gumball machine.

She skips through the check-stand,
runs toward the electric exit, passing
a fleet of shopping carts, bundles
of used-up magazines (*Ebony* and *Jet*)
stacked in pyramids in the far aisle,
reaches the bright globe of the vendor,
fumbles for her coins, and works the knob.

My father comes in from the Rainbow
across the street, ten hands of Jacks
or Better, five draw, a winner
with a few dollars to peel away
from grocery money and money to fix
the washer, a dollar for me to buy
four pounds of Pocket Wisdoms, Bantams,
a Dell that says *Walt Whitman, Poet
of the Open Road*, and hands it to me,
saying "We won, *Boy-san*! We won!"
as the final blast of sunset kicks through
plate glass and stained air, firing through
the thicket of neon across the street,
consuming the store, the girl, the dollar bill,

even the Rainbow and the falling night
in a brief symphony of candied light.

MAURICE KENNY

Joshua Clark
Three Mile Bay, N.Y. July 1979

> *"Kind and loving husband and tender to your flock."*
>
> . . .*gravestone epitaph*

I

name stained in colored glass
on the Baptist window erected
in the English spirit of your fervor

let me tell you, Pastor Joshua,
great-great-great grandfather,
bred in the clover spring of 1802,
bed to Sybil, sire of Mary
sire to the stones of this
seedy cemetery bloody from veins
opened to the summer breeze,
let me tell you, Joshua,
even your bones are dust.
the headstone chips in the sun
white asters climb
moisture of the grasses
wending across your name

yes, let me tell you, Joshua Clark,
your great-grandson married
the Seneca girl whose father's land
you stole, and his brother drunk
in the velvet parlor lifted cup
by cup the earth to the tavern keeper's smile
yes, my grandfather paid it away, too,
acre by acre to maids that came to dust
his wife's music room and to hired hands
who plowed his father's fields
until only your church and cemetary plot
were left and safe from their foolishness

Joshua, the apple trees have claimed
the house, sumac fill the cellar bins,
the stone foundations bed mice
and snakes prowl your yellow roses
where once you sat in the shade, counting souls
drinking ginger-beer
eyeing the westerly sun
black with barn swallows

your woods are cleared, hickory axed;
there is not a single creek
in those meadows, even bats
and hawks have fled;
your blood has thinned into a trickle . . .
I claim very little and pass nothing on . . .
not a drop to any vein.

your siring is finished, deeds done
and accomplishments or not only a name
remains penned into an old family Bible
and stained in glass, purple and green
of a church no one visits
but skunks and black spiders;
there's enough babies squawking anyway.

II

you were a strong man, strong as the elms
which once reared over the front lawn
and the white pine which fenced the fruit
orchard where ginghamed Sybil plucked
sweet cherry and damson plum
and teased your loins with her pretty English face
her thin ankle and narrow waist;
you were a strong man in the blood
your sap ran April
and you fathered our centuries, our wars
our treacheries, our lies,
our disappointing lives, loves; your fingers
coiled the rope which bound and trussed us all
on the hanging tree, the roots of our feet
dangling over the earth wet with blood
rockets exploding about our ears
deaf and blind as your drunken grandson
to the waste of blackberry brambles
and the loud gnawing of rats in the sweat

of your goose down mattress where Sybil birthed
Mary and all the dawns of your hairy thighs

old cats purr on the supper table
of cold beef; goats munch clean
meadows in the twilight of
birch bending to the rainbows of mornings past.

III

Patty-Lyn and Craig
never read your epitaph,
nor knelt in your Baptist church nor tasted
Sybil's plum preserves, nor haven't
the slightest thought that Ely Parker
was a great Seneca General who had little to do
with your Baptist God;
hands were unfinned, unwebbed for tools
to preserve and beget and protect
all that's beautiful in trout and mallard
all which is remarkable in fire and ice
all which is noble in blood and loin
all which births and dies
in the raging sunset, of dawn;

this half-blood Mohawk condemns your church
to ash and though I would not tamper with the earth
which holds your dust I would chip the stone
flake by flake that heralds your name and deeds

but carry pails of fresh water to the green cedar
rooting in your family plot where my bones
refuse to lay coiled and pithed in the womb
of a tribe which has neither nation nor reason nor drum

my father claims my blood
and sired in the shadow of a turtle my growls
echo in the mountain woods where a bear climbs down
rocks to walk across your grave to leave its prints
upon the summer dust and pauses to sniff a wild hyssop
and break open a bee hive for the honey of the years
and smack its lips on red currants

old cats should be wild and feed on field mice.
Joshua, I've nearly lost the essence of your name
and cannot hear the murmur of your time.
I stand throwing rocks at the stained glass
of your fervor knowing time ceases with the crash
the tinkle of the stones striking glass,
and all our blood between the installation
and the retribution has vaporized into the bite
of a single mosquito sucking my arm
in the summer breeze of this seedy cemetery

now sleep

RUSSELL LEONG

Aerogramme 1–5: Los Angeles

AEROGRAMME 1: Los Angeles

I confess
I did not open the first letter
for a week.
Not that I feared using a dictionary
but the eight-legged ideograms
were like crabs
scuttling after my past.

"Your cousins and nephews
were happy to scatter wine
with you
over the ancestral hillside. . . ."
the letter began.
(I see
them hack away
the green thicket
clearing a path
to bring gravestone markers
to light.
They hadn't climbed
here in months, or more.)

Later
Between spats
at tin spittoons
they splatter me
with questions.
"How old are you?
Are you married?
How many sons
did your father have?
Are they married?"
They press
bags of dried orange peel
at me
I answer with wine,
cigarettes & money.

AEROGRAMME 2.

"Your relatives
in Sunwui county
wish good health to you,
to your mother & brother.
By the way
you know that
free enterprise
is alive & well
in China, indeed
we would like
to open

a dry goods shop
but we lack capital.
Send as much as you can spare."

They did not name a figure
leaving it to my guilt or grace.
But I admitted none
for once, in Sunwui city
the county capital
I saw a photo exhibit
of toothy Chinese
from Indonesia,
Canada, Singapore,
San Francisco.

They had invested dollars
in a primary school here,
a textile factory there—
but I had no coined
compatriotism
to tender.

Instead
I xeroxed a photo
of my old uncle
the one in the polaroid
wearing the hand-me-down jacket,
earmuffs, and torn green sneakers.
"Buy him and auntie

winter coats
and divide the rest of the money,"
I wrote, alongside
the good side of his face
that was not twisted by stroke.

He looks me straight
in the eye
beyond a cold morning
to a day
right after the War.
"In 1947," he says
"I was sixteen.
Standing by the riverbank
I waited patiently
for the ferry
to come upstream
carrying U.N. rations
& your father.
He was the first
from California
to step upon village soil
after the Japanese
laid down their guns.
He came, ate, sprinkled
American scotch & water
on the gravestones
& left.
Months later, he

sent us that picture
of himself in a G.I. uniform—
We never heard from him again."

I blame the cold war.
My uncle nods.
And when I tell him that Father
has just died
he shakes his head
without surprise.

AEROGRAMME 3.

"Greetings
from the factory cooperative
in Sunwui City.
The family" my nephew began,
"hopes to buy a government condominium
Please send five thousand dollars—U.S.
Tomorrow."

I took it in stride.
Checked the horoscope
in the L.A. *Times*
but Virgo refused
to speculate that far.
Consulted close friends.
The ones from China said:
"Send the money,"

The ones from America said:
"Crazy, man."

I had split vision.
In my left eye—
a new village house
yellow tiles, concrete block walls
a slab floor without cracks.
Running water, interior pipes
& lightbulbs
electrifying every room.

In my right eye—
a Los Angeles barrio
red spanish tiles aglow
over a stucco bungalow
leaning from the last earthquake,
palm trees, taco trucks
smoggy orange sunsets—
At thirty times the price
of a condo in Canton.
I winced.
Waited.
Waivered.
Calculated
mortgage points
exchange rates:
Four U.S. dollars
to one Chinese.

Procrastination sped me

to the new year

forced open my hand.

I telexed money from L.A. Chinatown,

to Hong Kong, to Canton,

to Sunwui village.

A token, less

than what they wanted

after finding that

they stood second, or third

on the family tree—

not in direct line

from grandfather, but

offshoots

concocted further back.

AEROGRAMME 4.

"Dear cousin in Los Angeles

We pen this letter

on behalf of your aunt

who went with us

to sweep family graves

again.

We chopped our way

thru last year's branches

& wondered when

you would return.

For, as fate had it

as she climbed down the hill

Auntie met
a young lass,
still single
supple as a willow.
It's time to start a family
agreed?"

Struck by the thought
I slid
into my '71 Ford Maverick
and cruised down Hollywood Boulevard.
Hookers—of both sexes
were walking nowhere
squinting
against the sun
at four in the afternoon.

AEROGRAMME 5.

Differed from the rest.
The writing quicker.
"Sir
I know it's bold
of me to write you.
I'll be twenty-two this year.
Didn't your auntie tell you
we met on the mountain?
I apologize
for my lack of schooling

I'm a country girl.
But I'm healthy
and you're of age.
If you want to see
me the next time
you return
please answer
my letter."

On the upper left corner
a two-inch photo
of a ten-story hotel
topped by a revolving restaurant
above
the palmettos
& orange groves
caught my eye.
Where was her face?

This is the last aerogramme
I've received so far.
I never showed them
to anyone
though
upon my return
I had pressed
the polaroids, like leaves
into an album.

"They look like
real Chinese
peasants, don't they!"
my mother said.
"You should see
Sunwui one day,"
I told my brother.
"Someday," he said.

Flattened and forgotten
the aerogrammes
lost their edge
until yesterday
when the *New York Times*
reported that
the People's Republic—
through a U.S. Chinese businessman—
planned to export
Chinese workers
to harvest American farms.
This is what he said:
"exporting workers
is like exporting oil—
or silk slippers."
But what we need now is bodies—
he meant to say.

His words hit dirt
reviving my suspicions.
Maybe matters

like aerogrammes,

family reunions,

gravesweeping,

and revolving restaurants

rising from the delta mud—

were just

concessions for export—

like oil or silk slippers.

Only

after I returned

from China

did the idea collapse

in my head:

I swore off

grimy ancestral markers—

I wrote off

filial piety

as useless;

a fallen branch.

Yet

as keenly

as the blade

of the letter opener

that falls upon my hand

I await the arrival

of the next

immutable

aerogramme.

COLLEEN J. McELROY

This Is the Poem I Never Meant to Write

my grandmother
raised me Georgia style
a broken mirror
spilled salt
a tattered hemline
all add up to bad spirits
when she died, I learned to worship
stranger things
a faded textbook full of bad theories
has no spirit at all
now I've gone full circle
in a town some still call Bahía
the drumbeat of the alabés
echoes my grandmother's warnings
I watch the daughters of the candomblé
dance to the rhythms of ancient spirits
as the ceremony begins
my lungs expand
like gas-filled dirigibles
stretched latex-thin

my grandmother spoke
the language of this scene
the mystery and magic

of rich colors in a tapestry
of brown and black skin
white candles
a small reed boat
six bloody gamecocks
all bind this church to its African source
I follow my people past spirit houses
past tight Spanish streets
where houses are painted blue and white
like any Moorish town
when we reach the sea
water seems to flow uphill
tropical landscapes turn mustard yellow
and above us the moon swallows the night

this is the poem
I never meant to write
I am learning to worship
my grandmother's spirits
an old woman
splinters of wood embedded
in her black leathery cheeks
three crosses tattooed
on the fleshy black skin
of her upper arms
draws my picture upon her palm
in blue ink
then tells me we are all strangers
bound by the same spirit

I have gone home
in the dim light
my grandmother smiles

JOSEPHINE MILES

Doll

Though the willows bent down to shelter us where we played
House in the sandy acres, though our dolls,
Especially Lillian, weathered all the action,
I kept getting so much earlier home to rest
That medical consultation led to cast
From head to toe. It was a surprise for my parents
And so for me also, and I railed
Flat out in the back seat on the long trip home
In which three tires blew on our trusty Mitchell.
Home, in a slight roughhouse of my brothers,
It turned out Lillian had been knocked to the floor and broken
Across the face. Good, said my mother
In her John Deweyan constructive way,
Now you and Lillian can be mended together.
We made a special trip to the doll hospital
To pick her up. But, They can't fix her after all, my father
    said,

You'll just have to tend her with her broken cheek.
I was very willing. We opened the box, and she lay
In shards mixed among tissue paper. Only her eyes
Set loose on a metal stick so they would open
And close, opened and closed, and I grew seasick.

A friend of the family sent me a kewpie doll.
Later Miss Babcox the sitter,
After many repetitious card games,
Said, We must talk about bad things.
Let me tell you
Some of the bad things I have known in my life.
She did not ask me mine, I could not have told her.
Among the bad things in my life, she said,
Have been many good people, good but without troubles;
Her various stories tended
To end with transmigrations of one sort or another,
Dishonest riches to honest poverty; kings and queens
To indians over an adequate space of time.
Take this cat coming along here, she said,
A glossy black cat whom she fed her wages in salmon,
He is a wise one, about to become a person.
Come to think of it, possibly Lillian
Is about to become a cat.

She will have different eyes then, I said.
Obviously. Slanted, and what is more,
Able to see in the dark.

MURSALATA MUHAMMAD

Last Days of a Slow Cooker

Esau brought 13 halal chickens to her house last night
at 6:53a.m.,
right after Fajr, she
      started getting the birds ready
      for slow cooking over
      her 50-gallon drum grill, it cost her $80
      she still owes $20 to Kadija for helping her buy it
      she hasn't taken her medicine today
      it makes her *feel funny*
      she washes each piece
      feeling the barely cool flesh
      in every section of her hands except
      the fingertips of her left one
      an irritating reminder of her stroke last new year's eve
      she pokes holes in the pieces so the herbs soak in
      to the bone
      she places the bird into her special mixture:
      freshly mashed garlic plus garlic powder
      small cut pieces of onion plus onion powder
      curry, sage, lemon pepper, kosher salt, more garlic
by 10
she lights the coals, not too many because
she's slow cooking today
by 11
she and the coals are hot enough to begin grilling

she shifts back and forth from left-foot to right-foot, in front of
   the grill
she's too heavy for her current health status
     lying each browned-in-herb section of bird
     neatly on wire racks
     she looks sturdier than the back porch's dirty-gray
     foundation sloping dangerously
     towards the ground on the right
     it's a crooked house
     slowly word of mouth walks, rides bikes, buses, cars and
     uses cell phones, carrying smells of
     her slow cooking across Detroit
by 1:30pm
they arrive wordless, except for maybe
muffled "salaam-alaikum's," and one by one
pile food on the small green kitchen table
she knows who's been there by what they've left
     to be cooked
     for baking: pineapples—Marium; yams—Mustafa
     for frying: corn—Malik; okra—Kadija; squash (all colors)—
       Elijah
     for boiling: brown rice—Malika; more corn—Dawud
the steak is Rakman's there are only two because he knows
she doesn't like cooking beef
convinced mad cow disease is a plot
to kill poor people, especially black ones
he leaves only enough for himself with a note "it's halal"
she cooks it on a different grill
by 2:45
     the mysterious appearance of food stops

after all we do want to eat at some point today

the coals have reddened and their heat has risen almost as

high as the pressure pumping her blood

that continues to dumbfound Henry Ford Hospital's

ER doctors, who say

"we don't know why your mother is still conscious and able
    to talk, most people . . ."

ain't slow cookers, one of us replies

the doctors don't get it

by 6:15

her dicing, chopping, slicing, cutting has

brought by faces she hasn't seen in months, some years

all of them wanting to know "how you been?"and

commenting, "you look good as it smell in here"

by 7:30

the last of the slow cooked pieces of bird are

like her

done

by 7:33

children, grandchildren, great-grandchildren

expectant great-great-grandchildren, friends,

and friends of friends descend like

roaches on 254 pilgrim street, wearing

Muslim names like after-thoughts

no one notices

she has no appetite or if she did

there isn't one thing on the menu a

74 yr old high blood pressured, diseased heart

could safely ingest

by 9:15

she's dead

asleep when latecomers

    struggle to rouse her asking

    "when you cookin, agin?"

    she considers my offer to come

    live with me but

    would rather a massive stroke

    make that decision or

    death null and void that it

    completely

    she answers

    "I don't know, when I get some res' I guess"

    "Ok" they say, "see you next week"

NAOMI QUIÑÓNEZ

My Shattered Sister

Sister, I wish to be the waters
of insistent rivers
the long arms of the Colorado
that reach past those man-made borders
to the surging Amazon currents.

Is not your blood my blood
whether coursing through veins
of family I have never met
or spilled on the land
of a continent we share?
My blood is yours,
we are the bleeding twins.
You are the southern sister
veiled in oppressive shadow
that covers your enigmatic light,
I, the Northern twin,
watch angrily
with fists clenched tight
the cancer that invades
our ancestors' defiled dreams.
Your cries become deafening
as the distance disappears.
Deserts burn,
jungles part silent,
your broken body
appears before me
in a paid advertisement
on the 11 o'clock news
as you break the zombie stupor
of televised distraction.
You are the drumming noise
of my sleepless nights.
The dancing voices of children
become a mother's anguished cries

and ricochet off
the prefabricated fortresses
we have so carefully constructed.
You haunt me sister
when I pretend.
it could never happen here
or as I turn the pages
and read the countless headlines:
Latino family of 12 living in 2-room shack,
Health care denied campesinos,
Latino unemployment doubles.
Somewhere a warm wind whirls
past our neon-lit hopes,
it is your breath sister
carrying the scent
of ashes and blood
as your voice becomes the river
that connects us.
And we all walk quieter
in the clutches of the North
when we hear the splintered echoes
of America to the South.

LUIS J. RODRÌGUEZ

Hungry

My wife left me, taking the two kids
and everything
but the stereo, TV and a few dishes.
Later in this squalid hour,
I began an affair
with my wife's best friend.
But she already had three kids and no man
and talked about love and marriage,
and I didn't know how to get out of it,
being also an alcoholic.
Soon I couldn't pay the rent
so I kept getting notices in death tones,
insinuating broken bones or whatever.
My friend Franco helped me sneak
out of the place.
Franco and me arrived in the middle of the night,
and loaded what I had onto a pickup truck.
I would come back
on other late nights to get the mail.
And the woman, who was alone with three kids
and looking for a husband,
kept leaving notes,
and I kept throwing them away.
But the hunger had just begun.

My only property of value was a 1954
red Chevy in mint condition.
It had the original skirts, whitewalls,
and chrome hood ornament.
What a prize!
I never wanted to part with it,
even as layoff slips and parking tickets
accumulated on the dashboard,
even when I found myself living with Mom and Dad
and the '54 Chevy got stashed out in back.
But the hunger and the drinking
and looking for love in all the wrong faces
blurred into a sort of blindness.
I stared out the back window,
at that red Chevy,
and thought how it resembled a large steak
with egg yolks for headlights.
No, no, I couldn't do it;
I couldn't turn my back on it now.
The days withered away
and again I looked out that window,
with Mom yelling behind me
about getting a job,
and I could taste that last scotch,
that last carnitas burrito,
and perhaps take in the stale scent
of a one-room apartment somewhere.
Then the hunger became a fever.
The fever a pain in my head.

And as soon as some dude with 200 bucks came along,

I sold it. God almighty,

I sold my red Chevy!

For 200 bucks!

For nothing, man.

Oh, I thought it would help

stop my wife's face

in every reflection;

her friend's staring out of my coffee cup.

That it would help hold me

for more than a week,

and end the curses

ringing in my ears.

I sold it! My red Chevy.

Prized possession.

200 bucks.

Gone forever.

Days later, the 200 bucks spent,

I was still hungry.

BRYNN NOELLE SAITO

Turkey People

Other familiar monsters surface along with my white republican
    uncle
to tell me what they really think about guns and art.
In their arms, they carry love and chocolate.

My capri-clad mother balances on her skinny ankles,
while searching for anything interesting to say to her frumpy
    sister-in-law
who is coughing up sincere attempts at political correctness.

The Korean matriarch crosses her long legs, fiddles with her thick
    jewelry,
and runs her bony fingers through the hair of her newly born and
    nearly blonde
grandchild. Oh the wonder of acceptance.

Everyone and their perfect english will dance on the linoleum,
    smell like cinnamon.
Everyone will nibble the bird, inhale the tamales, dissect the sushi,
and breathe through the screaming in their peculiar heads.

JOAN SELF

Quill Holler Waller

Uncle Jimmy flies in from Hollywood,
suitcase full of dope, smiling wide and ready
to celebrate, or commiserate, Papa Jim's
dying day. September's timeless wake,
a weeklong wallow, we remember him.
White lightning mouths sing praise
in the crackling breeze of the bonfire waves.

Mama dresses up as Sadie in the night
Long black wig, buckteeth, she strums
her busted guitar, stuffs up her breasts,
asks us did we go to the church-meetin today.
Leaning into sister, brother, uncle, we
make up new verses for her songs, stare
at an empty whisky bottle in the flames,
listen for Russell's jaw-harp twang,
melt our voices across the banjo strings.

Wake up in early morning heat, dried grass
stuck to our eyelids. Smoky shirt-smell gets us
up to the porch for breakfast.
Buttermilk biscuits, fresh squeezed
orange and grapefruit juice.

Kids squeal from the tickle monster's arms
into the kitchen, under Tomi's apron,
round the cutting board, out the screen door.
Jimmie Rodgers yodels from a radio top the fridge.

Hor'shoes in the afternoon, steamy
rhubarb under the yellow maple
Appalachia sun sets Quill Hollow
plenty of time yet to say good-bye.

ANNE SEXTON

The Truth the Dead Know

For my mother, born March 1902, died March 1959
and my father, born February 1900, died June 1959

Gone, I say and walk from church,
refusing the stiff procession to the grave,
letting the dead ride alone on the hearse.
It is June. I am tired of being brave.

We drive to the Cape. I cultivate

myself where the sun gutters from the sky,
where the sea swings in like an iron gate
and we touch. In another country people die.

My darling, the wind falls in like stones
from the whitehearted water and when we touch
we enter touch entirely. No one's alone.
Men kill for this, or for as much.

And what of the dead? They lie without shoes
in their stone boats. They are more like stone
than the sea would be if it stopped. They refuse
to be blessed, throat, eye and knucklebone.

CHARLES SIMIC

The Elders

I go to great troubles.
Bareheaded,
I visit them first thing in the morning.
Their gloomy servant ushers me in.
I, the poor cousin—
They, my benefactors

Standing with their stove-pipe hats
In a circle of splendid bloodhounds,
In a circle of sharp-nosed women.

The rain is pouring down, the rain . . .
Inside, their steps are slow, arthritic.
A slight greeting and I'm shown into the corner
Where I sit watching their pale hands,
Their hands with many tiny blue veins,
With many long and sharp fingernails,
While the curtains billow and billow
As if birds, as if large birds were caught in them.

Sights that make everyone sigh,
Except for me, interested as I am
Only in their beautiful daughter
Who touched me on the way in
With the same finger
That will loosen the button above her breasts,
In the evening
When the lights are low.

SUSIE SILOOK

Uncle Good Intentions

He stepped off the plane shaking
and went to the nearest bar for a quick
one or two shots of medicine.

He said he was relieved
he was
to find his long lost sisters

even more relieved to find
they were not bow-legged
and pigeon toed little
Native women
as he had feared.

His half sisters.

all these years he hadn't seen them.
since their mother took to the sea
that day his, their, father caught her
beating him with his hip waders.

Said he was the reason they'd fought
Dad gave him permission to go fishing
but no one told that

mean little Eskimo woman
Susie
that

so she whipped him *good.*

My mother was born at sea
heading back to Alaska with a mother
who was a runner.

She was running from an Indian boarding school
when she begged my grandfather to help her escape
and he helped her and
himself to a mother for his sons.

My family predicament
according to half uncle Doug
read like this:
Carol was a shameful unwed mother
Johnny a no good womanizer
spreading his precious seed and
Rose was nothing but a nigger lover.

Said the only children he liked
were Barry and me.

The only children he never met were
Barry and me.

Asked my mother who she felt she
belonged to
her white
or Eskimo
side.

When she said Eskimo
he said didn't blame her
cause that's who raised her.

He liked his half brother Walter, though,
cause Walter could drink like a man,
you know.

Said only that no one was ever gonna
kill *him* in a bar
when asked what happened to
their father, Mr. Faegins,
that man with the accent
or their other brother Clairmont.

Told them their father had
searched high and low
for them after
Susie ran.

That mean little Eskimo woman.

My mother was happy to see
him coming
and happier to
see him going,
long lost
Uncle Doug of the
good Catholic intentions.

CATHY SONG

Easter: Wahiawa, 1959

1

The rain stopped for one afternoon.
Father brought out
his movie camera and for a few hours
we were all together
under a thin film
that separated the rain showers
from that part of the earth
like a hammock
held loosely by clothespins.

Grandmother took the opportunity
to hang the laundry
and Mother and my aunts
filed out of the house
in pedal pushers and poodle cuts,
carrying the blue washed eggs.

Grandfather kept the children
penned in on the porch,
clucking at us in his broken English
whenever we tried to peek
around him. There were bread crumbs
stuck to his blue gray whiskers.

I looked from him to the sky,
a membrane of egg whites
straining under the weight
of the storm that threatened
to break.

We burst loose from Grandfather
when the mothers returned
from planting the eggs
around the soggy yard.
He followed us,
walking with stiff but sturdy legs.
We dashed and disappeared
into bushes,
searching for the treasures;

the hard-boiled eggs
which Grandmother had been simmering
in vinegar and blue color all morning.

    2

When Grandfather was a young boy
in Korea,
it was a long walk
to the riverbank,
where, if he were lucky,
a quail egg or two
would gleam from the mud
like gigantic pearls.
He could never eat enough
of them.

It was another long walk
through the sugarcane fields
of Hawaii,
where he worked for eighteen years,
cutting the sweet stalks
with a machete. His right arm
grew disproportionately large
to the rest of his body.
He could hold three
grandchildren in that arm.

I want to think
that each stalk that fell
brought him closer
to a clearing,
to that palpable field
where from the porch
to the gardenia hedge
that day he was enclosed
by his grandchildren,
scrambling around him,
for whom he could at last buy
cratefuls of oranges,
basketfuls of sky blue eggs.

I found three that afternoon.
By evening, it was raining hard.
Grandfather and I skipped supper.
Instead, we sat on the porch
and I ate what he peeled
and cleaned for me.
The scattering of the delicate
marine-colored shells across his lap
was something like what the ocean gives
the beach after a rain.

PHILLINA SUN ·

Untitled

In the living room sit the men,
nuzzling glasses of fine amber cognac,
their murmuring
overwhelmed by feminine laughter
a honey seeping through
the crack of the kitchen door.

Not at all the naïve brides they had married
many babies ago,
once girls of virgin hips, now mothers,
many aunts,
priestesses all.

A kitchen is their temple,
their goddess is a stove,
their chants unwritten recipes
taught generation after generation,
from mother to daughter
(though this daughter is mute,
for she knows only English,
a language of frustration,
not Cambodian,
a flock of doves in flight)

A man stumbles in,
uneasy invader
in search of more cognac, another glass, ice cubes,
to flee, under a fusillade of teasing.

A noisy laughing procession of women exits the kitchen,
carrying the fragrant rewards of worship,
a feast to stretch bellies tight
delicate-boned deep-fried quail,
broiled fish (their skins crackling brown) in green tamarind
   sauce, pickled vegetables, to wrinkle tongues,
saffron-colored pancakes, stuffed with crumbled pork and sauteed
   onions,
my mother's special stew of tomatoes, peas, and slivered chicken.
Longan white and round and sweet,
Spoons to scrape the breast-soft insides of split canteloupes.

JANNIFER TRAIG

For My Sister

For the first two years of her life I tried to kill her:
sat on her doughy organs
pushed her stroller into traffic
and gave her plastic bags to play with.

But the pink blob would not turn blue.
She would not die.
My tyranny had only strengthened her.
I had made her stronger than myself.

When she learned to talk we called a truce.
Then she learned to swear and ruled the block, ruled especially me.
I chased behind her for years with love
the first born who didn't run as fast.

Now she comes home for holidays
flies in from LA wearing hip-boots and a swagger.
Then kisses our parents on both cheeks, European-style
and tells them we're taking the car.

I still don't have my license.
She drives like a demon and parks on the grade-school playground.
We sit on the swings while smoking cigarettes
then makes me kiss her once to see if she has Marlboro breath.

I think she must have usurped my birthright.
Maybe she mugged it from me
or maybe extorted it for a cereal-box prize; I don't remember
and anyway it doesn't matter.

I would have given it to her for nothing
for a kiss for free
we know by now
that I would do anything for her.

ERNESTO TREJO

The Cloud Unfolding

It starts with the picture of my grandfather,
machine gunned in his car, Packard De Luxe, 1923.
A snapshot with poor composition, slightly
out of focus, it holds the forty-three
bullets that pushed for light or air
& which now find their black spaces and obey
our eyes. His last curse will never leave
this picture, his body will never
leave that car, his blood will forever
cake on the red upholstery
(someone pulled you out of the car, someone else
unfolded a blanket over your face not knowing
that you wanted to see that cloud unfold
over the whole sky
or gather into rain & flood your eyes.
Your last curse gave way to visions of battle,
of other men, never yourself,
dying in the heat & the dust).
In El Paso my grandfather once stayed up
all night & when the sun rose he shaved the goatee,
tapped over his heart & felt the fake passport.
Later he emerged from the hotel a businessman,
like Lenis, & walked six blocks to the train station,
a black mushroom in the fog,

a piece of shit under the sky of El Paso
or Geneva, a sky that ate his shirts & sucked
his head into a chisel of anger.

Further back, in one autumn the Eiffel went up,
a symbol of itself, & every washerwoman
felt proud of her city
(But one night, in 1936, the tower would crack,
collapsing over Los Angeles, against the pavement
dressed with spit & yellow newspapers
that told the Negros *Burn, Generation of Vipers*
& the Mexicans *Go Back Where You Came From.*
Roosevelt, the syphilitic Jew, will sell
to the Germans tomorrow at 10:15. My father
is in his kitchen, dropping ice cubes in a glass
of water, when the phone rings & a man
tells him that his bar is in flames.
When my father arrives at the bar, nine years
of good luck go up in smoke & someone tells him
it was the Negroes, your brother refused them credit.
My father nods, not knowing why, & stands
there for hours following the slow cloud from his bar
until the sun silhouettes the church two blocks away
& he thinks *that shadow is a bad omen*).
Father, for the rest of your life, in Mexico,
you never mentioned the fire
but spoke of flappers, of Roosevelt, of Chaplin
devoured by a clock on his way to work.

RONALD WALLACE

The Fat of the Land

Gathered in the heavy heat of Indiana,
we've come from all over this great
country, one big happy family, back from
wherever we've spread ourselves too thin.
A cornucopia of cousins and uncles, grand-
parents and aunts, nieces and nephews, expanding.
All day we laze on the oily beach;
we eat all the smoke-filled evening:
shrimp dip and crackers,
Velveeta cheese and beer,
handfuls of junk food, vanishing.
We sit at card tables, examining
our pudgy hands, piling in
hot fudge and double-chocolate
brownies, strawberry shortcake and cream,
as the lard-ball children
sluice from room to room.
O the loveliness of so much loved flesh,
the litany of split seams and puffed sleeves,
sack dresses and Sansabelt slacks,
dimpled knees and knuckles, the jiggle
of triple chins. O the gladness
that only a family understands,
our fat smiles dancing

as we play our cards right.

Our jovial conversation blooms and booms

in love's large company, as our sweet

words ripen and split their skins:

mulberry, fabulous, flotation,

phlegmatic, plumbaginous.

Let our large hearts attack us,

our blood run us off the scale.

We're huge and whole on this simmering night,

battened against the small skinny

futures that must befall all of us,

the gray thin days and the noncaloric dark.

TERENCE WINCH

Six Families of Puerto Ricans

I guess it was the summer of nineteen

fifty five   I just got back from Rockaway

the first thing I heard when I got back

was the news that

six families of Puerto Ricans had moved

into nineteen fifteen Daly Avenue   the Mitchells'

building   as time went on

more and more pee ars moved into
the neighborhood   there was great hostility
on both sides   once on the fourth of July
Martin Conlon threw some cherry bombs
and ash cans through the windows of the Puerto
Ricans   they were just spics to us
I remember a Puerto Rican shooting
at me and some friends with a bee bee gun
from his roof   you could hear the bee bees
bouncing off the cars   bodegas opened
on Tremont Avenue   Spanish kids dropped
water balloons on Irish kids   there was
a Sunday mass in Spanish in the church basement
this was worse than a potato famine
and the Irish started moving out
Mr. Zayas moved in next door to us
where the Gormans had lived   Mr. Zayas
had a son named Efrain who married
a beautiful girl named Carmen   Puerto Rican men
played dominoes on the sidewalk
when me and my father left the block
in the fall of nineteen sixty eight
we were among a handful of Irish still
in the neighborhood   things were so bad
by then that even the respectable Puerto Ricans
like Mr. Zayas were long gone
we used to think Puerto Ricans
weren't too far from being animals
even if they were Catholics

NELLIE WONG

It's in the Blood

We never asked to be mysterious.
We never asked to be inscrutable.
Still untold stories, untold histories.
Still the unknown unknown.
Retrieve burnt letters, receipts, bills,
anything written, anything spoken?
Our dreams in bones and ashes?
To be seen and heard.
To be known but not merely by our many names.
Being presumptuous I speak for myself.
Others who remain silent own their own tongues.

Li Hong's ma ma died when Li Hong was an infant.
Ma said that Li Hong's ma ma was a little crazy.
The villagers said so. Li Hong likes to eat chicken feet.
Li Hong smiles, a childwoman.
Li Hong loves babies.
Li Hong is my sister.

Li Keng remembers Angel Island, the bright lights
of Oakland and San Francisco.
She said that Bah Bah sent fruit and candy
to cheer them up behind bars.
They were lucky, imprisoned

on Angel Island only four days.

The other immigrants waved goodbye,

some etched poems into the walls.

Li Keng learned to eat cheese and tomatoes

on the President Hoover.

To this day Li Keng cannot stomach butter or milk.

Li Keng is my sister.

Lai Wah remembers the ship. She was three years old.

The immigration officer asked her: What is your name?

Lai Wah answered: If you don't tell me yours,

I won't tell you mine.

Lai Wah smiled behind straight bangs.

Lai Wah remembers nothing of her years in China.

Lai Wah is my sister.

Seow Hong Gee is my father.

Suey Ting Yee Gee is my mother.

From 1933 to 1965 Suey Ting Gee was known as Theo Quee Gee,

a sister's name, a sister's paper that Bah Bah bought

!o bring his wife and daughters over.

Theo Quee Gee was supposed to be my father's sister,

my sister's aunt.

This was 1933. In 1924 the law said that Chinese men

could bring no wives to the United States.

Theo Quee Gee was unmarried but we knew better.

Nellie Wong is my name. I was never Nellie Gee

but we knew better.

When my sister's aunt, that is, Theo Quee Gee, my mother,
got pregnant, to bear a child out of wedlock
was out of the question.
So Theo Quee Gee got married, by faking
a marriage certificate, by *marrying* a man
named Sheng Wong who agreed to appear
on paper to be my father.
Shame to the outside world avoided.
Secrets depending on which side of the fence.
When I was five and entered Chinese school,
Lai Oy became my Chinese name.

Leslie Wong was born after me.
Ai yah, another girl! That was my mother's wail.
Ma and Bah Bah named Leslie Li Ying.
Her nicname was *thlom gawk ngon,*
three-corner eye.
Leslie Wong is my sister.

Florence Wong was born after Leslie.
Ai yah, another girl! That was my mother's wail.
So no more Li's, so no more daughters
with Chinese names beginning with Li,
beginning with *beautiful.*
So Florence was named Ling Oy to change my mother's luck.
Florence Wong is my sister.

William Wong was born after Florence.
Finally a boy! That was Ma's and Bah Bah's joy.

Thankful their daughter, Ling Oy,
brought them their son.
Bah Bah gave a month-old party
to shave William's head.
Eggs were dyed red, friends and relatives filled the house.
We drank chicken whiskey, gnawed vinegar pigs' feet.
Ling Oy was the magic that Ma and Bah Bah decided.
To beget (a son), to beget (a son) to love
and the heavens answered.
Wah Keung is William Wong's Chinese name.
William Wong is my brother.

I was never sure who I really was.
My school records showed that I was Nellie Wong,
that my father and Leslie's father
and Florence's father and William's father
was a man named Sheng Wong.
We told no lies, only the truth
as we were forced to.

My three older sisters were supposed to be my cousins.
My father was supposed to be my uncle.
My mother was supposed to be my father's sister.
When Theo Quee Gee *confessed* her illegal status,
she became Suey Ting Gee, my father's legal wife.
But it was too late. Bah Bah died in 1961.

Now I use the name, Nellie Wong.
Now I search for all the names that gave me life.

SPECKLED RED

The Dirty Dozens

Well I want all you women folks to fall in line
Shake your shimmy like I'm shaking mine
You shake your shimmy and you shake it fast
You can't shake your shimmy, shake your yes yes yes

      Now you's a dirty mistreater
      A robber and a cheater
      Slip you in the dozens
      Your poppy is your cousin
      Your mama do's the lawdy lawd

Yonder go your mama going out across the field
Running and a-shaking like an automobile
I hollered at your mama and I told her to wait
She slipped away from me like a Cadillac 8

      Now she's a running mistreater
      A robber and a cheater
      Poppy is her cousin
      Slip you in the dozens
      Her mama do's the lawdy lawd

I like your mama, I like your sister too
I *did* like your daddy, but your daddy wouldn't do

Met your daddy on the corner the other day
You know about that, that he was funny that way

> So now he's a funny mistreater
> A robber and a cheater
> Slip you in the dozens
> Poppy is your cousin
> Your mama do's the lawdy lawd

God made him an elephant, he made him stout
He wasn't satisfied until he made him a snout
He made his snout just as long as a rail
He wasn't satisfied until he made him a tail
He made his tail just to fan the fly
He wasn't satisfied until he made some eye
He made his eye just to look over the grass
He wasn't satisfied: he made his yes yes yes
Made his yes yes yes and didn't get it fixed
He wasn't satisfied until it made him sick
It made him sick, lord, it made him well
You know by that that the elephant caught hell

> Now he's a dirty mistreater
> A robber and a cheater
> Slip you in the dozens
> Your poppy is your cousin
> Your mama do's the lawdy lawd

Now now boys, say, you ain't acting fair

You know 'bout that, you got real bad hair
Your face is all hid, now your back's all bare
If you ain't doing the bobo, what's your head doing there?

> Now you's a dirty mistreater
> A robber and a cheater
> Slip you in the dozens
> Now your poppy is your cousin
> And your mama do's the lawdy lawd

Now your little sister, well, she asked me to kiss her
I told her to wait until she got a little bigger
She got a little bigger, says now I could kiss her
You know 'bout that, boy, that I didn't miss her

> She's a dirty mistreater
> A robber and a cheater
> Slip you in the dozens
> Now your poppy is your cousin
> And your mama do's the lawdy lawd

Now the first three months there she did very well
The next three months she began to raise a little hell
The next three months, said she got real tough
You know by that that she was strutting that stuff

> Now she's a dirty mistreater
> A robber and a cheater
> Slip you in the dozens

Now your poppy is your cousin
And your mama do's the lawdy lawd

Now I like your mama, but she wouldn't do this
I hit her across the head with my great big fist
The clock's on the shelf going tick tick tick
Your ma's out on the street doing I don't know which

Four five six seven eight nine and ten
I like your mama but she's got too many men
Ashes to ashes, now it's sand to sand
Every time I see her she's got a brand new man

She's a dirty mistreater
A robber and a cheater
Slip you in the dozens
Now your poppy is your cousin
And your mama do's the lawdy lawd

POLITICS

Politics and polemics: these days my students seem to think these are subjects that one is supposed to avoid when writing poetry. They've been told that politics, polemics, and real poetry don't mix by amnesiac middle-class critics whose grandfathers, grand-mothers, fathers, and mothers might well have participated in some of the bloodiest labor strikes on record, or spent their spare time in crowded rooms parsing obscure radical pamphlets. Do politics and art mix? That depends on the artist. Shelley, Byron, and Milton, touted as among the greatest writers in the English language, all wrote political poetry. Jesus of Nazareth, considered the founder of Western civilization, totally lost it when making speeches against hypocrisy. Although students are taught that you aren't supposed to be angry, traditionally poetry has conveyed a healthy dose of anger and invective. (Take a look at Milton's "In Defense of the English People," or his description of the pope as "the triple tyrant" in "On the Late Massacre in Piedmont.")

Political poetry is an honored tradition in Europe, Africa, and Asia. The poets in this collection continue that tradition. Cecil Brown writes about racial profiling in his "Integrating the Strawberry Swimming Pool in 1998," a work that employs irony and humor as it shows that the fight for public accommodations first waged by Frederick Douglass and Ida B. Wells continues. Brown also uses one of the country's homegrown verse forms, the Blues, to address the sort of humiliation that many African Americans, Native Americans, Hispanics, and Asian Americans are subjected to daily by people whose limited education makes them suspicious and often hostile to those who are different. Frank Marshall Davis also uses humor in "Giles Johnson, Ph.D.," a poem about a man who belonged to a generation of African Americans whose talents and potential were wasted in a racist society. Langston Hughes's brilliant and exciting "Advertisement for the Waldorf-Astoria," which was dismissed as a political poem and criticized by his patron, Carl Van Vechten, is as contemporary today as the day it was written. Hughes demands our attention as he draws a contrast between the lives of the rich and the famous and the downtrodden and obscure. Will Heford's and Kenneth Fearing's indictments of corporate greed are also timely as we witness continual examples of disgusting greed and excess by CEOs who've left thousands ruined. Muriel Rukeyser's and Cordelia Candelaria's comments about the media also ring true.

In "And in the U.S.A.," Miguel Algarín writes about the criminal injustice system that packs the prisons with blacks and Hispanics. He asks us to consider the humanity of the people who are jailed, some of whom confess to their crimes under coercion.

In "Centennial Year for the Spirits," Sister Goodwin writes about the cultural theft and imperialism that artists, from totem-pole carvers to Little Richard, know so well. The practice of mainstream artists, and scholars, helping themselves to the creations (and even, in certain museums, the body parts) of others, without the permission of the donors, is a denial of the donor's humanity.

Denise Levertov asks us to consider the humanity of those abroad who are often dismissed as "collateral damage" when the United States wages a high-tech, state-of-the-art, remote-control war against defenseless civilians. In "This Passover or the Next I Will Never Be in Jerusalem," Hilton Obenzinger uses dramatic dialogue to pose that eternal question: should one be loyal to one's convictions, or to one's "blood"? The head of the family tries to corral the skeptical narrator into conformity, but at the end of the meal, the skeptic still has questions.

Miguel Algarín

And in the U.S.A.
(State of emergency in New Brunswick, N.J.)

If something is not done
Criminal Justice will collapse,
or worse, there will be riots in jails
just like those in Essex, Union and Bergen Counties.
Prisons overflow, they can't hold,
there's no space, the courts dismiss everything,
only extreme cases are retained,
though it's still difficult to hold on to
people who react with brutal crimes.
The hitch is in the rapid dismissals,
can't keep up with those handcuffed,
the courts are jammed,
the list of fugitives grows.
If beds aren't found,
the jails'll explode,
set on fire by inmates
who yield to violent passions.

CECIL BROWN

Integrating the Strawberry Swimming Pool in 1998

Strawberry Canyon Swimming Pool,
ain't been there befo'
Strawberry Canyon Swimming Pool,
ain't been there befo'
I been once, they don't want no blacks up there
Ain't goin' there no mo'

In the merry month of May, 1998
I was swimming in the lane, at the Strawberry swimming pool,
When I saw two cops in blue, black Gestapo boots, waitin at the end
Isn't it strange, I'm thinking, how they now have cops everywhere
One of them beckoned to me, I thinking, it's a joke.
Can we speak to you, he demanded with twisted gesture
What is it? I asked
The short dark-haired one says, Are you a professor here?
Yes, I answer
Where's your office, the tall, old, yaller-haired one asked.
My office? I'm not teaching now. What's the beef?
We got a report that somebody's been tellin'
People they're a professor.
What has that got to do with me?

Strawberry Canyon Swimming Pool,
ain't been there befo'

Strawberry Canyon Swimming Pool,

ain't been there befo'

What's your status here?

I'm a researcher postdoctoral

With a Ph.D. from UC Berkeley

So what? the blonde one says, I ain't got nothing but a eight
    grade

Can you prove it?

I motioned to the bundle of clothes at the other end of the pool.

Strawberry Canyon Swimming Pool,

ain't been there befo'

Strawberry Canyon Swimming Pool,

ain't been there befo'

As we walk pass the white women in their bikinis

The short dark one glares at them and back at me.

Strawberry Canyon Swimming Pool,

ain't been there befo'

Strawberry Canyon Swimming Pool,

ain't been there befo'

I take out my wallet, show him my identification

Sit down, he told me in an icy voice, as he calls my

Name in on the phone.

Both stand with their hands on their guns Strawberry

Canyon Swimming Pool,

ain't been there befo'

Strawberry Canyon Swimming Pool,
ain't been there befo'

I am grilled, told by one cop
Don't be talkin' to anybody up here
We have complaints that somebody's
been actin' unsociable.
Somebody called us
Said, "There he goes again!"

But that's not me
No answer, but a stare
Finally, the short dark-haired one hands me back
My licenses and UC Berkeley identification
You can go on with your swim, he said.

Strawberry Canyon Swimming Pool,
ain't been there befo'
Strawberry Canyon Swimming Pool,
ain't been there befo'
They don't want no blacks up there
Ain't goin' there no mo'

I sat there in the blazing sun
Stunned.
Who called them? Which lifeguard?
Which one of the whites who guard the place
Who said, "There he goes again"?

Not more than a few hours
I asked the Department of _____
To teach a course in James Baldwin
No, we have no money to pay for a Baldwin course.

Now I see the connection.
The threshold guardians keep Baldwin out
The police guard the swimming pool.
The police are working for the professors,
My liberal collegues,
The heads of the departments, too
Grin in your face, how do you do
Baldwin is kept out, just's I am kept out

We pay taxes, they get the classes
We have the melanin in our skins, but they get to lie in the sun in
The Strawberry swimming pool

Strawberry Canyon Swimming Pool,
ain't been there befo'
Strawberry Canyon Swimming Pool,
ain't been there befo'
They don't want no blacks up there
Ain't goin' there no mo'

Cordelia Candelaria

Killers

The paper's merciless in reminding us
who shares the planet with our averageness.
They frighten and fascinate.
We have to read their stories.
We have to keep them in front of us
assaulting someone else, tearing her lingerie
to newsprint shreds, shooting his left ventricle
precisely. You wonder what they do. How
they live their lives. Up early? Late?
Flowered sheets? Jam on their toast?
When it rains like tonight heavy and cold
do they sit cozy somewhere
reading poems or writing them or plotting how
to kill you couplets of murder, cups of rum
in front of a snug fire somewhere
warming toes, making small talk, marking time.

LORNA DEE CERVANTES

Poem for the Young White Man
Who Asked Me How I, an
Intelligent, Well-Read Person,
Could Believe in the War
Between Races

In my land there are no distinctions.
The barbed wire politics of oppression
have been torn down long ago. The only reminder
of past battles, lost or won, is a slight
rutting in the fertile fields.

In my land
people write poems about love,
full of nothing but contented childlike syllables.
Everyone reads Russian short stories and weeps.
There are no boundaries.
There is no hunger, no
complicated famine or greed.

I am not a revolutionary.
I don't even like political poems.
Do you think I can believe in a war between races?
I can deny it. I can forget about it
when I'm safe,
living on my own continent of harmony

and home, but I am not
there.

I believe in revolution
because everywhere the crosses are burning,
sharp-shooting goose-steppers round every corner,
there are snipers in the schools . . .
(I know you don't believe this.
You think this is nothing
but faddish exaggeration. But they
are not shooting at you.)

I'm marked by the color of my skin.
The bullets are discrete and designed to kill slowly.
They are aiming at my children.
These are facts.
Let me show you my wounds: my stumbling mind, my
"excuse me" tongue, and this
nagging preoccupation
with the feeling of not being good enough.

These bullets bury deeper than logic.
Racism is not intellectual.
I can not reason these scars away.

Outside my door
there is a real enemy
who hates me.

I am a poet
who yearns to dance on rooftops,
to whisper delicate lines about joy
and the blessings of human understanding.
I try. I go to my land, my tower of words and
bolt the door, but the typewriter doesn't fade out
the sounds of blasting and muffled outrage.
My own days bring me slaps on the face.
Every day I am deluged with reminders
that this is not
my land
and this is my land.

I do not believe in the war between races.

but in this country
there is war.

FRANK MARSHALL DAVIS

Giles Johnson, Ph.D.

Giles Johnson
had four college degrees
knew the whyfore of this
the wherefore of that
could orate in Latin
or cuss in Greek
and, having learned such things
he died of starvation
because he wouldn't teach
and he couldn't porter.

W. E. B. DuBois

The Song of the Smoke

I am the Smoke King
I am black!
I am swinging in the sky,
I am wringing worlds awry;

I am the thought of the throbbing mills,
I am the soul of the soul-toil kills,
Wraith of the ripple of trading rills;
Up I'm curling from the sod,
I am whirling home to God;
    I am the Smoke King
    I am black.

    I am the Smoke King,
    I am black!
I am wreathing broken hearts,
I am sheathing love's light darts;
    Inspiration of iron times
    Wedding the toil of toiling climes,
    Shedding the blood of bloodless crimes—
Lurid lowering 'mid the blue,
Torrid towering toward the true,
    I am the Smoke King,
    I am black.

    I am the Smoke King,
    I am black!
I am darkening with song,
I am hearkening to wrong!
    I will be black as blackness can—
    The blacker the mantle, the mightier the man!
    For blackness was ancient ere whiteness began.
I am daubing God in night,
I am swabbing Hell in white:

I am the Smoke King

I am black.

I am the Smoke King,

I am black!

I am cursing ruddy morn,

I am hearsing hearts unborn:

Souls unto me are as stars in a night,

I whiten my black men—I blacken my white!

What's the hue of a hide to a man in his might?

Hail! great, gritty, grimy hands—

Sweet Christ, pity toiling lands!

I am the Smoke King

I am black.

MARI EVANS

Speak the Truth to the People

Speak the truth to the people

Talk sense to the people

Free them with reason

Free them with honesty

Free the people with Love and Courage and Care for their Being

Spare them the fantasy

Fantasy enslaves

A slave is enslaved

Can be enslaved by unwisdom

Can be enslaved by black unwisdom

Can be re-enslaved while in flight from the enemy

Can be enslaved by his brother whom he loves

His brother whom he trusts

His brother with the loud voice

And the unwisdom

Speak the truth to the people

It is not necessary to green the heart

Only to identify the enemy

It is not necessary to blow the mind

Only to free the mind

To identify the enemy is to free the mind

A free mind has no need to scream

A free mind is ready for other things

To BUILD black schools

To BUILD black children

To BUILD black minds

To BUILD black love

To BUILD black impregnability

To BUILD a strong black nation

To BUILD.

Speak the truth to the people.

Spare them the opium of devil-hate.

They need no trips on honky-chants.

Move them instead to a BLACK ONENESS.

A black strength which will defend its own
Needing no cacophony of screams for activation.
A black strength which attacks the laws
exposes the lies disassembles the structure
and ravages the very foundation of evil.

Speak the truth to the people
To identify the enemy is to free the mind
Free the mind of the people
Speak to the mind of the people
Speak Truth.

KENNETH FEARING

1933

You heard the gentleman, with automatic precision, speak the
     truth.
   Cheers. Triumph.
   And then mechanically it followed the gentleman lied.
   Deafening applause. Flashlights, cameras, microphones.
     Floral tribute. Cheers.

Down Mrs. Hogan's alley, your hand with others reaching
     among the ashes, cinders, scrapiron, garbage, you

found the rib of sirloin wrapped in papal documents.
Snatched it. Yours by right, the title clear.
Looked up. Saw lips twitch in the smiling head thrust from
the museum window. "A new deal."

And ran. Escaped. You returned the million dollars. You
restored the lady's virginity.
You were decorated 46 times in rapid succession by the
King of Italy. Took a Nobel prize. Evicted again, you
went downtown, slept at the movies, stood in the
breadline, voted yourself a limousine.
Rage seized the Jewish Veterans of Foreign Wars. In
footnotes, capitals, Latin, italics, the poet of the
Sunday supplements voiced steamheated grief. The
RFC expressed surprise.
And the news, at the Fuller Brush hour, leaked out.
Shouts. Cheers. Stamping of feet. Blizzard of confetti.
Thunderous applause.

But the stocks were stolen. The pearls of the actress, stolen
again. The bonds embezzled.
Inexorably, the thief pursued. Captured inexorably. Tried.
Inexorably acquitted.
And again you heard the gentleman, with automatic
precision, speak the truth.
Saw, once more, the lady's virginity restored.

In the sewers of Berlin, the directors prepared, the room dark
for the seance, she a simple Baroness, you a lowly
millionaire, came face to face with John D. Christ.

Shook hands, his knife at your back, your knife at his. Sat
down.

Saw issue from his throat the ectoplasm of Pius VIII, and
heard "A test of the people's faith." You said amen,
voted to endorse but warned against default, you
observed the astral form of Nicholas II, and heard
"Sacred union of all." Saw little "Safe for democracy"
Nell. Listened to Adolph "Safety of France and
society" Theirs.

And beheld the faith, the union of rags, blackened hands,
stacked carrion, breached barricades in flame,

no default, credit restored, Union Carbide 94 3/8, call
money 10%, disarm, steel five points up, rails rise,
Dupont up, disarm, disarm, and heard again,

ghost out of ghost out of ghost out of ghost,

the voice of the senator reverberate through all the
morgues of all the world, echo again for liberty in the
catacombs of Rome, again sound through the
sweatshops, ghettoes, factories, mines, hunger again
repealed, circle the London cenotaph once more
annulling death, saw ten million dead returned to life,
shot down again, again restored,

Heard once more the gentleman speak, with automatic
precision, the final truth,

once more beheld the lady's virginity, the lady's decency,
the lady's purity, the lady's innocence,

paid for, certified, and restored.

Crawled amorously into bed. Felt among the maggots for the
    mouldering lips. The crumbled arms. Found them.
Tumult of cheers. Music and prayer by the YMCA. Horns,
    rockets. Spotlight.
The child was nursed on government bonds. Cut its teeth
    on a hand grenade. Grew fat on shrapnel. Bullets.
    Barbed wire. Chlorine gas. Laughed at the bayonet
    through its heart.

These are the things you saw and heard, these are the things
    you did, this is your record,
you.

JACK FOLEY

Eli, Eli

> "It would be bad enough if I were the next door
> neighbor. But this is like God doing it. Jesus doing it."
> > "First Person: The Confession of Father X"

Father O'Fondle comes to town
Hoping that your pants are down
What's your sport, me lad, says he

Can you sit upon me knee
(I have sport enow for thee!)
Let me look upon your dangle
Try Confession from THIS angle
What I beat is not a drum
Who put the "cum" in "Vobiscum"?
(Which of you dare call me "scum"?)
Bishop, Bishop, though I'm lacking
I know you will send me packing
To another parish bright
Where I'm sure I'll do all right
I'll bring "God" to them and theirs
And they'll remember in their prayers
In the night when dreams are wet
They will see me smiling yet
Holding out God's helping hand—
There's a sweet and sacred band!
Till Hell turns to ice and freezes
You'll make Love to me—and Jesus
I'll apply the priestly arts
To your troubled private parts
Here, my lad's, a welcome solace
Let me touch your throbbing phallus
Hear the Sacred Choir thrumming
As I prepare my Second Coming!
Father O'Fondle, troubled man
Needing love, and under ban
In such desire for the Son,
Would I have done as you have done?

ROBERT FROST

A Semi-Revolution

I advocate a semi-revolution.
The trouble with a total revolution
(Ask any reputable Rosicrucian)
Is that it brings the same class up on top.
Executives of skillful execution
Will therefore plan to go halfway and stop.
Yes, revolutions are the only salves,
But they're one thing that should be done by halves.

SISTER GOODWIN (ELIZABETH HOPE)

Centennial Year for the Spirits

peering coyly, i said
look, you seem rather flushed
              open up from your
trance. i have returned
from your dimension
              my silent stiff plane

is a low beam shadow against
eight walls

many visitors
society conscious
grey haired aristocrats
some are misers
some are curious
they save up their money
to look around
empty senses do not seek
original life giver to
these amulets

my lips are behind
an ancient glass
case
ice melting to some old
man
as he h-hmmmed
nice arctic sample h-hmmm

i kiss the inuit
masks at night
after the ivory men perform
their trade ceremony
i kiss a
Kushdakaa mask stolen
from a grave

                    south of New Archangel
            his eyes jiggle shaking away
        a pretentious gaze

            i unlock
        a famous warrior from his
                    window cage
            he wears his Raven Helmet
        and dances the war of the lords
            in a glorious reconstruction
        of the Battle of 1804
                fierce pride is in his arms
                        reminding us he had
        victoried over the russians
        the man in the kayaq
                steps down to play a
        ragtime song on the 100 year old
                finnish lutheran organ
        soon he picks up the drum
        as the life picks up the dead
                    all the little men
                and a few little women
        take up their place of hierarchy
                    a pentatonic momentum
            slowly penetrates the Octagon House
                    we begin hooting and
            clapping
        vocals up in high pitch

dance   dance
        until our souls

overcome our bodies
     blissful and remote

               calm job
          in the stillness there was no
          need to search for the unknown
we danced for a good hunt
we danced for good weather
we danced for the happiness of others
we danced for peace
                    body exertion
               minds hypnotic from the beat
               minds thinking the same thing
calm joy
coming back from the unknown
we were there
we were there

               in the stillness
          a Pt. Hope whaler says
yai, nigipaaq manna
yai, a lot of food here
tea & vodka in the samovar
          herring eggs halibut
sweet roots salmon berries
          aqutuq caribou maktak

dried sheefish & seal oil
   a delicious feast
   for everyone's soul

   we never noticed
Bishop Viniaminov who popped out
of his 1797 photograph
     to guard the door with the
12 pounder carronade
     our language is now his
     our survival in his hands
     his subjects have named him
     Saint Innocent

at 8am, peering coyly, i said
i feel the energies exchanged
last night

WILL HEFORD

That God Made

This is the Earth that God made.
These are the Timber and Coal and Oil
And Water Powers and fertile Soil
That belong to us all in spite of the gall
Of the Grabbers and Grafters who forestall
The natural rights and needs of all
Who live on the Earth that God made.

These are the Corporate Snakes that coil
Around the Timber and Coal and Oil
And Water Powers and fertile Soil
Which belong to us all in spite of the gall
Of the Grabbers and Grafters who forestall
The natural rights and needs of all
Who live on the Earth that God made.

These are the Lords of Mill and Mine
Who act as if they were divine,
Who can't read the writing on the wall
But admire the skill and excuse the gall
Of the Grabbers and Grafters who forestall
The natural rights and needs of all
Who live on the Earth that God made.

These are the Parsons shaven and shorn
Who tell the workers all forlorn
To pray for contentment night and morn
And to bear and to suffer want and scorn
And be lowly and meek and humbly seek
For their just reward on the Heavenly shore,
But not on the Earth that God made.

BOB HOLMAN

1990

the taking of flash photos & use of recording devices of any kind,
including pens, pencils, eye & ears, is strictly encouraged.

It's 1990
& Nelson Mandela is free!

& people are looking at each other
They're going like "Wha?"
& the other people are looking back
& they're going like "Duh?"
& finally, after this deep interaction,
You hear the wild cry of:
"Excuse me, could you tell me the time?"

What time is it?

It's Wake & Shake Time

It's Death of the Decade Time

It's Turn of the Century Time

It's Gyrate the Millennium Time

It's the End of Time

"At the sound of the tone it will be the End of Time"

It's 1 PF—it's Post Future

It's 1 PT—it's post time

It's Post Time!

It's 1990

& Nelson Mandela is free!

History's on fast forward

Make that double-fast fast forward

That's where you run past the Future so fast you're back in the Past

Sure, it's the End of History

So how come all we can think is, "What comes next?"

One minute you're rolling in ecstasy because the Berlin Wall is
    tumbling down,

The next you think, a reunited Germany! Oh God no!

Here come the storm troopers! & I'm Jewish (Well, my father
    was Jewish, so I'm not Jewish enough for the Jews—but I'm
    Jewish enough for the Nazis!)

One minute it's survival tactics & the next it's where's the angle

It's 1990

& Nelson Mandela is free!

& everybody wants a little glasnost

We know we want it cause we see Frank Zappa smoking

  cigarettes with Vaclav Havel, who 6 months ago was in jail,

  an artist whose work was banned by the government,

  now he's the President of Czechoslovakia

So stop in for free baby burritos at the corner bar

Except suddenly it's a karaoke sushi bar specializing in

  piranha sushi, & everybody here's a star,

Because you get to stand in front of the massive TV screen

  showing an MTV-minus-one video clip & sing along with the

  bouncing ball—

Except the words are all in Japanese and how can you sing

  "Feelings" with feeling in Japanese?

Kanjiru! Watashiwa, kanjiru!

It's 1990

& Nelson Mandela is free!

Communism has collapsed

At last the Russians get to wear the "Happy Face" masks & stand

  in line for a Beeg Mek

The Azerbaijanis are finally free so they get to beat up on the

  Armenians

Yugoslavia has decided to go back to indigenous cave tribe

  groupings

In Italy the Communists have met & decided they're not
    Communists
They're gonna change their name to be more appealing to the
    Socialists and the Greens
But for the time being they're calling themselves simply The Thing
The Thing! Personally, I'm planning to vote for—The Thing
For the time being For the time being
There's nothing left anymore except for the time being
You live your whole life for the time being
While meanwhile—there is no meanwhile

It's 1990
& Nelson Mandela is free!

"Play ethics by ear"
Let me out of here—but which way is out?
I'm a part of the *food chain,* isn't that enough?
At night I snuggle up close to the warm blue glow of images
    provided for everyone by a select few
Listen, they've packaged a shopping mall so small you can only
    visit it with a Video Walkperson, a cellular phone and a Visa card
The world is changing, but we're not
We're stuck in a commercial for Life
Trying to figure out who to give the money to
When, surprise! There is no money

It's 1990
& Nelson Mandela is free!

Señor Yuppie! Phone call for Señor Yuppie!

Pardon me, have to step over these homeless people to close on
  my Home Equity Loan, sorry

"Our bodies are still tender & not full-grown & the prospect of
  dying frightens us all, but history calls us & we must go"

But where did they go, the Chinese students on their bicycles
  riding towards the tanks at Tiananmen Square,

It can't happen here because it's already happened here

AIDS epidemic grabs Life till we don't even see it, gone like holes
  in heart,

Surrounded by ghosts, meeting Death in the middle of Life

While lesbians and gay men still have to fight for the right to love

& be sure to send your poetry to the Department of Official
  Bullshit to get labelled

So it just has to be—time to get a Co-op!—
  buy the place you used to rent, and still get to pay the rent

It's time to be a great parent—
  work extra hours to pay for the best childcare while you're away

My kid is majoring in Nikes

Don't worry! Don't be happy! Explode!

The decision of birth from her body is solely & privately that of
  the woman herself

It's 1990
& Nelson Mandela is free!

And everything used to be something else

Now it's *1,000* words a minute, & Times Square is just so much
  more interesting

We're hellbent on something, sort of positive in a senile way

I can't even keep up with my life

It's a secret between me & my stunt double

Honey, I'm home—nuke me

Hop to it, ban cigarettes before it's too late

It's Earth Day again, if you can find any earth left

Paranoia used to be a psychosis, now it's a national pastime

Try the new fashion: the bare-breast style of no clothes at all, &
   it's not cheap, either

& poetry is the Newspaper of the Future

Except it's locked out of the media

You know things! Think them!

There's optimism at the yacht club

The salad bar is open

Excuse me, isn't it time to mow your head?

I hate you! Thank you very much, have a nice day

They don't even know what it is, but they've already got an
   option on it

They're buying into it! Let's Not Make A Deal!

It's 1990

& Nelson Mandela is free!

& there's a guy at the microphone & he's yelling at me

& he's not using language that makes any sense from where I
   come from

It all rhymes & it all starts with capital letters

& it's all intense italics underlined three times in boldface headlines

& all I can remember is the part about

It's 1990
& Nelson Mandela is free!

& around the world a sense of possibility
As women slowly ease the old gray dinosaur poobahs from their
   penile thrones
The universal remote control is being passed into your hands

Zap it! Zap it!
Zap it! Zap it! Zap it!

It's 1990
& Nelson Mandela is free!

LANGSTON HUGHES

Advertisement for the Waldorf-Astoria

Fine living . . . à la carte??
Come to the Waldorf-Astoria!

LISTEN, HUNGRY ONES!
Look! See what *Vanity Fair* says about the
   new Waldorf-Astoria:

"All the luxuries of private home. . . ."
Now, won't that be charming when the last flop-house
    has turned you down this winter?
    Furthermore:
"It is far beyond anything hitherto attempted in the hotel
    world. . . ." It cost twenty-eight million dollars. The fa-
    mous Oscar Tschirky is in charge of banqueting.
    Alexandre Gastaud is chef. It will be a distinguished
    background for society.
So when you've got no place else to go, homeless and hungry
    ones, choose the Waldorf as a background for your rags—
(Or do you still consider the subway after midnight good
    enough?)

ROOMERS

Take a room at the new Waldorf, you down-and-outers—
    sleepers in charity's flop-houses where God pulls a
    long face, and you have to pray to get a bed.
They serve swell board at the Waldorf-Astoria. Look at this menu,
    will you:

GUMBO CREOLE

CRABMEAT IN CASSOLETTE

BOILED BRISKET OF BEEF

SMALL ONIONS IN CREAM

WATERCRESS SALAD

PEACH MELBA

Have luncheon there this afternoon, all you jobless.
    Why not?

Dine with some of the men and women who got rich off of
    your labor, who clip coupons with clean white fingers
    because your hands dug coal, drilled stone, sewed garments,
    poured steel to let other people draw dividends
    and live easy.
(Or haven't you had enough yet of the soup-lines and the bit-
    ter bread of charity?)
Walk through Peacock Alley tonight before dinner, and get
    warm, anyway. You've got nothing else to do.

EVICTED FAMILIES

All you families put out in the street:
    Apartments in the Towers are only $10,000 a year.
       (Three rooms and two baths.) Move in there until
       times get good, and you can do better. $10,000 and $1.00
       are about the same to you, aren't they?
    Who cares about money with a wife and kids homeless, and
       nobody in the family working? Wouldn't a duplex
       high above the street be grand, with a view of the rich-
       est city in the world at your nose?
"A lease, if you prefer, or an arrangement terminable at will."

NEGROES

Oh, Lawd, I done forgot Harlem!
Say, you colored folks, hungry a long time in 135th Street—
    they got swell music at the Waldorf-Astoria. It sure is a
    mighty nice place to shake hips in, too. There's dancing
    after supper in a big warm room. It's cold as hell
    on Lenox Avenue. All you've had all day is a cup of
    coffee. Your pawnshop overcoat's a ragged banner on

your hungry frame. You know, downtown folks are just
crazy about Paul Robeson! Maybe they'll like you, too,
black mob from Harlem. Drop in at the Waldorf this
afternoon for tea. Stay to dinner. Give Park Avenue a
lot of darkie color—free for nothing! Ask the Junior
Leaguers to sing a spiritual for you. They probably
know 'em better than you do—and their lips won't be
so chapped with cold after they step out of their closed
cars in the undercover driveways.

    Hallelujah! Undercover driveways!

    Ma soul's a witness for de Waldorf-Astoria!

(A thousand nigger section-hands keep the roadbeds smooth,
    so investments in railroads pay ladies with diamond
    necklaces staring at Sert murals.)

    Thank God A-mighty!

(And a million niggers bend their backs on rubber planta-
    tions, for rich behinds to ride on thick tires to the
    Theatre Guild tonight.)

    Ma soul's a witness!

(And here we stand, shivering in the cold, in Harlem.)

    Glory be to God—

    De Waldorf-Astoria's open!

EVERYBODY

So get proud and rare back; everybody! The new Waldorf-
    Astoria's open!

(Special siding for private cars from the railroad yards.)

    You ain't been there yet?

(A thousand miles of carpet and a million bathrooms.)

    What's the matter?

You haven't seen the ads in the papers? Didn't you get a card?

Don't you know they specialize in American cooking?

Ankle on down to 49th Street at Park Avenue. Get up

off that subway bench tonight with the evening POST

for cover! Come on out o' that flop-house! Stop shivering

your guts out all day on street corners under the El.

Jesus, ain't you tired yet?

CHRISTMAS CARD

Hail Mary, Mother of God!

the new Christ child of the Revolution's about to be

born.

(Kick hard, red baby, in the bitter womb of the mob.)

Somebody, put an ad in *Vanity Fair* quick!

Call Oscar of the Waldorf—for Christ's sake!!

It's almost Christmas, and that little girl—turned whore

because her belly was too hungry to stand it anymore—

wants a nice clean bed for the Immaculate Conception.

Listen, Mary, Mother of God, wrap your new born babe in

the red flag of Revolution: the Waldorf-Astoria's the

best manger we've got. For reservations: Telephone EL.

5-3000.

CYNTHIA HWANG

The Potato Manifesto

How long has our kind been marginalized
Ostracized at supermarkets
With a dismissive wave of hand
As poor folks' food

My origins are humble
But like me the Truffle also comes from the ground.
I'm the butt of jokes, derided,
Likened to lazy sit-abouts—"couch potatoes."
My skin devoured with beer by potbellied men of no distinction.

So I issue a call to you, many-eyed brethren
Fellow discontents and maltreated Amer-potatoes
to migrate to Russia
where, blended together, we will be appreciated
in fine-aged
vodka.

Yusef Komunyakaa

Facing It

My black face fades,
hiding inside the black granite.
I said I wouldn't,
dammit: No tears.
I'm stone. I'm flesh.
My clouded reflection eyes me
like a bird of prey, the profile of night
slanted against morning. I turn
this way—the stone lets me go.
I turn that way—I'm inside
the Vietnam Veterans Memorial
again, depending on the light
to make a difference.
I go down the 58,022 names,
half-expecting to find
my own in letters like smoke.
I touch the name Andrew Johnson;
I see the booby trap's white flash.
Names shimmer on a woman's blouse
but when she walks away
the names stay on the wall.
Brushstrokes flash, a red bird's
wings cutting across my stare.
The sky. A plane in the sky.

A white vet's image floats
closer to me, then his pale eyes
look through mine. I'm a window.
He's lost his right arm
inside the stone. In the black mirror
a woman's trying to erase names:
No, she's brushing a boy's hair.

DENISE LEVERTOV

What Were They Like?

1) Did the people of Viet Nam
     use lanterns of stone?
2) Did they hold ceremonies
     to reverence the opening of buds?
3) Were they inclined to rippling laughter?
4) Did they use bone and ivory,
     jade and silver, for ornament?
5) Had they an epic poem?
6) Did they distinguish between speech and singing?

1) Sir, their light hearts turned to stone.

It is not remembered whether in gardens
stone lanterns illuminated pleasant ways.

2) Perhaps they gathered once to delight in blossom,
but after the children were killed
there were no more buds.

3) Sir, laughter is bitter to the burned mouth.

4) A dream ago, perhaps. Ornament is for joy.
All the bones were charred.

5) It is not remembered. Remember,
most were peasants; their life
was in rice and bamboo.
When peaceful clouds were reflected in the paddies
and the water buffalo stepped surely along terraces,
maybe fathers told their sons old tales.
When bombs smashed the mirrors
there was time only to scream.

6) There is an echo yet, it is said,
of their speech which was like a song.
It is reported their singing resembled
the flight of moths in moonlight.
Who can say? It is silent now.

WALTER LOWENFELS

The Execution

And after Governor Faubus led his army against Little Rock
and General Walker led his troops against the
Supreme Court and Governor Wallace led his
bombers against Birmingham
and after 300 years of *if you're white alright, but if you're
black, step back*
and after 20 millions of us said *now, right now,* and a quarter
million of us marched on Washington
and after the secret army of Governor X and Senator Y
bombed the Constitution 41 times in Birmingham
and nobody was arrested
we cornered four girl hostages in the basement at Sunday
School and executed them using the secret dynamite
formula.
And their names were Denice McNair, 11, Carrol Robertson,
Addie Mae Collins and Cynthia Wesley, all 14.
And Cynthia was identified only by her clothing and a ring.
And they never said a mumbling word, only their memory
lies uneasy in us wondering
will we love them as long as the grass shall grow and carry
them in our hearts when we shall overcome some
day
and really believe they died for us to live?
and the date of the execution was Youth Day at the 16th
Street Baptist Church, Birmingham.

Nancy Mercado

Milla
Mi abuela, Puerto Rico

Milla lived eons ago
When sandals pounded dirt roads
Blazing hot under palm tree lined skies.
Milla's long dark hair flowed side to side,
Glistened in the noon light.
Mahogany skinned, she shopped;
Platanos, yucas, a bark of soap.
Milla worked,
Striking clothes against wooden boards,
Gathering wood for evening meals,
Feeding chickens, hogs, dogs,
And roosters at dawn.
Milla traveled only once
To Chicago.
A color-faded photograph serves as document.
Smiles and thousands of hugs
For the grandchildren on a park bench.
Milla's a century old
And still remembers every one of us
Even those left over in the U.S.
She still carries a stick
Certain of her authority
Over four generations.
Milla outlived two world wars,

Saw the first television,

The first electric bulb in her town,

Hitler, segregation,

The Vietnam War,

And Gorbachev.

Milla can speak of

The turn of the century land reforms,

Of the blinded enthusiasm

For a man called Marín

And the mass migration of the 1950's.

Milla can speak of her beloved husband,

Sugar cane cutter for life.

She can speak of the love of a people,

Of the pain of separation.

Milla can speak of the Caribbean Ocean,

The history of the sun and sand

And the mystery of the stars.

Milla maintains an eternal candle lit

Just for me.

Milla will live for all time.

HILTON OBENZINGER

This Passover or the Next I Will Never
Be in Jerusalem

The clan is all together, eating Passover matzoh, joking.
At the head, the old Patriarch makes his blessing; he collars
me, & he imparts wisdom:
"Is it so bad to be a Jew?
In Israel even the street sweeper is a Jew, not that anyone
should be a street sweeper, but
nobody yells 'Dirty Jew!'
After 2,000 years we have something finally. Isn't it about time?
We are not taking any Arab land from anybody.
This is the land that belonged to our forefathers,
& we came only to take up our inheritance.
Can anyone say we are *stealing* what is already *ours*?
Why don't you go to Israel, learn something about your people?
Can it be nothing but good?"

I fidget & nod politely at his references to Abraham & other
        long-lost relatives.

"So you move so far away from your parents in New York,
you move to California to live with the Indians.
You decide to be so noble to be a schoolteacher with the Indians.
Nu, I wish them well, but what is this with the Indians,

aren't they so different & so wild?"

"Actually,

Indians are not what you see on TV . . ."

"Nu, but are they your own people? Your own flesh & blood?
Do you hate New York so much you have to live with Indians?
What is this Indians? You can work in your father's store,
make a good life. He is getting old, and you need gelt in life,
right?
Is it so bad selling rags?
Can't you be writer all you want, love Indians all you want,
    & make money too?
What's this, Indians and California?
If not Israel, shouldn't you think New York maybe to live?"

The young couple across the table from me, recently married
(& living just a few blocks away as does all the family
peppered throughout the Brooklyn neighborhood
so as better to visit one another on Shabbas when one can onl
walk & by injunction is forbidden to drive),
these young marrieds smile good-naturedly & ask,

"Don't you feel strange living so far away from your family?"

Why is this Jew different from all other Jews?
I sip my wine. The white tablecloth is a vast Jordan.
This Passover or the next I will never be in Jerusalem.
The Jordan flows between me and the land I never remember
        anyone promising me.

No sound can be heard except the occasional wail of some
    wild animal.
I will never step across the shore. *Am I the anti-Moses?*

I jump up from my plate, startled.

"Uh, no, I don't feel strange at all. . . ."

JOHN REED

from *America in 1918*

I have watched the summer day come up from the top of a
    pier of the Williamsburgh Bridge,
I have slept in a basket of squid at the Fulton Street Market,
Talked about God with the old cockney woman who sells
    hot-dogs under the Elevated at South Ferry,
Listen to tales of dago dips in the family parlor of the Hellhole,
And from the top gallery of the Metropolitan heard Didur
    sing "Boris Godunov". . .
I have shot craps with gangsters in the Gas House district,
And seen what happens to a green bull on San Juan Hill. . .
I can tell you where to hire a gunman to croak a squealor,
And where young girls are bought and sold, and how to get
    coke on 125th Street

And what men talk about behind Steve Brodie's, or in the
    private rooms of the Lafayette Baths. . .

Dear and familiar and ever-new to me is the city
As the body of my lover . . .
All sounds—harsh clatter of the Elevated, rumble of the subway,
Tapping of policemen's clubs on midnight pavements,
Hand-organs plaintive and monotonous, squawking motorhorns,
Gatling crepitation of airy riveters,
Muffled detonations deep down underground,
Flat bawling of newsboys, quick-clamoring ambulance gongs,
Deep nervous tooting from the evening harbor,
And the profound shuffling thunder of myriad feet. . .

All smells—smell of sample shoes, second-hand clothing,
Dutch bakeries, Sunday delicatessen, kosher cooking,
Smell of damp tons of newspapers along Park Row,
The Subway, smelling like the tomb of Rameses the Great,
The tired odor of infinite human dust-drug-stores,
And the sour slum stench of mean streets. . .

People—rock-eyed brokers gambling with Empires,
Swarthy insolent boot-blacks, cringing push-cart peddlers,
The white-capped wop flipping wheat-cakes in the window of Childs',
Sallow garment-workers coughing on a park-bench in the
    thin spring sun,
Dully watching the leaping fountain as they eat a handful of
    peanuts for lunch . . .
The steeple-jack swaying infinitesimal at the top of the
    Woolworth flag-pole,

Charity workers driving hard bargains for the degradation of
    the poor,

Worn-out snarling street-car conductors, sentimental prize
    fighters,

White wings scouring the roaring traffic-ways, foul-mouthed
    truck-drivers,

Spanish longshoremen heaving up freight-mountains, hollow-
    eyed silk workers,

Structural steel workers catching hot rivets on high-up
    spidery girders,

Sand-hogs in hissing air-locks under the North River, sweating
    subway muckers, hard-rock men blasting beneath Broadway,

Ward-leaders with uptilted cigars, planning mysterious
    underground battles for power,

Raucous soap-boxers in Union Square, preaching the everlasting
    crusade,

Pale half-fed cash-girls in department stores, gaunt children
    making paper-flowers in dim garrets,

Princess stenographers, and manicurists chewing gum with a
    queenly air,

Macs, whore-house madams, street-walkers, touts, bouncers,
    stool-pigeons. . .

All professions, races, temperaments, philosophies,

All history, all possibilities, all romance,

America . . . the world. . .!

WENDY ROSE

For the Angry White Student Who Wanted to Know If I Thought White People Ever Did Anything Good for "the Indians"

O yes I told her.
First of all
there's Häagen-Dazs
though
we had to supply
the flavors
and Siberians learned
to freeze it.
I would not
forget
the wheat and raisins
for cinnamon rolls,
the English dough
into which
is put
our sweet potato
or pumpkin sauce,
whipped cream on top
from tough Highland cows.
And bluejeans are good
though it was
our cotton they used

with staple long enough
to be spun and dyed
with indigo from India.
<blockquote>

And the horse

was a good thing

I like horses
</blockquote>
big enough to pull
the tipi poles,
drag travois across
the cratered plain
so punched with holes
that wheels bog down.
<blockquote>

And coffee, canned peaches,

oranges and sugar
</blockquote>
from reeds selected and cut
by our sea—going cousins
<blockquote>

and melons

so like our gourds

but soft and sweet,
</blockquote>
the oasis
within August.
<blockquote>

Computers, boots, baroque music,

paper more fragile than birch
</blockquote>
to replace Mayan books burned
by Spanish tantrums.
<blockquote>

Typewriters, trucks, rock 'n' roll,

electric lights, polished steel
</blockquote>
for the knife and the ax. And guns, outboard motors,

customers

willing to be silent

as we auction off the days

remaining.

MURIEL RUKEYSER

Poem (I Lived in the First Century)

I lived in the first century of world wars.

Most mornings I would be more or less insane,

The newspapers would arrive with their careless stories,

The news would pour out of various devices

Interrupted by attempts to sell products to the unseen.

I would call my friends on other devices;

They would be more or less mad for similar reasons.

Slowly I would get to pen and paper,

Make my poems for others unseen and unborn.

In the day I would be reminded of those men and women

Brave, setting up signals across vast distances,

Considering a nameless way of living, of almost unimagined
    values.

As the lights darkened, as the lights of night brightened,

We would try to imagine them, try to find each other.

To construct peace, to make love, to reconcile
Waking with sleeping, ourselves with each other,
Ourselves with ourselves. We would try by any means
To reach the limits of ourselves, to reach beyond ourselves,
To let go the means, to wake.
I lived in the first century of these wars.

RICHARD WRIGHT

Between the World and Me

And one morning while in the woods I stumbled suddenly
upon the thing,
Stumbled upon it in a grassy clearing guarded by scaly oaks
and elms.
And the sooty details of the scene rose, thrusting themselves
between the world and me. . . .

There was a design of white bones slumbering forgottenly
upon a cushion of ashes.
There was a charred stump of a sapling pointing a blunt
finger accusingly at the sky.
There were torn tree limbs, tiny veins of burnt leaves, and a
scorched coil of greasy hemp;

A vacant shoe, an empty tie, a ripped shirt, a lonely hat, and
a pair of trousers still with black blood
And upon the trampled grass were buttons, dead matches,
butt-ends of cigars and cigarettes, peanut shells, a
drained gin-flask, and a whore's lipstick;
Scattered traces of tar, restless arrays of feathers, and the
lingering smell of gasoline.
And through the morning air the sun poured yellow surprise
into the eye sockets of a stony skull. . . .
And while I stood my mind was frozen with a cold pity for
the life that was gone.
The ground gripped my feet and my heart was circled by
icy walls of fear—
The sun died in the sky; a night wind muttered in the grass
and fumbled the leaves in the trees; the woods poured
forth the hungry yelping of hounds; the darkness
screamed with thirsty voices; and the witnesses rose
and lived:
The dry bones stirred, rattled, lifted, melting themselves into
my bones.
The grey ashes formed flesh firm and black, entering into my
flesh.
The gin-flask passed from mouth to mouth; cigars and cigarettes
glowed, the whore smeared the lipstick red
upon her lips,
And a thousand faces swirled around me, clamoring that
my life be burned. . . .

And then they had me, stripped me, battering my teeth into

my throat till I swallowed my own blood.

My voice was drowned in the roar of their voices, and my
black wet body slipped and rolled in their hands as
they bound me to the sapling.

And my skin clung to the bubbling hot tar, falling from me in
limp patches.

And the down and quills of the white feathers sank into my
raw flesh, and I moaned in my agony.

Then my blood was cooled mercifully, cooled by a baptism
of gasoline.

And in a blaze of red I leaped to the sky as pain rose like
water, boiling my limbs.

Panting, begging I clutched childlike, clutched to the hot
sides of death.

Now I am dry bones and my face a stony skull staring in
yellow surprise at the sun. . . .

HEROES & SHEROES,
ANTI & OTHERWISE

Politicians, artists, athletes, gods, goddesses, legends, even entire countries and continents have been worshipped, condemned, and commented on by poets, probably since the first verses were recited. Some excellent examples below include Sarah Webster Fabio paying homage to the late Duke Ellington, Sam Hamod to Joe Williams, and Bob Kaufman in "Crootey Songo" to Bebop (a legendary art form) with his scat poem. Vachel Lindsay and Edward Sanders pay poetic tribute to the iconic twentieth-century politicians William Jennings Bryan and Robert Kennedy. Jerry Leiber and Mike Stoller's rock and roll classic "Searchin'" alludes to old radio and movie heroes like Bulldog Drummond and Boston Blackie. There are tricksters, too, old as the literature of the totem poles. Roland Legiardi-Laura does a killer job on the trickster rabbit. He brings this classic character up to date, while beat poet Ted Joans does a film take on a contemporary trickster in his "Skip the Byuppie."

Angela Martin probes the mystery of that perennial icon, Mona Lisa, while Linda Hogan's "La Llorona" and Joy Harjo's "The Wolf Warrior" explore legends that have been passed down through generations.

While Hogan and Harjo draw their inspiration from the past, other writers are inspired by modern legends. Long before African-American Fortune 500 CEOs appeared on the cover of *Time*, we got a day off to celebrate Martin Luther King Jr.'s birth date, and a black American was considered worthy enough to be considered for the presidency, athletes were the most prominent African-American heroes—athletes like Quincy Troupe's Magic Johnson and Calvin Hernton's Joe Louis. And not only have poets treated individuals as legends; they have honored cities and continents, too. For Julia Vinograd, Jerusalem is a legend; in Askai M. Touré's "Dawnsong!" the legend is Africa.

Peter Blue Cloud

Coyote Makes the First People

Coyote stopped to drink at a big lake and saw his reflection. "Now there's a really good-looking coyote," he said, leaning farther over.

And of course he fell in. And of course you will think this is a take-off on an old theme.

But what happened was, he drank up the whole lake to keep from drowning. And because he didn't really like the taste of certain fish, he spat them out. And because he felt sorry when he saw them flopping around, he sang a song to give them legs.

"Maybe they'll become the first people," Coyote mused aloud.

"Oh, no you don't," said the headman of that tribe of fish, "if it's all the same with you, could you just put us back where we were? And could you please take away these stupid legs?"

So Coyote regurgitated the lake and put everything back the way it was.

Again he saw his reflection and said, "Okay, you're pretty good-looking, but are you smart? I've been trying to make the first people for a long time now, but nothing wants to be people. So, what do I do, huh, can you tell me?"

His reflection studied him for a long time, then it squatted and dropped a big turd.

"Okay," said Coyote, "I guess that's as good an answer as any."

Then he himself squatted, and began to fashion the first people.

JAYNE CORTEZ

Ogun's Friend

I saw your eyes like bumps of flint
i saw your shoes like high-top boulders
i saw your hands like faces of fire
i saw your fingers like axes of Shango
i saw your body like a rocker of steel

Yo
i heard a hum down there
i heard a rumble down there
i heard a ghost down there
i heard a thunderbolt expel down there
i heard a anvil in the night go hummmmmmmmm
down there

Hey whose metals are shouting so loud
they must be the tapper that Ogun knows

whose are those beads so hot and black
they must be brass for Ogun to fill

who's that worker with corrugated gums
it must be the worker that Ogun chose

who's that one with feet like flames
it must be the welder that's Ogun's friend

Yo
i smell a chicken in here
i smell some charcoal in here
i smell a goat in here
i smell some wax in here
i smell a dog in here
i smell some clay and some oil and some blood in here

Hey i see your chains like links of teeth
crow-bars
i see your coils like female pouches
barbwire
i see your grills like braided snakes
fish-net
i see your ladder like a totem of pliers
crocodiles
i see your pipes like razors on tusks
wine bottles
i see your scissors and your keys on the table in there
uh-huhn

Yo
you got pant legs made into hats
you got diamond plates made into walls
you got straightening combs made into steps

you got hammer-heads made into skulls
you got flat-rings made into ears

Pant legs diamond plates
straightening combs hammer-heads
flat-rings
yo

I feel your flux
i feel your sander
i feel your drill bit
i feel your grinder
i feel your drill press
i feel your hack saw
i feel your brick ax

Yo
i saw your windows like sheets of steel
i heard a gong down there
i saw some navels like bushes of wire
i heard a bird down there

Hey
you got lizard tongues made into tongs
i feel your bald spot
you got snakeskins covered in bronze
i feel your chin marks
lizard tongues bald spots
snakeskins chin marks

Yo
i smell some fish in here
i see a rail down there
i smell some toes in here
i see a horn down there
i smell some funk in here
i see a knife down there
i smell some ratheads in here
i see a person down there

Whose that one so brown and fine
Ogun's friend
whose that one in green on green
Ogun's friend
whose that one who eats so fast
Ogun's friend
whose that one with toothpaste lips
Ogun's friend
whose that one who spits on tools
Ogun's friend
Yo Ogun's friend

VICTOR HERNÀNDEZ CRUZ

Song 1 from "Three Songs from the 50's"

Julito used to shine the soul
of his shoes before he left for
the Palladium to take the wax
off the floor while Tito Rodriguez
flew around the walls like a
parakee choking maracas
It was around this time that
Julito threw away his cape
because the Umbrella Man and the
Dragons put the heat on all the
Ricans who used to fly around
in Dracula capes swinging canes
or carrying umbrellas
Even if there was no rain
on the horizon
That same epoca my mother
got the urge to paint the
living room pink and buy a
new mirror with flamingoes
elegantly on the right hand
corner because the one we had
was broken from the time that
Carlos tried to put some respect
Into Julito and knock the
party out of him.

THULANI DAVIS

Skin of Clouds

Goddess of the Waters:
And one day they began
to fall, to rain,
rain down
into my endless, my watery,
unknowing reach.
They began to fall,
these people,
creations of the gods,
fall
like petals, strands of palm,
into my endless
unknowing body.
The people always gave me honor.
They came to the water's edge,
bringing sweets and flowers
as offering.

I have a taste for honey,
sweet amber hidden in trees,
and tree blossoms, bright colored
and fragile,
fragrant, and short-lived.
They grow in the earth,
unknown to me.

But, they come as if from the heavens,
creatures of the earth,
falling into my body,
passing through my
dancing and gleaming,
my skin of mirrors and clouds,
spittle and sky,
blood and sinew,
pulled down by my heaving waves.
I am the waters
that run through their hands,
through their skin and
back into the vast within.

They come as if from the heavens,
creatures of the earth,
seeds spit from me onto the land,
not like an offering,
not like the honey, the blossoms,
the sweet smells I crave
but screaming,
flung like wasted dead leaves,
broken tree limbs,
lifeless shells.

Give them to the fire first.
When they come to me,
the fire is still inside them,

burning from within.
Give them to the fire first.
Sear them from memory.
Do not offer them to me
half-lit and screaming.
Let them know fire's emptiness.
Let me soothe them with my fullness.

Give them to the air first.
Let them fly till life is gone.
Suck the air from their lungs,
and clear their souls of all regret.
Let them be clean of the pain.
Do not offer them to me
bellowing with fear and sorrow.
Let them know the air's loneliness.
So I may soothe them with my embrace.

I tell the heavens,
I tell the earth,
gods of all the living
and the dead,
the waters will rise up
with the moon
and crush the rims of earth.
This howling is not of the seas.
The death defiles my body,
dares to take my children,
rip them from the land.

This howling is not of the seas.
It is a madness,
not of nature,
not of the gods,
but of men.

H. D. (HILDA DOOLITTLE)

Helen

All Greece hates
the still eyes in the white face,
the lustre as of olives
where she stands,
and the white hands.

All Greece reviles
the wan face when she smiles,
hating it deeper still
when it grows wan and white,
remembering past enchantments
and past ills.

Greece sees unmoved,
God's daughter, born of love,
the beauty of cool feet
and slenderest knees,
could love indeed the maid,
only if she were laid,
white ash amid funereal cypresses.

SARAH WEBSTER FABIO

Tribute to Duke

Rhythm and Blues   *Ohh, Ooh, Oh,*
sired you; gospel's   *moaning low,*
your mother tongue: *I got*
that of a MAN   *the blues.*
praying in the
miraculous language   *Sometimes I'm*
of song—soul   *up; sometimes*
communion with   *I'm down.*
his maker,
a sacred offering   *Sometimes I'm*
from the   *down; sometimes*
God-in-man.   *I'm up*

to the
God-of-man

Oh happy day
When Jesus washed
my sin away.

You reigned King
of Jazz before
Whiteman imitations
of "Black-Brown and
Beige" became the
order of the day.
Here, now, we but add
one star more to
your two-grand
jewel-studded crown
for that many tunes
you turned the world
onto in your
half-centuried
creative fever riffed
in scales of color
from "Black Beauty"
to "Creole Rhapsody"
and "Black and Tan
   Fantasy."
All praises
to Duke,
King of Jazz

(musical background
with a medley of
tunes)

Boss, boss
tunes in
technicolor
SOUL—
Black-
Brown-
Beige-
Creole-

Black

and

Tan

is

the color
of my fantasy.

To run it down
for you. That
fever that came on
with that "Uptown Beat"
caused Cotton when
he came to Harlem
that first time to
do a "Sugar Hill
Shim Sham."

When things got down
and funky
you bit into the blues
and blew into the air,
"I Got It Bad and
That Ain't Good,"
And from deep
down into your
"Solitude," you
touched both
"Satin Doll" and
"Sophisticated Lady"
wrapped them in
"Mood Indigo" and made
each moment
"A Prelude
to a kiss."

Way back then, Man,

When things
got down
and really
funky
fever, fever,
light
my fire.

Down,
   down,
     down
Nee-eev-eer
treat me
kind
and gentle—
BLOW
   (music in the
     background)
   the way you
     should
BLOW, MAN
Ain't
I
Got
it
Bad.

Break it down.

you were doing   *Break*
your thing.   *it down*
Blowing minds with   *Right on down*
riffs capping   *to*
whimsical whiffs of   *the*
lush melody—   *Real*
changing minds   *nitty gritty.*
with moods and   *("Solitude"*
modulations,   *as background*
changing minds,   *sound)*
changing faces,   *Blow,*
changing tunes,   *blow,*
                                         blow

changing changes,
tripping out with   *Do your thing.*
Billy to "Take the
A Train," making it   *Change, change, change*
your theme—   *your 'chine*
your heat—   *and Take*
coming on strong   *the*
with bold dissonance   *A Train.*
and fast, fast, beat
of the early, late
sound of our time.

"Harlem Airshaft"   *Ain't*
"Rent Party Blues"   *got no*
jangling jazzed tone   *money*
portraits of life   *Ain't got no bread.*

in the streets.
"Harlem"—a symphony
of cacaphonous sound,
bristling rhythms,
haunting laments
trumpeting into the air
defiant blasts blown solo
to fully orchestrated
folk chorus.
World Ambassador,
translating Life
into lyric; voice
into song; pulse
into beat
the beat, the beat,
a beat, a beat, a beat,
beat, beat, beat, beat
Do it now.
Get down,
"A Drum Is a Woman,"
and what more
language does
a sweetback need
to trip out to
"Mood Indigo,"

Right on, Duke
Do your thing,
your own thing.

Ain't got
no place
to lay my Afro head.
  I got
    those low down
    blues.
Chorus: Hot-and-Cold-
Running- Harlem
"Rent Party Blues."

Break it down,
down
    down
        down
Right on down
to the
    Real
    nitty gritty.
    (drums in the
    background become
      drum solo)

(Theme song)

And, Man,   *Take*

the word's out

when you   *the*

get down   *A*

Bad   *Train*

it's good,

Real good,

And as you   *Right on.*

go   *Right*

know   *on*

you're tops,   *out*

and whatever   *of*

you do,   *this*

"We love you   *funky*

madly."   *world.*

Jessica Hagedorn

Latin Music in New York

made me dance with you
tito eddie n ray
somewhere with plumjam eyelids
i danced with you
in a roomful of mirrors
in miss harlow's house

the white girl's in town
and i smell death
the poet dying in a bar
body shaking in time
to lady day's song
  he's dying in a nod
  in a lullaby
  of ambulance haze
  and chloral hydrate
  they burned his brain

somewhere
i saw the white girl smiling
la cucaracha was up all night
hiding her spoons her mirrors her revolutions
in the morning

the trace of vampires
still there
in the blood   even after a bath

you can't wash it away
you can't hide it
again and again
i looked under my bed
    inside a perfume box
        in the argentinian dagger
            the baby wolf gave me
                in your eyes
                    in a furtive smile
                        in a good fuck
                            in the boogaloo i do
there's no escaping it
        somewhere   with plumjam eyelids

i danced the tasty freeze shuffle with you
the reds   the blues   the tango con tu madre
it's there
in town for the night
a guest appearance   a quick solo
death gets hyped
and i'm in love again

latin music in new york
made me dance with you
azúcar y chocolaté

the alligator dream
of a tropical night

death makes a quick run
to las vegas
trying to take the poet
with him

latin music in new york
made me dance with you
tito eddie n ray

revolutions are creeping out
from under my bed!
and i sing a song for you
    and you
        and
            you

SAM HAMOD

Joe Williams at the Blue Note/Chicago, 1955; March 30, 1999

> "Everyday, everyday, everydaayyy
> I got the blues,
> talking of bad luck and sorrow
> Well you know I had my share . . ."
>
> — *Joe Williams with the*
> *Count Basie Band*

Tonight, they tell me you died
on a Vegas street,
Walked several miles from a hospital
Just checked yourself out and escaped toward home—
No, no—
I don't want to believe it, rather, we're
back at the Blue Note, Chicago, 1955
You're standing on the bandstand, light green rolled collar, your
Big white teeth smile as the Count says,
"Now here's a young man whose recently joined our band—
we think you're going to like his singing"
then you smacked it out, like a 1x12 smacking water, "*Everyday*"
"Everyday, everyday, everyday I got the blues"
and now, hearing that you've passed into that other side of the song,
everyday we'll have the blues, talking of bad luck and sorrow, well
you

know this will add to our share—but let me hear you, let me look at that big

smile again—swinging uptempo with the band "The *Comeback*"— telling your girl, hold tight,

hold tight baby, and we could hear the pleading in your voice as you asked her

to hang on, to just wait a while longer because you'd be back—and then you were

sliding into "*Rollem Pete*" you made us all jump for joy, and you were up there

just like a rollin' baby boy—and we were up on our feet dancing and clapping

Basie just kept smiling and the band kept blaring, trumpets High-cresting, the saxes laying down that harmonic line and the trombones

filling the background, their slides darting in and out of the the light then you're joined by Lambert, Hendrix and Ross and you make the Blue Note shake

with "*Going To Chicago*"—and you tell it like it is, cause ain't nothin' in Chicago

that a monkey woman can do—and we were like that, hometown people, full

of good folks from home, and you knew it, and we knew it when you sang it,

and the Count said it, "Chicago is always like home to me" and somehow,

you up there with that big rolled collar have always stayed in my mind, in

my heart, now tonight, I refuse to believe

that you stole out of that hospital late at night

I don't want to remember you struggling down that road

Struggling for breath, each slight step a pain, a

Gasp, a pulling for air, just wanting to get back home

To those lights, to get back to that stage, to get back

Among your friends—why was it no one understood

A singer like you can't be kept away from your people, you

Were given that voice to sing, to get out among people, to make

Them laugh, to feel wistful, to remember when they were in love, and what

Love is, that special feeling that embraces us with its happiness and sorrow,

That love in all its configurations is still that warmth, that warmth in your voice

In your broad smile, and in that way you held the mike and moved from jet black to silver hair

All in an instant—almost too fast for any of us to remember how it all changed—none of us

Noticed the time passing because there was always you, Ella, Sarah, Dinah, Count, Duke,

Hamp, Diz—now we have only Nancy Wilson, and I know she'll cry tonight and a lot of days

And nights as she remembers your big wide voice pleading,

   "*Please Send Me Someone To*

Love," and she'll ask the lord to send you to the right place, where you'll join the others

Singing with the angels—and we'll be earthbound, having you in vinyl, on cassette, on CD and in

our memories—so tonight, I know they speak their truth

That you have died, but my truth is that you are there at the Blue
Note in Chicago
You are there at Blues Alley in Washington, DC, a little hoarse, and
you are there with your arm
around Nancy Wilson singing another love song—but now, you
    slip just slightly
Off stage, but we hear you singing, singing those long deep notes,
long
After the lights have gone out . . .

JOY HARJO

Wolf Warrior

> For all the warriors

A white butterfly speckled with pollen joined me in my prayers
yesterday morning as I thought of you in Washington. I didn't want
the pain of repeated history to break your back. In my blanket of
hope I walked with you, wolf warrior, and the council of tribes to
what used to be the Department of War to discuss justice. When a
people institute a bureaucratic department to serve justice, then be
suspicious. False justice is not justified by massive structure, just
as the sacred is not confinable to buildings constructed for the
purpose of worship.

I pray these words don't obstruct the meaning I am searching to give you, a gift like love so you can approach that strange mind without going insane. So we can all walk with you, sober, our children empowered with the clothes of memory in which they are never hungry for love, or justice.

An old Cherokee who prizes wisdom above the decisions rendered by departments of justice in this world told me this story. It isn't Cherokee but a gift given to him from the people in the North. I know I carried this story for a reason, and now I understand I am to give it to you. A young man, about your age or mine, went camping with his dogs. It was just a few years ago, not long after the eruption of Mount St. Helens, when white ash covered the northern cities, an event predicting a turning of the worlds. I imagine October and bears fat with berries of the brilliant harvest, before the freezing breath of the north settles in and the moon is easier to reach by flight without planes. His journey was a journey toward the unknowable, and that night as he built a fire out of twigs and broken boughs he remembered the thousand white butterflies climbing toward the sun when he had camped there last summer.

Dogs were his beloved companions in the land that had chosen him through the door of his mother. His mother continued to teach him well, and it was she who had reminded him that the sound of pumping oil wells might kill him, turn him toward money. So he and his dogs traveled out into the land that remembered everything, including butterflies, and the stories that were told when light flickered from grease.

That night as he boiled water for coffee and peeled potatoes he saw a wolf walking toward camp on her hind legs. It had been generations since wolves had visited his people. The dogs were awed to see their ancient relatives and moved over to make room for them at the fire. The lead wolf motioned for her companions to come with her and they approached humbly, welcomed by the young man who had heard of such goings-on but the people had not been so blessed since the church had fought for their souls. He did not quite know the protocol, but knew the wolves as relatives and offered them coffee, store meat, and fried potatoes which they relished in silence. He stoked the fire and sat quiet with them as the moon in the form of a knife for scaling fish came up and a light wind ruffled the flame.

The soundlessness in which they communed is what I imagined when I talked with the sun yesterday. It is the current in the river of your spinal cord that carries memory from sacred places, the sound of a thousand butterflies taking flight in windlessness.

He knew this meeting was unusual and she concurred, then told the story of how the world as they knew it had changed and could no longer support the sacred purpose of life. Food was scarce, pups were being born deformed, and their migrations, which were in essence a ceremony for renewal, were restricted by fences. The world as all life on earth knew it would end, and there was still time in the circle of hope to turn back the destruction.

That's why they had waited for him, called him here from the town a day away over the rolling hills, from his job constructing offices for the immigrants. They shared a smoke and he took the story into his blood, his bones, while the stars nodded their heads, while the dogs murmured their agreement. "We can't stay long," the wolf said. "We have others with whom to speak and we haven't much time." He packed the wolf people some food to take with them, some tobacco, and they prayed together for safety on this journey.

As they left the first flakes of winter began falling and covered their tracks. It was as if they had never been there.

But the story burned in the heart of this human from the north and he told it to everyone who would listen, including my elder friend who told it to me one day while we ate biscuits and eggs in Arizona. The story now belongs to you, too, and much as pollen on the legs of a butterfly is nourishment carried by the butterfly from one flowering to another, this is an ongoing prayer for strength for us all.

CALVIN HERNTON

A Ballad of the Life and Times of Joe Louis
The Great Brown Bomber

I

Know I must and think I will
Sound the gong and make a song of shimmering steel
And make it real
For the Great Brown Bomber born on the Buckalow Mountains
among the Alabama Hills!

Lesser men

who raving
who babble senility
who name lakes after themselves who eyes glint
who lips twitch
Are not abandon to shipwreck cold and naked shock
   but are
   paraded before the world
   and live in mansions
If not in peace.

So come and go
Ye throngs of thousands, ye mermaids of cognition
Hail! Hail! Hail!
Come and go back to fireside chats and the gospel songs
   of the Golden Gate Quartet,
Come and go
   when I was a boy down in Chattanooga, Tennessee
   when black folks congregate in Big Mable's bootlegged
   liquor joint
   and children hovered outside against the storefront
   windows painted black all the way up to the heights of our
   wool-laden heads
   when the entire ghetto street grew quiet
   in open daylight
   when pride quelled beating hearts still
   and over the only wireless in the neighborhood
   we stood as though around a throne
And all ears awaited the sound of the gong.

II

Hail! Hail! Hail!

JUNE 22ND 1938

YANKEE STADIUM

ROUND ONE

LOUIS COMES OUT MAKING A WINDING MOTION WITH HIS RIGHT

FOREARM

Just like the first time

AND HE SENDS A RIGHT TO SCHMELING'S JAW THAT STAGGERS

THE BIG GERMAN

NOW LOUIS SENDS ANOTHER, A THIRD, A FOURTH, ALL HITTERS!

And unlike the first time

LOUIS DOES NOT DROP HIS GUARD AFTER HITTING THE GERMAN

UNLIKE THE FIRST TIME

NOW SCHMELING TRIES TO COUNTER WITH A FUSILLADE OF RIPPING

RIGHTS AND LEFTS.

BUT JOE JERKS BACK

SCHMELING BORES IN AND TOUCHES A LIGHT ONE LOUIS IGNORES IT

NOW THEN BUT LOUIS SMASHES HOME A RIGHT THAT SHOULD

HAVE DENTED CONCRETE DENTED CONCRETE DENTED CONCRETE!!!

And the nation exploded: "Beat That German, Brown Bomber,
Beat That German!"

As if to himself the crippled man in the White House in the fire-
side chair murmured: "Beat The Nazi, Beat Him For The
Morale Of The American Democracy!"

And in big Mabel's bootlegged liquor joint up and down the street
everywhere shouted to the sky: "Whop Him, Joe, Baby, Whop

Him For The Sake Of Colored Folks All Over Dis Forsaken
Land!

WHEELING SCHMELING FACE FRONT TO THE ROPES JOE LOUIS SENDS

A VICIOUS RIGHT TO THE KIDNEY

Why does the announcer call Joe's punch "Vicious"?

Were it the other way around . . .

A VICIOUS RIGHT TO THE KIDNEY VICIOUS TO THE KIDNEY AND

SCHMELING SCREAMS LADIES AND GENTLEMEN

SCREAMS IN PAIN PAIN PAIN WHEELING SCHMELING FACE FRONT

TO THE ROPES OH MY COUNTRY ROPES OF THEE BLACK NECKS HANGING

FROM THE POPLAR TREES MY COUNTRY TEARS OH VICIOUS RIGHT

TO THE KIDNEY AND THE GERMAN BLOND SCREAMS IN AGONY

ONE OF THE MOST TERRIFYING SOUNDS HEARD IN THE RING

LADIES AND GENTLEMEN

In the first round of the first fight when the Brown Bomber entered
the ring and took off his robe
there was another scream sounded the same
hysterical scream from a WOMAN at ringside:

EEEEEEEEEEEOOOOOOOOOOOOOOOOOOOWWWWWWWWW!!!!!!

WHAT'S THAT HE GOT IN HIS PANTS OH GOD WHAT'S THAT BIG BULGING

IN HIS JOCKSTRAP

The Most Terrifying Sound Ever Heard In The Ring!

MAX SCHMELING STRUGGLES TO LIFT HIS RIGHT ARM TO GRAB

THE SIDE THE RIB THE GOOD OLD BAR B QED RIB BUT MAX IS

PARALYZED PARALYZED

REFEREE ARTHUR DONOVAN STEPS BETWEEN LOUIS AND THE GERMAN

AND THE BROWN BOMBER IS POISING ANOTHER BOMB

Get Away, Joe! screams Referee Donovan

LOUIS BLINKS AND BACKS AWAY GLARING ANGRILY AT THE WRITHING

GERMAN. . . *scenes of flashing back images montage what a ball*

of cotton with a great dictator mustache walking arrogantly

from the olympic stands vowing he's never recognize no black

coon even if he were the fastest man alive!. . . PEOPLE YELL FOR

THE COUNT START THE COUNT THE COUNT BUT NO COUNT BEGINS

MAX IS UTTERLY HELPLESS AND BUT FOR THE ROPES HE WOULD BE

FLOPPED ALREADY HIS BLOND HEAD IS ROLLING LIKE RUBBER

NOW THEN LOUIS HITS HIM WITH A SWISHING HOOK WITH A RIFLE

TWIST TO IT SCHMELING DROPS BUT BEHOLD STAGGERS UP ON KNOCKING

KNEES WITHOUT TAKING A SINGLE COUNT WOO WOO WOO THE GERMAN

MUST REALLY BE SUPERMAN

NOW THEN BUT LOUIS AGAIN FLOORS THE GERM. . . SOMETHING WHITE

AN ILLEGAL TOWEL HAS BEEN THROWN INTO THE RING FROM SCHMELING'S

CORNER THE REFEREE IS THROWING THE TOWEL BACK OUT OF THE

RING . . . BUT SCHMELING HAS CRUMPLED . . . FOR KEEPS . . .

REFEREE DONOVAN BREASTROKES WITH BOTH ARMS AND THE MASSACRE

IS ENDED WHERE SCHMELING WAKES UP IN THE HOSPITAL

Down in Chattanooga, Tennessee black men and women and
   children sang
and wept and danced and prayed and rejoiced
And my grandmother said: "Lawd, childe, aint neber seed black
   folks
be so proud, naw, not eben when ole Abraham Lincoln freed us
aint neber seed black folks so hopeful, naw, not even when ole
Abe promised forty acres and one mule."
Hail! Hail! Oh, Hail!

III

I know I'm right and can't be wrong
Come along children and sang this song
And let it live
For the Great Brown Bomber born on the Buckalow Mountains
    among the Alabama Hills.

A pot of lye will sting and a bullet will kill
"Maw, I glad I win, I glad I win," quot the heavyweight champeen
O come along while the moon is shining bright
Gie me a pig feet and a bottle of gin
We gon raise the ruckus tonight!

IN EVERY MAIN BATTLE NO PERSON WHATEVER SHALL BE UPON THE
STAGE EXCEPT THE PRINCIPALS AND THEIR SECONDS: THE SAME RULE
TO BE OBSERVED IN THE BY-BATTLES, EXCEPT THAT IN THE LATTER
MR. BROUGHTON IS ALLOWED TO BE UPON THE STAGE TO KEEP DECORUM
AND TO ASSIST GENTLEMEN IN GETTING TO THEIR PLACES THESE ARE
MR. BROUGHTON'S RULES 1743

Fifty-nine heavyweight champeen fights fifty-one by knockout!
Flat feet stalker! Yo mamma wusnt no Mississippi delta queen
1619 nineteen Africans rattled their chains on the shores of
    Jamestown Virginia didnt come to America on no flower of
    May seeking no dream for

The white dream is a black nightmare.

ON THE MEN BEING STRIPPED IT SHALL BE THE DUTY OF THE SECONDS

TO EXAMINE THEIR DRAWERS, AND IF ANY OBJECTION ARISES AS TO

THE INSERTIN OF IMPROPER SUBSTANCES THEREIN THEY SHALL APPEAL

TO THEIR UMPIRES WHO WITH THE CONCURRENCE OF THE REFEREE SHALL

DIRECT WHAT ALTERATIONS SHALL BE MADE THESE ARE LONDON PRIZE

RING RULES 1838 REVISED 1853

And a white woman screamed at ringside . . . *Here are the fruits*
  for the
  wind to such and the buzzards to pluck
  seeds often thousand black men dripping blood
  from the magnolia tree . . .
STOPPING A FIGHT A MOMENT TOO SOON MAY BE UNFAIR TO

A GAME MAN: STOPPING IT A MOMENT TOO LATE MAY BE A TRAGEDY

SO SAITH ARTHUR DONOVAN

Runt fat men hallucinating jungle hunters, playing tough guys
Writing novels of wild life and statuesque imperialists
  with shotguns in their mouths
Jack London switching alongside the stout black legs of Jack
  Johnson
Burnt-out Hebrew novelist jerking off his dukes at the bicep pistons
of the baddest black man ever to leap out of the criminology
    books
Who fought his way from nothing and nobody to the Heavyweight
  Champeenhood of the known world, alas, to be
Found "mysteriously" dead for seven nights and seven days

Oh Hail! Hail! Hail!
Jersey Joe Sugar Ray Floyd Patterson Kid Gavaland Archie Moore
Gentleman Jim John G. Chamber and the Marquis of Queensberry—
Oh, Hail to the Contest of Endurance!

IV

Maybe I'm wrong and don't care if I am
But I believe I will
Sound the gong *Flam Flam Flam*
For the Great Brown Bomber who rose above the Buckalow
    Mountains and the hills of Alabam.

BORN: 1914 May 13th TAURUS:
First decanate: Sub-ruler, Venus
Constellation: LEPUS
Of African Indian and Caucasian blood
Making money making money making money FOR WHOM

The gong tolls?
MARVA! Fine brownskin middle-class fashion-struck woman
    prancing through celluloid cities of Paris, London, Madrid
Hanging out with Josephine Baker
    scream of a woman at ringside. . .

Jockstrap of the Bull!
Stalking Jabbing Stalking Jabbing Stalking Chunking bomb after
    bomb
    after bomb into the bodies of other men
    fighting as many as eight fights a year!
1937 Chicago Knock out James J. Braddock
1937 New York defeated Tommy Farr
1938 New York Knock out Nathan Mann
1938 New York Knock out Harry Thomas
1938 New York Knock out Max Schmeling

1939 New York Knockout John H. Lewis

1939 Los Angeles Knock out Jack Roper

1939 New York Knock out Tony Galento

1939 Detroit Knockout Bob Paster

1940 New York defeated Arturo Godey

1940 New York Knock out Johnny Paycheck

1940 New York Knock out Arturo Godey

1940 Boston Joe Louis Knocked out Al McCoy

1941 New York Joe Louis Knocked out Red Berman

1941 Philadelphia Joe Louis Knocked out Gus Derazio

1941 Detroit Joe Louis Knocked out Abe Simon

1941 St. Louis Joe Louis Knocked out Tony Muste

1941 Washington D.C. Joe Louis whipped Buddy Baer

1941 New York Joe Louis Knocked out Billy Conn

1941 New York Joe Louis Knock out Lou Nova

1942 New York Joe Louis Knock out Buddy Baer

1942 New York Joe Louis Knock out Abe Simon

And then

  around the world

BROOM... BROOM. BRRRRROOOOOOOOMMMMMMMMMMMM

                    PEARL HARBOR!

       UNCLE SAM WANTS YOU   boy

Uncle Sam God Damn Hush! yo mouf.

      SLIP OF THE LIP MIGHT SINK A SHIP

      TODAY EUROPE TOMORROW THE WORLD

Exhibition fights for Uncle Sam's morale

But do not go near the white frenchy women, boy

Or you'll find your neck swinging from the ropes

scream of a woman. . .

      NOTHING TO FEAR BUT FEAR ITSELF

PATHE NEWS: Knockout Tojo: PATHE NEWS: all chickens cackle when
    the ROOSTER crows: One down Two to go
PATHE NEWS: Atomic Bomb!
Hey, boy, you may be the Brown Bomber but we got a Bomb
    that gonna knock out ten million chinks before you can
    throw a punch
Oh, Hail! Hail! Hail!
ATOMIC BOMB!

V

Stars and Stripes forever!
Five winters past
Stars and Stripes
Name a bottle of gin "Joe Louis"
      Spirit of Lightning
      The Knock Out Liquor
Five summertimes in the matador's ring
Taurus possessor of healing powers divinely given
Whom shall you fight five winter ages gone, Ole!

WEDNESDAY NIGHT JUNE 19TH 1946

YANKEE STADIUM

45,266 SPECTATORS FAN THE WITNESS BOX
1,925,564 DOLLARS RESIDE AT THE BOX OFFICE
Give us pause: Arthur Donovan all time fight referee
        Jo Humphreys all time fight announcer
    having died during the interim of the duration
Before the fight give them pause.

BILLY CONN FOOT FLEET NIMBLE FOR EIGHT ROUNDS

BACKING AWAY DANCING SIDE TO SIDE BACKPEDDLING BICYCLING

NEW REFEREE EDDIE JOSEPH AS WELL AS THE NEW ANNOUNCER ARE

OUT OF BREATH TRYING TO KEEP APACE WITH THE SKATING BUTTERFLY

OF THE RING LADIES AND GENTLEMEN

BUT NOW EARLY IN THIS ROUND BILLY AINT MOVING FAST ENOUGH

AND JOE CATCHES HIM WITH A WICKED LEFT HOOK AND A SHARP

TEARING RIGHT HANDER

"He Can Run But He Can't Hide"

THE SECOND PUNCH, THE SHARP, TEARING RIGHT HANDER, RIPPED

OPEN A GASH UNDER THE BUTTERFLY'S LEFT EYE AND BILLY IS HURT

BUT NOT IN REAL TROUBLE NOT YET

NEVERTHELESS CONN'S LEGS DO NOT CARRY HIM BACKWARDS WITH THE

SAME EARLIER SPEED AND JOE IS ON TOP OF HIM ON TOP OF HIM

AND LOUIS HITS CONN FIVE FIVE FIVE FIVE FIVE PUNCHES IN

A BLISTERING FUSILLADE ALL IN THE SPACE OF SECONDS

AND ALL TO THE HEAD. . .

[Hey, Joe! Joe of Louis, why don't you come and go with me
Back down to Chattanooga Tennessee
I aint got a dime and I dont own a buffalo
But you and me Joe we are Tauruses We got hearts full of magnolias
    and lilacs and green grass in our loins
Face it everybody loves a winner but when you lose you lose alone
And it is cold out here among the pale stone
Please Joe
Come with me, do not let them drive you too like the rest

into those anonymous ruins where

haggard nurses stalk the silence

And forgotten men sit idle exhuming wisdom in

Oblivion's concern]

. . .ALL TO THE HEAD

THE LAST ONE IS A MURDEROUS RIGHT CROSS AND BILLY CONN SAGS

LOUIS FIRES A HARD LEFT THAT STAGGERS CONN, AND FOLLOWS WITH

A HARD LEFT AND RIGHT THAT STRETCHES CONN ON HIS BACK ON THE

FLOOR WHERE REFEREE JOSEPH COUNTS HIM OUT FULL "TEN" AT TWO

MINUTES NINETEEN SECONDS OF THE EIGHT AND FINAL ROUND

Final for Conn Final for Conn and Finally

An omen for you too Joe.

VI

So now we sit here in the year of nineteen hundred and seventy

   one.

What happened to all that money you made

What happened to your fortune

Oh, Birds! Birds! Birds!

We stand idle inside of trembling fists

   where no gongs

But the ringing in our spines limp and old

Yes, Old!

When first I journeyed from Chattanooga seeking strange

   insistent voices

To New York, expecting to actually find you walking the streets
    of Harlem, strong and proud and hear you speak to me alone
    characterisitically as Billie Holiday might have spoken
    had she escaped,
I was disappointed.
Not with you but with the world!
For you are not merely my hero of old but hero of all time
    for all black men and women whiriwinding within the
    gift outraged;
But your friends, your wives, the multitude of hangers-on
Where are they—are they with you flow?

I am with you Joe Louis
I am with you in your strange surroundings and in your fears,
    for, unbeknowing to those who write copy and those who put
    on parties,
Your fears are *my* fears—Oh, God! How real they really are?

Hail! Hail! Hail!
I walked with you when you were up and in
I walk with you now although you are out you are not down
    and never will
Oh, Hail? Great Brown Bomber born on the Buckalow Mountains
    among the Alabama Hills!

LINDA HOGAN

Tiva's Tapestry: La Llorona

For Tiva Trujillo, 1979

White-haired woman of winter,
la Llorona
with the river's black
unraveling
drowned children from her hands.

At night frozen leaves
rustle the sound of her skirt.
Listen and wind comes spinning
her song from the burning eyes of animals
from the owl
whose eyes look straight ahead.
She comes dragging
the dark river
a ghost on fire
for children she held
under water.

Stars are embroidered on the dark.
Long shadows, long like rivers
I am sewing
shut the doors

filling the windows in with light.
This needle pierces a thousand kisses
and rage
the shape of a woman.
I light this house,
sprinkle salt on my sleeping child
so dreams won't fly her into the night.

These fingers have sewn a darkness
and flying away
on the white hair growing
on the awful tapestry of sky
just one of the mothers
among the downward circling stars.

LAWSON INADA

Filling the Gap

When Bird died, I didn't mind:
I had things to do—

polish some shoes, practice
a high school cha-cha-cha.

I didn't even know
Clifford was dead:

I must have been
lobbing an oblong ball
beside the gymnasium.

I saw the Lady
right before she died—

dried, brittle
as last year's gardenia.

I let her scratch an autograph.

But not Pres.

Too bugged to boo, I left
as Basie's brass
booted him off the stand
in a sick reunion—

tottering, saxophone
dragging him like a stage-hook.

When I read Dr. Williams
poem, "Stormy,"
I wrote a letter of love and praise

and didn't mail it.

After he died, it burned my desk
like a delinquent prescription . . .

I don't like to mourn the dead:
what didn't, never will.

And I sometimes feel foolish
staying up late,
trying to squeeze some life
out of books and records,
filling the gaps
between words and notes.

That is why
I rush into our room to find you
mumbling and moaning
in your incoherent performance.

That is why
I rub and squeeze you
and love to hear your
live, alterable cry against my breast.

Ted Joans

Skip The Byuppie

He the ultimate shady dark Right

winger

Either a Newt-negro

Or growling Sambo t.v. talk

Show is pitbull fist swinger

He in a double breasted

Bathing suit of sweat

Trying like all he

Hell to do well

In his newly media

Plastic office crack

Tight assed taught to

Perform his token tongue

Tap dance of loose lips

Him be drum stick stuck

And drum major of

Byuppie minor parade

Him stays in step

Unhip and aloof

Imitating Wasp ways

Publishing his quick slick

Instructions for those

Who prepare his grave

He is the first

As well as America's worst

Byuppie by far

No big loaves of bread

Like the Yuppie Gates

This goody boy Gates is grim

He cant even swing

A lucrative campus opening

For worthy Black—cause

Jivey League may downsize him!

Certain Whites amongst themselves

Say that he's their crazy lap dog

Faculty members welcome him

He be just the N-word they need

An intellectual seedy glib tongued

University nice negro number one

Byuppie invited as dinner guest

Blatant lies as he chews the food

His dark face radiates his joy

Being adressed as

Mister-Professor 'boy'

Byuppie eyebrows stay arched

As he disguises his stress

Nevertheless he mouths and writes

What his master knows best

Byuppie is the

Vomit vermillion coloured boy

A dickless N-word media

Golliwog toy

Ubiquitous dull and unhip thus

Un-golden gate to skip
Byuppie is the puppy of the Yuppie
Byuppie is the puppy of the Yuppie
A grotesque gate that must he shut
Skip the byuppie gate

BOB KAUFMAN

Crootey Songo

DERRAT SLEGELATIONS, FLO GOOF BABER,
SCRASH SHO DUBIES, WAGO WAILO WAILO.
GEED BOP NAVA GLIED, NAVA GLIED NAVA
SPLEERIEDER, HUYEDIST, HEDACAZ, AX–, O.O.

DEEREDITION, BOOMEDITION, SQUOM, SQUOM, SQUOM.
DEE BEETSTRAWIST, WAPAGO, LOCOEST, LOCORO, LO.
VOOMETEYEREEPETIOP, BOP, BOP, BOP, WHIPOLAT.

DEGET, SKLOKO. KURRITIF, PLOG, MANGI, PLOG MANGI,
CLOPO JAGO BREE, BREE, ASLOOPERED, AKINGO LABY.
ENGPOP, ENGPOP, BOP, PLOLO, PLOLO, BOP, BOP.

ALAN CHONG LAU

Sun Yat Sen Comes to Lodi

for my great grandfather, ou ch'ü-chia

1

SUN YAT SEN COMES TO LODI
grandfather in pinstripes
mouth sporting a toothpick
tells friends, "no sin, no sin,
no sir, no sin to get excited"

mr. yee's four-year-old beaming in a pink meenop
hair's done up in pinktails
sam wo has closed his laundry
only day of the year he would do this
excepting new year's

the good doctor smiles
from a sedan's back seat
cheers resound
delta dust flies

there is the speech
"china will be china again"
this brings tears

not losing a minute
to sip
he tells us all that money buys arms
money drives out manchus

most people understand, there is little hesitation
the new york yankees have not yet won the pennant
it is too early to predict weather or the lucky number
but money is dug from pockets
pulled from cloth bags
when the time comes
he says thank you
a cry of genuine sadness
a rush to take seats for a last picture

photographer tong yee
fumbles underneath a black shroud like a soul leaving body
poses change legs shift position
nobody seems to mind too much
only local banker wong hesitates
meeting the public often, he declines
offering a bigger contribution instead

grandfather sits by the doctor's side
pausing only to doff his hat
remove a coin from the ear
and drop a wet toothpick in a spittoon

2

he is proud of that picture
brown and bent in one corner
the only photo left in the family album
since big sister's marriage

there is also a newspaper clipping
with the headline
"SUN YAN SEN COMES TO LODI"
spread out all in characters
that could be relatives telling a story
or scales of a black bass dripping evidence of water

never having learnt the language
i just have to go by hearsay

ROLAND LEGIARDI-LAURA

Trickster Rabbit

I am your trickster rabbit
I accept this role in society
        with gracious humility
I will wreak havoc forever on you all

I will shit on the table of my host
>while singing grateful praise of the meal
I will bleed the hand that bites me

I am trickster rabbit
>the crusader of rags
I will rewrite all the messages on your fortune
>cookies
instructing you to dial ecstasy for the
>dialectic
I am the furry little clawed foot
>you keep in your back pocket
>the one that cuts deep into your butt
>every time you sit down too fast
I am your Uncle Steve and Crazy Eddie
>if you undersell me I'll break
>that Panasonic coda-phone over
>your head
I am trickster rabbit,
>I'll hop down your
throat and suck your lungs dry . . .
>you'll spit and cough and yell
>Uncle.
I am your neighbor who plays trumpet and
>tap dances and yodels
and when you complain yells art in your
>face.
I am the silent deadly digital watch
>that tells you the date, time, lunar phase
>and astrological sign.

My tick is your tick

       tickless cold dead feather rubbing up against the

soft spot on the inside of your left nostril.

I am your therapist and lover

     curing you once and for all of your

     fears of riding up in elevators at the

     Hyatt Regency

I am your dance teacher

   explaining the secrets of the pelvis

   your disks all slipped

     you lie prostrate before me

       while I demonstrate the

boogaloo, the twist, the shimmy and the most mysterious

mouse.

I am your Clint Eastwood you are my

   Sunshine, my only sunshine.

I come to you disguised as rabbit stew,

     Lapin Roti,

all ears, pink furry cutesy ears

    my carrot in hand.

    I ask you to tell me all

without hesitation. "What's up, Doc!!!"

   I am your conductor on the L

   Canarsie line who tells you

that because of construction, that's right

   new construction the train you are

    on will pass its regularly scheduled

    stop on Bedford Avenue and a changeover

    has been arranged for you at Montauk Point

I am your cab driver
      your museum curator
      your arts council auditor
I am judgment day in a plastic no break no mess
          bottle.
I am lead guitar for the Clash
      I am page 74 of The German Ideology
      and babies are my business
          my only business
I go to sleep with you naked
      and wake up wrapped in the
          biggest pampers you ever saw
I am Trickster Rabbit, Ricochet Rabbit,
      Crusader Rabbit and Bugs Bunny.
I am a rotten Easter egg on the White House
      lawn
painted day glo brown
I'm hung like a guinea pig and
      I like to watch.
When you're walking home late, about
      to enter Tompkins Square Park
      I am the street lamp that
        flickers—
"Whitey you a sucker, your ass is mine
      gimme your wallet."
I am your wallet with your YMHA
membership card   your plastic Eye and
      Ear Infirmary card
and a faded picture of Roy and Trigger

the wonderhorse
I am your green, sweaty crumbling
wallet with twenty-two
dollars, a cancelled check and two ticket
stubs to the Kitchen.
I am your trembling hand that wants to
take the mugger's knife away from him
do a back flip, land on his shoulders
and whisper gently into his ear
"Home James or I'll slice the smile right outta
your face."
I'm your panic button that says 'no'
I'm your logic button that says 'wooah'
I'm your belly button that says 'ho ho ho'
I am your trickster rabbit's foot
pressed between your wallet
and your ass
I am the font of wisdom
the hole that passes gas
You know now I have power
over you
I am your report card
your telephone bill
the meter maid
the Good Humor man
I am a goddamn fudgesicle in July
I am your change of address card
I am the seven arms of Shiva
the six hammers of Thor

the hot lips of Hera
the fox lock on your door.
I am a bag of Pepperidge Farm cookies
and a quart of milk,
Dylan's born-again christianity
and a dress made of blue silk.
I am heart of rabbit
and my pump will never stop
I am heart of rabbit
hop hop hop hop
        hop hop hop
          hop.

VACHEL LINDSAY

Bryan, Bryan, Bryan, Bryan

The Campaign of Eighteen Ninety-six, as Viewed at the Time by a Sixteen-Year-Old, etc.

I

In a nation of one hundred fine, mob-hearted, lynching,
   relenting, repenting millions,
There are plenty of sweeping, swinging, stinging, gorgeous

   things to shout about,
And knock your old blue devils out.

I brag and chant of Bryan, Bryan, Bryan,
  Candidate for president who sketched a silver Zion,
  The one American Poet who could sing outdoors,
  He brought in tides of wonder, of unprecedented splendor,
Wild roses from the plains, that made hearts tender,
All the funny circus silks
  Of politics unfurled,
Bartlett pears of romance that were honey at the cores,
And torchlights down the street, to the end of the world.

There were truths eternal in the gab and tittle-tattle.
There were real heads broken in the fustian and the rattle.
There were real lines drawn:
Not the silver and the gold,
But Nebraska's cry went eastward against the dour and old,
The mean and cold.

It was eighteen ninety-six, and I was just sixteen
And Altgeld ruled in Springfield, Illinois,
When there came from the sunset Nebraska's shout of joy:
In a coat like a deacon, in a black Stetson hat
He scourged the elephant plutocrats
With barbed wire from the Platte.
The scales dropped from their mighty eyes.
They saw that summer's noon
A tribe of wonders coming
To a marching tune.

Oh, the longhorns from Texas,

The jay hawks from Kansas,

The plop-eyed bungaroo and giant giassicus,

The varmint, chipmunk, bugaboo,

The horned-toad, prairie-dog and ballyhoo,

From all the newborn states arow,

Bidding the eagles of the west fly on,

Bidding the eagles of the west fly on.

The fawn, prodactyl and thing-a-ma-jig,

The rakaboor, the hellangone,

The whangdoodle, batfowl and pig,

The coyote, wild-cat and grizzly in a glow,

In a miracle of health and speed, the whole breed abreast,

They leaped the Mississippi, blue border of the West,

From the Gulf to Canada, two thousand miles long:—

Against the towns of Tubal Cain,

Ah,—sharp was their song.

Against the ways of Tubal Cain, too cunning for the young,

The longhorn calf, the buffalo and wampus gave tongue.

These creatures were defending things Mark Hanna never
   dreamed:

The moods of airy childhood that in desert dews gleamed,

The gossamers and whimsies,

The monkeyshines and didoes

Rank and strange

Of the canyons and the range,

The ultimate fantastics

Of the far western slope,

And of prairie schooner children

Born beneath the stars,

Beneath falling snows,

Of the babies born at midnight

In the sod huts of lost hope,

With no physician there,

Except a Kansas prayer,

With the Indian raid a howling through the air

And all these in their helpless days

By the dour East oppressed,

Mean paternalism

Making their mistakes for them,

Crucifying half the West,

Till the whole Atlantic coast

Seemed a giant spiders' nest.

And these children and their sons

At last rode through the cactus,

A cliff of mighty cowboys

On the lope,

With gun and rope.

And all the way to frightened Maine the old East heard them call,

And saw our Bryan by a mile lead the wall

Of men and whirling flowers and beasts,

The bard and the prophet of them all.

Prairie avenger, mountain lion,

Bryan, Bryan, Bryan, Bryan,

Gigantic troubadour, speaking like a siege gun,

Smashing Plymouth Rock with his boulders from the West,

And just a hundred miles behind, tornadoes piled across the sky,

Blotting out sun and moon,

A sign on high.

Headlong, dazed and blinking in the weird green light,

The scalawags made moan,

Afraid to fight.

II

When Bryan came to Springfield, and Altgeld gave him greeting,

Rochester was deserted,

Divernon was deserted,

Mechanicsburg, Riverton, Chickenbristle, Cotton Hill,

Empty: for all Sangamon drove to the meeting—

In silver-decked racing cart,

Buggy, buckboard, carryall,

Carriage, phaeton, whatever would haul,

And silver-decked farm wagons gritted, banged and rolled,

With the new tale of Bryan by the iron tires told.

The State House loomed afar,

A speck, a hive, a football,

A captive balloon!

And the town was all one spreading wing of bunting,

   plumes, and sunshine,

Every rag and flag, and Bryan picture sold,

When the rigs in many a dusty line

Jammed our streets at noon,

And joined the wild parade against the power of gold.

We roamed, we boys from High School,

With mankind,

While Springfield gleamed,

Silk-lined.

Oh, Tom Dines, and Art Fitzgerald,

And the gangs that they could get!

I can hear them yelling yet.

Helping the incantation,

Defying aristocracy,

With every bridle gone,

Ridding the world of the low down mean,

Bidding the eagles of the West fly on,

Bidding the eagles of the West fly on,

We were bully, wild and woolly,

Never yet curried below the knees.

We saw flowers in the air,

Fair as the Pleiades, bright as Orion,

—Hopes of all mankind,

Made rare, resistless, thrice refined.

Oh, we bucks from every Springfield ward!

Colts of democracy—

Yet time-winds out of Chaos from the star-fields of the Lord.

The long parade rolled on. I stood by my best girl.

She was a cool young citizen, with wise and laughing eyes.

With my necktie by my ear, I was stepping on my dear,
But she kept like a pattern, without a shaken curl.

She wore in her hair a brave prairie rose.
Her gold chums cut her, for that was not the pose.
No Gibson Girl would wear it in that fresh way.
But we were fairy Democrats, and this was our day.

The earth rocked like the ocean, the sidewalk was a deck.
The houses for the moment were lost in the wide wreck.
And the bands played strange and stranger music as they
   trailed along.
Against the ways of Tubal Cain,
Ah, sharp was their song!
The demons in the bricks, the demons in the grass,
The demons in the bank-vaults peered out to see us pass,
And the angels in the trees, the angels in the grass,
The angels in the flags, peered out to see us pass.
And the sidewalk was our chariot, and the flowers bloomed
     higher,
And the street turned to silver and the grass turned to fire,
And then it was but grass, and the town was there again,
A place for women and men.

III

Then we stood where we could see
Every band,

And the speaker's stand.
And Bryan took the platform.
And he was introduced.
And he lifted his hand
And cast a new spell.
Progressive silence fell
In Springfield,
In Illinois,
Around the world.
Then we heard these glacial boulders across the prairie rolled:
'The people have a right to make their own mistakes. . . .
You shall not crucify mankind
Upon a cross of gold.'

And everybody heard him—
In the streets and State House yard.
And everybody heard him
In Springfield,
In Illinois,
Around and around and around the world,
That danced upon its axis
And like a darling broncho whirled.

IV

July, August, suspense,
Wall Street lost to sense.
August, September, October,

More suspense,
And the whole East down like a wind-smashed fence.

Then Hanna to the rescue,
Hanna of Ohio,
Rallying the roller-tops,
Rallying the bucket-shops.
Threatening drouth and death,
Promising manna,
Rallying the trusts against the bawling flannelmouth;
Invading misers' cellars,
Tin-cans, socks,
Melting down the rocks,
Pouring out the long green to a million workers,
Spondulix by the mountain-load, to stop each new tornado,
And beat the cheapskate, blatherskite,
Populistic, anarchistic,
Deacon—desperado.

V

Election night at midnight:
Boy Bryan's defeat.
Defeat of western silver.
Defeat of the wheat.
Victory of letterfiles
And plutocrats in miles
With dollar signs upon their coats,

Diamond watchchains on their vests

And spats on their feet.

Victory of custodians,

Plymouth Rock,

And all that inbred landlord stock.

Victory of the neat.

Defeat of the aspen groves of Colorado valleys,

The blue bells of the Rockies,

And blue bonnets of old Texas,

By the Pittsburg alleys.

Defeat of alfalfa and the Mariposa lily.

Defeat of the Pacific and the long Mississippi.

Defeat of the young by the old and silly.

Defeat of tornadoes by the poison vats supreme.

Defeat of my boyhood, defeat of my dream.

VI

Where is McKinley, that respectable McKinley,

The man without an angle or a tangle,

Who soothed down the city man and soothed down the farmer,

The German, the Irish, the Southerner, the Northerner,

Who climbed every greasy pole, and slipped through every crack;

Who soothed down the gambling hall, the bar-room, the church,

The devil vote, the angel vote, the neutral vote,

The desperately wicked, and their victims on the rack,

The gold vote, the silver vote, the brass vote, the lead vote,

Every vote? . . .

Where is McKinley, Mark Hanna's McKinley,
His slave, his echo, his suit of clothes?
Gone to join the shadows, with the pomps of that time,
And the flame of that summer's prairie rose.

Where is Cleveland whom the Democratic platform
Read from the party in a glorious hour,
Gone to join the shadows with pitchfork Tillman,
And sledge-hammer Altgeld who wrecked his power.

Where is Hanna, bulldog Hanna,
Low-browed Hanna, who said: 'Stand pat'?
Gone to his place with old Pierpont Morgan.
Gone somewhere . . . with lean rat Platt.

Where is Roosevelt, the young dude cowboy,
Who hated Bryan, then aped his way?
Gone to join the shadows with mighty Cromwell
And tall King Saul, till the Judgment day.

Where is Altgeld, brave as the truth,
Whose name the few still say with tears?
Gone to join the ironies with Old John Brown,
Whose fame rings loud for a thousand years.

Where is that boy, that Heaven-born Bryan,
That Homer Bryan, who sang from the West?
Gone to join the shadows with Altgeld the Eagle,
Where the kings and the slaves and the troubadours rest.

ANGELA MARTIN

Viewing Mona Lisa

She has left behind a smooth blank space, fuckable and pure in the Louvre. I have taken her and her smirking mouth and locked her in a room. I take a look through a hole in the wall; she seems to glance and almost see. I long to watch her from behind. Some nights I imagine her Stone Age and grunting; sometimes Bedouin, wind-whipped and unheard. I often worry she will disappear into the mists of the landscape behind her. I wonder whether to lie her in a coffin or a marriage bed to keep her safe. I wish she would speak. Does she not love me? I fear she will bleed on our wedding night. I worry she will bleed spots and dashes onto the sheets that only she can read. I worry that those revolting scarlet hieroglyphs might mock me, like her silence, like her eyes. I worry she will repaint herself red. I whisper through the hole telling her everything is fine. Telling her: All I do is for her alone. I etch her surface, her gold-white flesh, with the weight of my tongue. ◆ I whispered there. I said: beautiful. I said: precious. Strangely, my last look was not a view of my beloved in a room, but of an eye stretched open.

"When the Mona Lisa was stolen from the Louvre in Paris in 1911 and was missing for two years, more people went to stare at the blank space than had gone to look at the masterpiece in the 12 previous years."

—Barbara Cortland, Book of Useless Information

SANDRA MCPHERSON

Six Movements for Portraits of Erzulie

Two images of love: one, a child artisan's, abstract,
with antennae, feelers; the other, something a child
couldn't make—

sharp swords to the heart.

The child's swords float loose, exterior, aim toward earth—

crutches that don't reach

Vapors from a rum cup. Flash from rectangular goat's eyes.

Child's goddess of love. Adults' salty deity.

In the child's, the heart is the face.

When the initiate rolls awake on the bed in her sanctuary
goose quills working through the pillow
scratch her eyelids and cheeks. Erzulie looks
brokenhearted, sinister.
As the boy sewed on her fingernails
(each a sole clear sequin
fixed with a glass bead,

the same as tears only
tears are pinker and more drawn out,
thinner in the calipers)
he glittered.

Who gores her heart seven times?
1 think she does, working the cutlery in
as one inserts thermometers to cook,
then folding her hands crisply away, blood
on her cuffs.
Oh that color—of blood rinsed
from a man's shaving sink.
Never far from her hand,
busy gold hilts collect no dust.

Pleasurable, promiscuous, passionate—
the heart that doesn't know
how to be a widow.

But sunset reflecting in the face
shows otherwise—there's a scowl
to sensuality.

When the heart and the face are separate,
you have to keep your eye on both.
Modestly, the flame of love's candle blows to the side
It is never clear and pure, never straight ascension.

And it's not because we're breathing on it
that it slants away.
Flame has to be our sloping, dwindling mirror,
our exact wax features
burning up.

Maybe you think it makes a difference
how she is expressed; as a heated human figure.
or, vaguer, as pigment and power.
What kind of portrait did you go to bed with,
wive, cheat on, and miss as a symbol
of your promising years?

And for women it is the same:
She is the idea
that beauty is rich, love poor and bare,
she is thinking that way,
flying to get out of
the single life of doctrine.

Finally she leaves you.
Only her abstraction is coming home.

SYLVIA PLATH

Lady Lazarus

I have done it again.
One year in every ten
I manage it—

A sort of walking miracle, my skin
Bright as a Nazi lampshade,
My right foot

A paperweight,
My face a featureless, fine
Jew linen.

Peel off the napkin
O my enemy.
Do I terrify?—

The nose, the eye pits, the full set of teeth?
The sour breath
Will vanish in a day.

Soon, soon the flesh
The grave cave ate will be
At home on me

And I a smiling woman.
I am only thirty.
And like the cat I have nine times to die.

This is Number Three.
What a trash
To annihilate each decade.

What a million filaments.
The peanut-crunching crowd
Shoves in to see

Them unwrap me hand and foot—
The big strip tease.
Gentleman, ladies,

These are my hands,
My knees.
I may be skin and bone,

Nevertheless, I am the same, identical woman.
The first time it happened I was ten.
It was an accident.

The second time I meant
To last it out and not come back at all.
I rocked shut

As a seashell.

They had to call and call
And pick the worms off me like sticky pearls.

Dying
Is an art, like everything else.
I do it exceptionally well.

I do it so it feels like hell.
I do it so it feels real.
I guess you could say I've a call.

It's easy enough to do it in a cell.
It's easy enough to do it and stay put.
It's the theatrical

Comeback in broad day
To the same place, the same face, the same brute
Amused shout:

"A miracle!"
That knocks me out.
There is a charge

For the eyeing of my scars, there is a charge
For the hearing of my heart—
It really goes.

And there is a charge, very large charge,
For a word or a touch
Or a bit of blood

Or a piece of my hair or my clothes.
So, so, Herr Doktor.
So, Herr Enemy.

I am your opus,
I am your valuable,
The pure gold baby

That melts to a shriek.
I turn and burn.
Do not think I underestimate your great concern.

Ash, ash—
You poke and stir.
Flesh, bone, there is nothing there—

A cake of soap,
A wedding ring,
A gold filling.

Herr God, Herr Lucifer,
Beware
Beware.

Out of the ash
I rise with my red hair
And I eat men like air.

TENNESSEE REED

Disney's Cinderella

She would wake up every morning
to an evil stepmother and jealous stepsisters
She was treated like a slave, doing the cooking and cleaning
Her stepmother always complained about her food:
"Cinderella, the pasta is too sticky, and the salad has ice burn"
or "Cinderella, the potatoes are a bit too hard"
Then Cinderella had to make her dinner again
One of the stepsisters accused her of stealing
her dark blue boot-cut jeans and white cotton blouse by Guess?
The other stepsister accused her of driving her Chevy Cavalier
without asking her when she went to pick up Ivory soap at
Duane Reade
(It turns out that her stepsister's ugly boyfriend
had borrowed it)
Her punishment was to go upstairs to her stepmother's room
to hear a long list of new chores
like changing her new baby stepsister's Pampers
Baby Dry disposable diaper, cleaning the kitchen with
Clorox wipes and wiping down the bathroom
with Windex and Pine-Sol
Despite all of this, Cinderella was an upbeat young woman,
she did what she was told, and she was very pleasant

There were times when Cinderella would give up,

like when her animal friends had made
her a dress for the ball
that was superior to Versace and Miyake
and it was ripped apart by her stepsisters
There were other times when she would
lose her temper or her patience
like when her name was called every two seconds
"Cinderella, it's Tuesday night, take out the garbage,"
or "Cinderella, the hamper is full"
She had people/animals in her corner
like her mice, her dog, horses and birds
as well as her Fairy God Mother

Because of the Fairy God Mother's storied enchantment
Cinderella was able to attend the ball
which was RSVP only
It was held at the Pierre Hotel
and Peter Duchin's band performed
The prince had his eye on her
even though there were hundreds of others in the room
including her stepsisters who had crashed the gate
One was eating Krispy Kreme doughnuts
even though she was diabetic
The other was eating a big bag of
Cool Ranch Dorito chips
She licked the remainders off of her fingers
The Blue Book Crowd was thinking,
"How grotesque"
The prince was stunned by Cinderella's beauty

and disappointed that she vanished
all except for her slippers
He arrived at her house in his shiny, gold Lexus
and slipped a shoe on her, which was more fancy
than the latest shoe by Giuseppe Zanotti
They flew off in his private jet
to honeymoon in Walt Disney World
and Disney's private island in the Bahamas
The angry stepsisters and mother showed up at the gate
but it was too late
His plane was taxying out to the runway

CORIE ROSEN

Madonna for the Damned—a 1980s Heroine

You stretched out your hungry voice
And grabbed Music Television
With fingerless black lace back-beats
And shocking pink lyrics.
From nowhere-nobody-nothing
New York
—sweaty streets full of Italian girls just like you—
You claimed your fame.

The teenybopper soul of the nation,

Your hollow trophy,

Moved to the music of big blonde hair

Moved by the bitter flavor,

The thin white lines

Of jagged, sweet cocaine.

Excommunicated matriarch of underage millions,

A sexual, bisexual, polyamorous parent of two,

America's own Eva Peron

In a black vinyl bodysuit,

You shoved the world into open-sided boxes

As you saw fit

And wouldn't take "no" for an answer.

The holy mother of pop,

You televised, musicalized, revolutionized,

For the very first time,

The spike-heeled sexual longing of fresh young girls.

Aching midnight dancers,

Free at last

To wear big cheap earrings.

EDWARD SANDERS

A Flower from Robert Kennedy's Grave

> *During demonstrations at Nixon's second*
> *inauguration, we watched his limo pass, on*
> *the way to the White House; then I drove*
> *over to Arlington Cemetery.*
>
> January 20, 1973

After
a winding walk
up past the white stones
of snuff,

past the guardhouse
circling circling
around the Catholic henge
to John Kennedy's bright taper
burning on the ground
in windy cold winter after-speech
afternoon

    then walk down
    to the left-hand

        edge of the hill-
ock—there in speechless serenity,

built onto the steepness
a small
elegant
perfectly proportioned
white cross 'bove
white flat marble marker

Robert Francis Kennedy

nearby a fount jets horizontal
over a slab o' stone

water curving down abruptly on the
rock front lip

R.F.K.'s words of race heal
writ upon the rock above
the flat-fount.

Across the walkway
by the grave
a long red rose
with a vial of water
slipped upon the stem end
& wrapped with shiny tape
lay singly
& to the left of it a
basket of yellow chrysanthemums

and this: that
only a whining hour past,
Richard Nixon
oozed down Pennsylvania Avenue
flashing V's from a limousine
behind a stutter-footed wary pack of Marines
                              their
    bayonets stabbing the January
in a thickery of different directions
like small lance hairs
    pricked up on the forehead of a
hallucinated drool fiend
      during a bummer

but big enough to stab the
    throats of hippie rioters
                              buddy.

    I picked a yellow petal
    from thy grave
      Mr. Robert Kennedy

    & brought it home
    from Arlington, where many young mourners
    stood crying quietly this inauguration day

Picked a dream
    Mr. Robert Kennedy

brought it home in our hearts
burning like a brand in a fennel stalk

Picked a thought-ray
Robert Kennedy

  brought it back from this
  hedge of park-side
  eternity

buses of protesters parked
in the lots beneath your hill

  Tears splash
  in the vessels
  of the sun

  Picked yellow
  molecules bunched
  in beauty
  from the beauty fount
  Mr. Robert Kennedy

The peace-ark
glides in the vastness,
though weirdness clings to your death.

But nothing can touch the ark

sails through the trellis of evil
brazen American wrought of light hate

Nothing can touch it
not even pyramidal battlements of gore-spore
nor tricky's pitiless flood
of dungeonoid luciphobian losers.

FRANK STANFORD

*

from *The Battlefield Where the Moon Says I Love You*

I still got hope Tang says
Jimmy was looking at the pictures trying to read James Dean's lips
there were for real tears coming out his eyes
the man turned up the volume folks we want you to remember
   our sunrise service
tomorrow morning we'll stop whatever is showing as soon as the
   preacher
gets here we would ask your cooperation in picking up the
   bottles and cans
under your vehicles before the preacher arrives
there will be he asked me to announce a collection taken up
aw shut up Clyde Miller a kid says

hymnals will be passed out at the concession stand after five
   o'clock this
morning thank you now back to our feature
honk honk honk he switched the mike off
and with a quick glance he reached in the till and got the two
   dollars Jimmy
give him and give it back to Jimmy saying sorry you can't bring
   those niggers
in here tonight son we got a religious service at daylight
and turned his back to Jimmy and says to his wife
Ronnie don't pay no tention to what the customers say I'm
   running this Drive Inn
Jimmy yelled what'd you say
the man's wife said honey you should a heard what some those
   people called you
the man turned around said get it they ain't coming in here
this woman said colored night was last night
Jimmy said we drove a long way ma'am
sorry she smacked her gum
Tang said uh uh what I say now what I say
the woman said y'all come back on another night and me and
   Clyde will be happy
to let you in see tomorrow's Easter and it just wouldn't be right
be too much scuttlebutt wouldn't honey say boy didn't Ray
   Charles record that
I just love Ray Charles he's one of my favorites next to Hank
did you know he's not really blind I read in a magazine it was a
   gimmick
hey Jimmy I said tell that mother fucker who I am

and tell that lady Ray Charles's blind as a bat

and while you're at it tell her she's bat fuck too

Jimmy said

sorry but you can't bring them boys in here I don't care what your
    name is

that didn't work either

the woman chewing gum said the others are welcome to come in
    she smiled

y'all go head and go Charlie said

Jimmy rattled the two bills in his hand like he was going to lay
    down and bet

ask him if we can come in just to see Baby Doll I said

what about me Tang said

ask him about Hallelujah too I said

he asked Clyde Miller

he was getting mad at Jimmy he said get on out the niggers
    couldn't come

they was having a revival service in the morning he said

the man said hold on cause his wife says it's time honey

he picked up the microphone and was about to talk

but Jimmy yelled out why don't you and Mrs. Miller go get
    fucked

the both of you I added Amen Tang and Charlie B. said

it carried over the sound system to every white man's car and
    truck

I know there must have been a tense moment for a moment

in the moom pitchu Drive Inn

cause all the peoples turned around and looked out they cars

I figured we'd be dead inside a minute but those folks had more
    sense

than I ever give them credit for I know them like the back of my
    hand I thought

but I guess I don't cause they just passed they two brown faces on

they must of knowd who we was although I'd like not to think so

yessiree they commenced to honking and yelling and laughing at
    Clyde Miller

it was a sight to see Tang looks over in my direction he says
    smart cracker jacks

Jimmy shoved it in reverse and scratched out backwards

he left two dollars worth a rubber in the man's Drive Inn
    driveway

he runned into his ticket shed on account of the slipping and
    sliding

then he hit another man's car he said get your ass out the way

Jimmy should never have riled the white man like that cause it
    riled all of them

he peeled out forward and we tore up some dead bushes Clyde
    Miller had planted

Jimmy was mad I guess before long we was doing a hundred
    miles an hour

fucking shithooks he was mumbling

I didn't think that car would do a hundred you drunk Jimmy I
    said

sorry bout that he told Charlie B.

Tang was laughing to himself saying told you so

he touched Jimmy on the shoulder slow this thing down boy he
    hit him in the head you crazy or something

we cruised on some more

boy that pisses me off Charlie B. says

don't it though Charlie Jimmy says

shuckit I says

goddamn motherfuckers Jimmy says

be what I told you wouldn't it Tang said y'all won't listen to an
    old man

shit y'all just whipsnaps I rode a hundred mules

you want to go back and shoot him Jimmy I said

nah could of done that then

open me nothun Tang said

say what about my supper

we stopped off on the way home about the time he said it

can a buy some firecrackers with the change Tang I said

yea but you better get me some soda crackers

I got some under the seat Jimmy says

good then they'll do he said

Jimmy gave me a dollar and told me pick some shells up

they had a sale on fishing worms and hooks so I took advantage
    of the bargain

I got enough to eat alright

so did Tang and the rest

drive up to the levee I want to yell a little bit Charlie B. says

the night got darker and we drove up there and parked

turn the damn radio back on Tang said

going to run down the battery if I do Jimmy said

piss on it you can coast start it if you have to

I got out the car and drunk me a lemon lime

lemme have the pistol I want to shoot tin cans

don't shoot yoself Charlie B. said

give me that box of shell too I just bought

don't shoot up all my bullets Jimmy said

I walked down the levee the high road

now it is getting colder and I am getting madder but an idea will
   come I thought

I'll dream something up

here I am saying this and still ain't off the mule yet

I ain't hit ball one ain't caught one either

I kept shooting at the can keeping it on top of the levee sometime
   having

to reel off some might quick shots to keep it from rolling down

whenever I missed I yelled missed

I didn't miss too much

after I'd shoot a full round I'd eject the empty cartridges out of
   the chamber

into my palm I'd warm my hand on them and smell the gun-
   powder smoke

it curled out of the brass like a garbage fire

I walked way down to a place I hadn't been before

some clearing had been done

the remains of snakes that had been cut in two by the bulldozer
   blade

stunk to high heaven the flies was buzzing like a radio station
   that won't come

in the trees were like wounded soldiers bent over on a battlefield

men that knew they had lost the fight and were going to die to
   boot

I can't see it but I know its there

gaunt and gallant like an old man with a pistol and an ace up his sleeve

reserved and noble with a silver moustache

mean as a convict's widow the river

I can smell it

ASKIA M. TOURÉ

Dawnsong!

(for the Ancient Anu/Nubians: founders of
Nile Valley Civilization)

Ethiopia and the African interior have always been
considered by Egyptians as the holy land from which
their forebears had come . . . The priestess of Amon at
Thebes, the Egyptian holy site par excellence, could
not be other than a Meroitic Sudanese [a Nubian].

—Cheikh Anta Diop
The African Origins of Civilization

Bennu bird, emerge from your ashes,
broadcast ecstatic cries
to the ibis, your kindred;
welcome a new sun rising from
Nile waters, like a bright flamingo
shrieking with joy . . .

Dawnsong. Jubilee. My bones and fossils
powder this proud land mankind
reclaims as Mother.
The Great Rift Valley, the Mountains
of the Moon, the Great Lakes region
blessed by a million mornings of legendary
dreamtimes, visions, times of living

gods, demons, royal ancestors: chants
which fertilized
    the humid atmosphere
      human aeons ago—fifty thousand years!
Yea. The swamps and wide savannahs
of the stellar people pregnant with
myriad myths and magic rituals; resounding
drumsongs giving birthchants and birthpangs
to create the lunar people:
    indigo tribes with lyre-horned
    cattle, scarification litanies,
    braided hair crowning
    prognathous silhouettes;

Matrilineal clans honoring goddesses
as "Great Mother" steatopygic
with natural, Nubian grace.
Cornrows: rituals of braided hair above
jewel-like scarifications, implying
numerous icons of feminine status
among families/clans/tribes.
Mattocks mating with the earth,
as warriors mate with holy
matriarchs, ritualizing love

Observe, in the human dawn,
the inner dawn
    break across horizons
    of Nubian minds, grappling

    with the soil, learning
      cycles of seasons;
growing crops, computing star charts,
moon charts, primordial innovation,
leading to mathematics
and solar calendars these
melanin millennia.
Moving, growing, migrating north,
gaining spiritual rhythms: vision
mirroring Cosmic principles:
—"As Above, So Below"—
from the moon and stellar jewels
glowing against the night, like
diamonds against indigo skin.

Cornrows moving sinuously
over the skull; hair as
the Primal Art Form—kinky,
rhythmic, erotic, twisted with
cowries over long skulls,
woven braids of farming rhythms:
these myriad rows of bending
women defining the soil,
mothering seeds, creating
harvests, nourishing
nations to come . . .

Night: copper moon-in-mist,
talking drums, as griots, relate

the magical awe, hideous beauty, written
in bloody icons of human sacrifice.
She—chant/scream/Mask—
the Oracle task;
　　　Speak, Spirits, Now!
Nude body oiled, voluptuous,
leaping, shrieking, dancing,
being ridden by the gods—
through ecstatic sunbursts,
comets, shooting stars—
prophesying wars, plagues,
miracles of birth and rebirth;

Dancing amid the gathered clans
in their thousands, shadows and
silhouettes relate the magic:
She changing shape into
　　　a cobra, a lioness, a hawk,
before the hypnotized multitudes.
Ostrich plumes, royal umbrellas,
gleaming jewelry, reflections
of firelight in the eyes, glistening
teeth, sighs fill thousands of
throats, as quickened hearts
witness the presence of the gods.
Totems with firelight blazing
on their banners:
the lion people, jackal people,
sparrow-hawk and crocodile;

Clans—majestic, silent,
frightened—enchanted
by the dancing queen.

O sing of the God-people!
The mighty Nubians, rooted in origins
South, beneath the Mountains of the Moon.
The "blameless Ethiopians" of the Greeks,
feasting with the gods; expanding serpent-
power, primordial energy, opening

> the Horus Eye, in
> grand temples of
> the Winged Scarab,
> Mind!

Those majestic, dusky clans
in lionskins and plumes:
fierce warriors, nubile maids,
dark hordes of sacred, dance,
and magical, lyre-horned cattle.
Sibyllic those statuesque queens,
who with farming, herbs and lore,
birthed pharoahs, priests, emerged
from towns to gleaming cities,
riding the Bird of Myth:
Bennu ruling sacred realms
of transcendental Truth! . . .

Hazy, amber dawns creating
torrid, blazing Suns,

birthing Isis, Osiris
and their kin . . .
dreaming Ta-Sili, Ta-Seti,
On, Abydos, Dendera—and
Pyramids to come!

QUINCY TROUPE

A Poem for "Magic";
for Earvin "Magic" Johnson, Donnell Reid,
and Richard Franklin

take it to the hoop, "magic" johnson
take the ball dazzling down the open lane
herk & jerk & raise your six foot nine inch
frame into air sweating screams of your neon name
"magic" johnson, nicknamed "windex" way back in high school
'cause you wiped glass backboards so clean
where you first juked & shook
& wiled your way to glory
a new styled fusion of shake & bake energy
using everything possible you created your own space
to fly through—any moment now we expect your wings
to spread feathers for that spooky take-off of yours
then shake & glide till you hammer home

a clotheslining deuce off glass

now, come back down with a reverse hoodoo gem

off the spin, & stick it in sweet popping nets

clean from twenty feet right side

put the ball on the floor, "magic"

slide the dribble behind your back, ease it deftly

between your bony stork legs, head bobbing everwhichaway

up & down, you see everything on the court, off the high

yoyo patter, stop & go dribble, you shoot

a threading needle rope pass sweet home to kareem

cutting through the lane, his skyhook pops the cords

now lead the fastbreak, hit jamaal on the fly

now blindside a behind the back pinpointpass for two more

off the fake, looking the other way

you raise off balance into tense space

sweating chants of your name, turn 360 degrees

on the move your legs scissoring space like a swimmer's

yoyoing motion in deep water, stretching out now

towards free flight, you double pump through human trees

hang in place, slip the ball into your left hand

then deal it like a Las Vegas card dealer off squared glass

into nets living up your singular nickname, so 'bad'

you cartwheel the crowd towards frenzy

wearing now your electric smile, neon as your name

in victory we suddenly sense your glorious uplift

your urgent need to be champion

& so we cheer, rejoicing with you for this quicksilver, quicksilver,

  quicksilver

moment of fame, so put the ball on the floor again, "magic"
juke & dazzle, shaking & baking down the lane
take the sucker to the hoop, "magic" johnson
recreate reverse hoodoo gems off the spin
deal alley-oop-dunk-a-thon-magician passes, now
double-pump, scissor, vamp through space, hang in place
& put it all in the sucker's face, "magic" johnson
& deal the roundball like the juju man that you am
like the shonuff shaman man that you am
"magic," like the shonuff spaceman you am

SAMIRA VIJGHEN

Fallen

I see you as victim of your own virtue. You have given your life to
humanity, and thus the world praises you. Your virtue must be so
large now. So convincing, it is the mockery of natural instinct to pre-
serve the species. A noble cause. But I mourn your one mistake,
and that is Batman. Your failure lies in losing your self by creating
a fiction and then becoming it. They love you, Bruce—Right now
they do. How can they not? You are better than a god; you
intercepted the rhetoric. You materialized an ideal in a world of
words and immaterial gods. You are the illusion of Batman built
upon the illusion of purpose and certainty. You live for the world.

But how, Bruce? All you have done is inventively reinforce the same story; in the name of morality, of good and evil. I see you selfless, and defined by the world, caught in a tragic dependency from the moment you wore the costume and became an icon for order. You gave them Batman; they expect it now. And what have you now but fear? Is your function really to protect the species, or to avoid the potential disappointment and scorn of the world? You, Batman, are the symptom of an ideology. Your good and their good are as much a lie as their God. If you reject the fiction you entered, the world will lean closer to the stage to hear the word. If you disillusion them now, you will become their next evil. Remember, first there was the word, then there was God. It's all lies, Bruce, all lies. You are Batman. And in pursuit of Truth and goodness for all, you lost the one thing you can be sure of.

JULIA VINOGRAD

Jerusalem Walked thru War

Jerusalem walked thru war
whistling for a pack of dogs
barking like guns,
whistling for a pack of guns
barking like dogs
to relieve themelves by firehydrants

and spilled brains.

"M16, you pretty little thing,

wag your tail and do your business."

Jerusalem walked thru war

among crumpled bodies

and stole their bloody clothes.

"My lovers should always be naked," she explained.

"I bury them in a soft shroud of kisses

but my lips cannot forgive

that none of them kiss me back.

Am I not beautiful?"

Jerusalem walked thru war,

thru burning ruins:

from a little Arab market

with scorched oranges rolling in the dust,

to the Church of the Nativity

where saints' stained glass faces

cough from the smoke,

to the child's empty stroller at the Passover massacre.

Fire is a ragged child Jerusalem sings to,

Clapping her hands to make the flames dance,

to make the smoke smile,

to make the fire grow up to be big and strong,

to rub the back of her hand against charred wood

and draw sooty black hearts

on any wall still standing.

Jerusalem walked barefoot on ashes,

like sand on the beach, wriggling her toes.

Jerusalem walked thru war.

War walked thru Jerusalem.

MARGARET WALKER

For Malcolm X

All you violated one with gentle hearts;
You violent dreamers whose cries shout heartbreak;
Whose voices echo clamors of our cool capers,
And whose black faces have hollowed pits for eyes.
All you gambling sons and hooked children and bowery bums
Hating white devils and black bourgeoisie,
Thumbing your noses at your burning red suns,
Gather round this coffin and mourn your dying swan.

Snow-white moslem head-dress around a dead black face!
Beautiful were your sand-papering words against our skins!
Our blood and water pour from your flowing wounds.
You have cut open out breasts and dug scalpels in our brains.
When and Where will another come to take your holy place?
Old man mumbling in his dotage, or crying child, unborn?

JERRY LEIBER & MIKE STOLLER

Searchin'

Gonna find her
Gonna find her

I been searchin', uh huh searchin'
Oh yeah searchin' every which a-way
Oh yeah I been searchin', searchin'
Searchin' every which a-way
I'm like that Northwest Mountie
You know I'll bring her in someday

Gonna find her

Well now if I have to swim a river, you know I will
And if I have to climb a mountain, you know I will
And if she's hidin' up on a blueberry hill
Am I gonna find her child, you know I will

Well now Sherlock Holmes, Sam Spade gonna nothin', child on me
Sergeant Friday, Charlie Chan, and Boston Blackie
No matter where she's hidin' she gonna hear me coming
I'm gonna walk right down that street like Bulldog Drummond

'Cause I been searchin', uh huh searchin'
Oh yeah searchin' every which a-way

Oh yeah I been searchin', searchin'
Searchin' every which a-way
I'm like that Northwest Mountie
You know I'll bring her in someday

Gonna find her
Gonna find her

MANIFESTOS

In the following appendix I have reprinted, in roughly chronological order, a selection of manifestos and poetic commentaries about key movements in American writing: Amy Lowell and others on the Imagists; the proletariat writers from the American Writers' Congress on "Revolutionary Symbolism in America"; Haki K. Madhubuti representing the Black Aesthetic movement in his tribute to the great Gwendolyn Brooks; Frank Chin and company representing the multicultural renaissance with their "Introduction to Chinese- and Japanese-American Literature"; Lawrence Ferlinghetti and Carolyn Kizer, poets who have consistently produced excellent work and paid their dues, contributing poems that comment on the goals and styles of some Beat and feminist poets; Geary Hobson writing about the rise of Native American cultural sovereignty; Alicia Suskin Ostriker's introduction to *Stealing the Language, the Emergence of Women's Poetry in America;* Leslie Scalapino addressing some of the issues raised by the controversial Language Poets, and Tata Lavieri's "Tito Madiera Smith," a poem that epitomizes the Nuyorican style. From these manifestos, and others described or quoted below, one can begin to gauge the trends of American poetry through the twentieth century.

Black writers have used the term *renaissance* to characterize each new generation of writers to come on the scene. The generation of the 1920s belonged to the Harlem Renaissance, the generation of the 1960s was referred to as the Second Renaissance (though a more accurate description might be the Third Renaissance, the second having come with writers of the 1930s and 1940s—Richard Wright, Margaret Walker, Gwendolyn Brooks, Melvin B. Tolsen and others). The Harlem Renaissance was guided by a manifesto, Alain Locke's 1925 book *The New Negro,* in which he wrote, "In the last decade something beyond the watch and guard of statistics has happened in the life of the American Negro and the three norms who have traditionally presided over the Negro problem have a changeling in their laps. The Sociologist, the Philanthropist, the Race-leader are not unaware of the New Negro, but they are at a loss to account for him. He simply cannot be swathed in their formulae. For the younger generation is vibrant with a new psychology; the new spirit is awake in the masses, and under the very eyes of the professional observers is transforming what has been a perennial problem into the progressive phases of contemporary Negro life."

These young writers were influenced not only by Broadway shows but also by a new militancy that energized the black middle class in the wake of the race riots of 1919. Those riots were immortalized by Claude McKay in his sonnet "If We Must Die," a protest poem later invoked by Winston Churchill during a BBC broadcast when London was being besieged by Nazi bombers.

Perhaps the most pioneering of the Harlem Renaissance writers were Langston Hughes and Zora Neale Hurston. Hughes became the predecessor of the multicultural poets by writing poetry with a Southwest setting, and of the feminist writers with his poems about the oppression of women. He was also a writer who helped lend prestige to popular poetry like the blues, jazz, and rock and roll (he was one of the first to read poetry to jazz—a performance style later picked up by the Beats). For her part, Zora Neale Hurston made important investigations into African-American religion ("Voo Doo and Hoo Doo") and in doing so anticipated a revival of interest in this topic by poets of the 1960s.

During the 1930s there occurred a power struggle within the American left that resulted in the ascendancy of literary elitism (represented by New York City's *Partisan Review*) over that of working-class populism (which found a voice in Chicago's *The Anvil*). The populists lost. This conflict is apparent in the agenda of the 1935 American Writers Congress (see p. 357). Of this struggle, Douglas Wixon writes in his book *The Worker Writer in America:* "It was a tragic loss if one believes that there is a room in American letters for cultural diversity reflecting class, race, gender, and ethnic differences. Yet it is still possible to study this neglected and often maligned episode and to find useful models for future experimentation." Among the proletariat writers was Louis Ginsberg, father of Allen Ginsberg, one of the leaders of a future revolt in American letters, the Beats. (*Beats* was a derivative of the word *beatnik,* which was said to have been coined by San Francisco columnist Herb Caen, playing on the term *Sputnik.*)

Continuing the social concerns of the proletariat writers and borrowing from Native-American, African-American, and Asian cultures, the Beats became among the most publicized writers in American history; like the writers of the 1930s, they could be credited for bringing writing from the parlor to Main Street, but on a much larger scale. Among the Beats was also a writer named LeRoi Jones (aka Amiri Baraka), who became one of the leading figures of the Black Aesthetic poets of the 1960s.

In a manifesto written by Larry Neal in 1968, the Black Aesthetic writers of the Second Renaissance called for a return to the and official establishment writer to become a populist voice for the newly found militancy of the 1960s. (During what might be called a counterrevolution, the more ornamental, European-influenced style made a comeback in the 1970s and was favored by white critics during the 1980s and 1990s; it is significant that the practitioners of this style seem to feel obligated to attack the Black Aesthetic writers of the 1960s.) Although some critics credit African-American writers from the New York scene for the Black Aesthetic revolution, Eugene B. Redmond's very worthwhile *Drumvoices: Mission of African-American Poetry* proves that black writers throughout the nation, among them the late Sarah Webster Fabio, were experimenting with the language of the streets.

Some of the multicultural writers of the 1970s trace their early experimentation with fiction to the influence of the Civil Rights movement. One contemporary Puerto Rican Slam poet has referred to the Black Aesthetic writers of the 1960s as his older brothers. Chinese-American writer Genny Lim also credits the Civil Rights movement for inspiring her. And Native American writer Mary Brave Bird writes, "We all had a good mouth, were good speakers and wrote a lot of poetry, though we were all dropouts who could not spell. We took some of our rhetoric from the blacks, who had started their movements before we did."

A younger generation of Native-American writers began to assert an aesthetic self-determination during the 1970s. In a classic work entitled "Old Time Indian Attack," novelist and poet Leslie Marmon Silko accused "white shamans" of participating in a form of cultural imperialism by appropriating Native American materials. Geary Hobson followed with his "The Rise of the White Shaman as a New Version of Cultural Imperialism."

The Asian-American Renaissance began in the mid-1970s, when Shawn Wong, Jeffery Chan, Frank Chin, and Lawson Inada began collaborating. They met at a party in Berkeley to celebrate the publication of *19 Necromancers from Now,* an anthology that I edited. Shawn Wong has said that at the beginning of the seventies, Asian-American students couldn't identify a single Asian-American writer, but by the mid-seventies they were writing themselves. Wong, Chan, Chin, and Inada went on to edit three landmark volumes: *Yardbird Reader, Vol. III, Aiiieeee,* and *The Big Aiiieeee.* These manifestos not only define new Asian-American writing but they also challenge what the writers contend to be the assimilationist, missionary literature of a former generation of Asian-Americans— just as Black Aesthetic writers of the 1960s challenged their predecessors who, during their own time, challenged the work of their antecedents.

As seems to be the pattern in American writing, toward the end of the 1980s yet another generation appeared and threw down the gauntlet to the rebels of the 1960s and 1970s. Trey Ellis and Greg Tate, young black writers, challenged the black manifestos of the 1960s in "The New Black Aesthetic." And challenging the concerns of Chin, Chan, Inada, and Wong, the more conservative Garrett Kaoru Hongo, editor of *The Open Boat,* writes, "At this historical moment, the issues surrounding Asian-American poetry could be characterized as a generation conflict between those who wish to uphold the notion of a personal subjectivity and poetics within the American experience, minority or mainstream, and those who make their priority the production of a politicized critique of general ideological domination within our culture."

Though women poets were included in and ranked among the pioneers of the major movements of American literature, the publicity and credit for these movements usually went to men. Alicia Suskin Ostriker launched a blistering attack on the sexism inherent in this attitude in her book *Stealing the Language,* and, as black and yellow and brown writers have done, attacked the double standards used by the largely white, male critical establishment when evaluating the works of writers different from them. Black, Asian, Hispanic, and Native American male writers can identify with some of Ms. Ostriker's observations, but even these writers were not let off the hook. Male domination of political and cultural life was sharply contested by feminists from these groups. Michele Wallace's landmark *Black Power and the Myth of Super Woman* and Toni Cade Bambara's *The Salt Eaters* were powerful indictments of male chauvinism.

Perhaps the most exciting and democratic poetry movement of today is that of the Slam poets (poetic cousins to the hip-hop lyricists). Some trace the origin of Slam poetry to the Nuyorican Poet's Cafe, located on the Lower East Side of Manhattan. Nicolàs Kanellos writes, "The Nuyorican writers created a style and ideology that dominates urban Hispanic writing today: working-class, unapologetic, and proud of its lack of schooling and polish—a threat not only to mainstream literature and the academy, but also, with its insistence on its outlaw and street culture elements, to mainstream society. . . . In capturing the sights and sounds of their 'urban pastoral,' it was an easy and natural step to cultivating bilingual poetry, capturing the bilingual-bicultural reality that surrounded them, and reintroducing their works into their communities through the virtuosity that live performance demands of folk culture."

One of the writers mentioned by Kanellos was Tato Laviera. I conclude this introduction with Tato Laviera's poem about the trickster, "tito madera smith." It is a perfect illustration of the points made by Kanellos about the Nuyorican poem.

for Dr. Juan Flores

he claims he can translate palés matos'
black poetry faster than i can talk,

and that if i get too smart,
he will double translate pig latin
english right out of webster's
dictionary, do you know him?

he claims he can walk into east harlem
apartment where langston hughes gives
spanglish classes for newly-arrived
immigrants seeking a bolitero-numbers
career and part-time vendors of cuchi-
fritters sunday afternoon in central
park, do you know him?

he claims to have a stronghold of the
only santería secret baptist sect in
west harlem, do you know him?

he claims he can talk spanish styled in
sunday dress eating crabmeat-jueyes
brought over on the morning eastern
plane deep fried by la negra costoso
joyfully singing puerto rican folklore:
"maría luisa no seas brava,
llévame contigo pa la cama," or
"oiga capitán delgado, hey captain delgaro,
mande a revisar la grama, please inspect
the grass, que dicen que un aeroplano,
they say that an airplane throws marijuana
seeds."

do you know him? yes you do,
i know you know him, that's right,
madera smith, tito madera smith:
he blacks and prieto talks at the same time,
splitting his mother's santurce talk,
twisting his father's south carolina soul,
adding new york scented blackest harlem
brown-eyes diddy bops, tú sabes mami,
that i can ski like a bomba soul salas
mambo turns to aretha franklin stevie
wonder nicknamed patato guaguancó steps,
do you know him?

he puerto rican talks to las mamitas
outside the pentecostal church, and
he gets away with it, fast-paced i
understand-you-my-man, with clave
sticks coming out of his pockets hooked
to his stereophonic 15-speaker indispensable   .
disco sounds blasting away at cold reality
struggling to say estás buena baby
as he walks out of tune and out of
step with alleluia cascabells,
puma sneakers,
pants rolled up,
shirt cut in middle chest,
santería chains,
madamo pantallas,
into the spanish social club,

to challenge elders in dominoes,
like the king of el diario's
budweiser tournament
drinking cerveza-beer
like a champ,
do you know him?
well, i sure don't,
and if i did, i'd
refer him to 1960
social scientists
for assimilation
acculturation
digging
autopsy

Finally, the polyrhythmic Nuyorican poetry style and that of such groups as the Last Poets seemed to be begging for an accompaniist. The rhythm section was provided by the sampling technology of rap DJs. From that marriage arose one of the most dynamic movements in the last hundred years of poetry. Hip-hop not only has popular appeal, but has made its way into academia and museums. I conclude the Manifestos section with a lyric by two of hip-hop's most avid and well-known practitioners: Dead Prez.

AMY LOWELL

The Imagists' Manifesto (1915)

1. To use the language of common speech, but to employ always the *exact* word, not the nearly-exact, nor the merely decorative word.

2. To create new rhythms—as the expression of new moods—and not to copy old rhythms, which merely echo old moods. We do not insist upon "free-verse" as the only method of writing poetry. We fight for it as a principle of liberty. We believe that the individuality of a poet may often be better expressed in free-verse than in conventional forms. In poetry, a new cadence means a new idea.

3. To allow absolute freedom in the choice of subject. It is not good art to write badly about aeroplanes and automobiles; nor is it necessarily bad art to write well about the past. We believe passionately in the artistic value of modern life, but we wish to point out that there is nothing so uninspiring nor so old-fashioned as an aeroplane of the year 1911.

4. To present an image (hence the name: "Imagist"). We are not a school of painters, but we believe that poetry should render particulars exactly and not deal in vague generalities, however magnificent and sonorous. It is for this reason that we oppose the cosmic poet, who seems to us to shirk the real difficulties of his art.

5. To produce poetry that is hard and clear, never blurred nor indefinite.

6. Finally, most of us believe that concentration is of the very essence of poetry.

Henry Hart

The Introduction to *American Writers' Congress* (1935)

Economic decay, affecting the whole world, has splintered all those human relationships which the educated classes of the West, for generations, have assumed to be normal and eternal.

The crisis began in colonial areas like Asia and South America, then broke upon Europe. For a brief period of wishful thinking, Americans hoped (therefore believed) they would escape the collapse of the old culture and the accompanying disintegration of material and spiritual life.

Reality awakened us from such self-satisfied fantasies, and, as an integral part of that section of the world which continues to endure the private ownership of the means of production and distribution, we shared the general fate.

Many of us began to see, amid the violences of rapid social change, the true nature of the society in which we live. Two cultures were struggling in mortal combat. Partisans and beneficiaries of the old order desperately strove to maintain it, with blood and iron, at the expense of the vast majority of men in all countries, *and at the expense of all that is best in human civilization.* Poverty, unemployment, fascism, the preparation for war—all revealed the real purpose beneath the vicious reaction of Mussolini in Italy, Hitler in Germany, Hearst in America.

From 1930 on, more and more American writers—like their fellow craftsmen in other countries—began to take sides in the world struggle between barbarism (deliberately cultivated by a handful of property owners) and the living interests of the mass of mankind. Within the last five years, those whose function is to describe and interpret human life in novel, story, poem, essay, play have been increasingly sure that their interests, and the interests of the propertyless and oppressed are inseparable.

American letters have begun to depict the aspirations, struggles and sufferings of *the mass* of Americans. Even those writers who continue to cling to the old aesthetic attitudes begin to be aware that, if culture is to survive, all men and women who create it, absorb it and cherish it, must *unite* with those social forces which can save the world from reaction and darkness. In various fields, in various ways, American writers had been aligning themselves with the forces of progress against the prevailing dangers of war, fascism and the extinction of culture. It soon became clear that the writer, like other members of the American community, must organize in his own defense. In January 1935, a group of writers issued the following call:

"The capitalist system crumbles so rapidly before our eyes that, whereas ten years ago scarcely more than a handful of writers were sufficiently far-sighted and courageous to take a stand for proletarian revolution, to-day hundreds of poets, novelists, dramatists, critics and short story writers recognize the necessity of personally helping to accelerate the destruction of capitalism and the establishment of a workers' government.

"We are faced by two kinds of problems. First, the problems of effective political action. The dangers of war and fascism are everywhere apparent; we all can see the steady march of the nations towards war and the transformation of sporadic violence into organized fascist terror.

"The question is: how can we function most successfully against these twin menaces?

"In the second place, there are the problems peculiar to us as writers, the problems of presenting in our work the fresh understanding of the American scene that has come from our enrollment in the revolutionary cause. A new renaissance is upon the world; for each writer there is the opportunity to proclaim both the new way of life and the revolutionary way to attain it. Indeed, in the historical perspective, it will be seen that only these two things matter. The revolutionary spirit is penetrating the ranks of the creative writers.

"Many revolutionary writers live virtually in isolation, lacking opportunities to discuss vital problems with their fellows. Others are so absorbed in the revolutionary cause that they have few opportunities for thorough examination and analysis. Never have the writers of the nation come together for fundamental discussion. "We propose, therefore, that a congress of American revolutionary writers be held in New York City on April 26, 27 and 28, 1935; that to this congress shall be invited all writers who have achieved some standing in their respective fields; who have clearly indicated their sympathy with the revolutionary cause; who do not need to be convinced of the decay of capitalism, of the inevitability of revolution. Subsequently, we will seek to influence and win to our side those writers not yet so convinced.

"This Congress will be devoted to exposition of all phases of a writer's participation in the struggle against war, the preservation of civil liberties and the destruction of fascist tendencies everywhere. It will develop the possibilities for wider distribution of revolutionary books and the improvement of the revolutionary press, as well as the relations between revolutionary writers and bourgeois publishers and editors. It will provide technical discussion of the literary applications of Marxist philosophy and of the relations between critic and creator. It will solidify our ranks.

"We believe such a Congress should create the League of American Writers, affiliated with the International Union of Revolutionary Writers. In European countries, the I.U.R.W. is in the vanguard of literature and political action. In France, for example, led by such men as Henri Barbusse, Romain Rolland,

André Malraux, André Gide and Louis Aragon, it has been in the forefront of the magnificent fight of the united militant working class against fascism.

"The program for the League of American Writers would be evolved at the Congress, basing itself on the following: fight against imperialist war and fascism; defend the Soviet Union against capitalist aggression; for the development and strengthening of the revolutionary labor movement; against white chauvinism (against all forms of Negro discrimination or persecution) and against the persecution of minority groups and of the foreign-born; solidarity with colonial people in the struggles for freedom; against the influence of reactionary ideas in American literature; against the imprisonment of revolutionary writers and artists, as well as other class-war prisoners throughout the world.

"By its very nature our organization would not occupy the time and energy of its members in administrative tasks; instead, it will reveal, through collective discussion, the most effective ways in which writers, as writers, can function in the rapidly developing crisis."

The call was signed by the following: Nelson Algren, Arnold B. Armstrong, Nathan Asch, Maxwell Bodenheim, Thomas Boyd, Earl Browder, Bob Brown, Fielding Burke, Kenneth Burke, Robert Coates, Erskine Caldwell, Alan Calmer, Robert Cantwell, Lester Cohen, Jack Conroy, Malcolm Cowley, Theodore Dreiser, Edward Dahlberg, Guy Endore, James T. Farrell, Kenneth Fearing, Ben Field, Waldo Frank, Joseph Freeman, Michael Gold, Eugene Gordon, Horace Gregory, Henry Hart, Clarence Hathaway, Josephine Herbst, Robert Herrick, Granville Hicks, Langston Hughes, Orrick Johns, Arthur Kallet, Lincoln Kirstein, Herbert Kline, Joshua Kunitz, John Howard Lawson, Tillie Lerner, Meridel Le Sueur, Melvin Levy, Robert Morss Lovett, Louis Lozowick, Grace Lumpkin, Lewis Mumford, Edward Newhouse, Joseph

North, Moissaye J. Olgin, Samuel Ornitz, Myra Page, John Dos Passos, Paul Peters, Allen Porter, Harold Preece, William Rollins Jr., Paul Romaine, Isidor Schneider, Edwin Seaver, Claire Siiton, Paul Sifton, George Sklar, John L. Spivak, Lincoln Steffens, Philip Stevenson, Genevieve Taggard, Alexander Trachtenberg, Nathaniel West, Ella Winter, and Richard Wright.

This call was unique in American letters. It was sent by writers of considerable achievement and standing, to all American writers, regardless of their aesthetic or political views, who were willing to unite on a general program for the defense of culture against the threat of fascism and war. The response resulted in the first congress of writers ever held in American history.

When the congress opened in Mecca Temple, New York City, on the night of April 26, 1935, there were present as delegates 216 writers from twenty-six states, and 150 writers who attended as guests, including fraternal delegates from Mexico, Cuba, Germany and Japan. The hall was crowded with 4,000 spectators—intellectuals, professionals and workers who came to greet this unprecedented event in American literature.

The fact that the struggle for the defense of culture against the threats of reaction is worldwide, was indicated by the honorary presiding committee for the congress chosen by the American writers:

> Louis Aragon, Henri Barbusse, André Gide, André Malraux and Romain Rolland, of France.
>
> Johannes Becher, Heinrich Mann, Theodore Plivier, Ludwig Renn and Anna Seghers, of Germany.
>
> Giovanni Germanetto, of Italy.
>
> Martin Andersen-Nëxo, of Denmark.
>
> Rafael Alberti, of Spain.
>
> Juan Marinello and Rejino Pedroso, of Cuba.

Juan de la Cabada and José Mancisidor, of Mexico.

Jacques Rournain, of Haiti.

Hu Lan Chi, Hwa Han, Liu Pen-Shu and Li Sing, of China.

Kirohata Kurahara, of Japan.

Sergei Dinamov, Maxim Gorky, Feodor Gladkov, Mikhail Sholokhov and Sergei Tretiakov, of the Soviet Union.

Messages and greetings were received from all parts of the world. Romain Rolland wrote: "We of Europe and you of America must coördinate our efforts. I am looking forward to a movement which shall not only participate in the necessary social action for the reconstruction of the world upon broader and more just foundations, but also for the renovation of the human spirit and an ensuing renaissance of art."

The German Writers' League (*Schutzverband Deutscher Schriftsteller*), the headquarters of which is in Paris, and whose executive committee includes Johannes R. Becher, Lion Feuchtwanger, Bruno Frank, Rudolf Leonhard, Heinrich Mann, Anna Seghers and other leading German writers cabled: "We feel sure that the American writers, who have convened this congress, will—with the earnest sense of responsibility which the hour demands—devote all their energies to the preservation of the great cultural treasures of humanity from the assaults of barbarism."

The great Soviet writer, Maxim Gorky, said in a cable: "My brotherly greetings to the congress of American writers organized for intellectual struggle against fascism and a new bloody war. We are with you, dear friends. With joy and approval we see how the forces of honest people who courageously oppose class exploitation and racial oppression are growing throughout the world."

The International Union of Revolutionary Writers wrote: "Separated by oceans, seas and thousands of miles of land, the revolutionary writers are connected by the common struggle for a new world. Now, when the shadow of fascism is over the earth, when the drums of war are being heard, the revolutionary writers, with increasing clarity, must realize there is but one force able to suppress fascism and abolish war—the force of the revolutionary proletariat. To-day the flower of humanity has rejected the old world and hails the revolution. We must see our aims clearly and understand the great, historical purposes of the fighting masses of workers. In this hour the writer's weapon is his creative work. To conquer, the weapon must be sharp and strong. Sharpen your weapon! Develop the art of revolution! Strengthen the courage and heroism of the masses and their will to victory! May your congress be the impetus to a wide front of struggle against fascism, against imperialist wars, and for the defense of the Soviet Union, the fatherland of the toilers of the world. Ardent revolutionary greetings to the first American congress of revolutionary writers."

Letters, telegrams and cablegrams were also received from Andersen Nëxo, the Danish novelist; Agnes Smedley, from China; Johannes Becher and Anna Seghers, both in exile in Paris; Boris Pilnyak, Sergei Tretiakov, Fcodor Gladkov, Dinamov, Apletin and others from the Soviet Union; the editors of *International Literature*; the China League of Left Writers; the Union of Soviet Writers; and from many organizations in the United States. Henri Barbusse sent a cablegram, the last sentence of which urged intellectuals to "follow the mass of workers as well as teach them." And from Madame Sun Yat-Sen in China, the Congress received a long letter, which included the following:

"We in China are among the latest sufferers from the reaction that is destroying culture and scientific progress. Innumerable cultural and scientific institutions, which took us centuries to build, have been wiped out in a few hours by the Japanese imperialists. Darkest reaction reigns in China and, while the Japanese militarists plunder and pillage our country, the Nanking traitors become Japanese henchmen in order to prolong their power. Now, almost daily, there are wholesale arrests and torture of workers, professors, writers and students who have joined our Association."

Some of these messages were read at the first meeting of the Congress—the only one open to the public—by the man who presided. This was Granville Hicks, who, a month later, was discharged from the Rensselaer Polytechnic Institute, where he had been teaching English, because of his participation in just such activities at the Congress typified.

Some of the papers which compose this volume were delivered that night those by Waldo Frank, Friedrich Wolf (the first speech of the Congress), Earl Browder, Langston Hughes and Moishe Nadir. Malcolm Cowley was among the speakers, but the ideas he presented that night were more extensively treated in the paper which is part of this book and which he delivered at a subsequent session of the Congress. Josephine Herbst spoke of "the stirring movement" she has witnessed in such disparate places as Iowa and Cuba, where she has lately been, and in Pennsylvania, where she lives, among workers and farmers.

"The talk is the same," she said, "though the language, inflection and rhythm vary. These men and women are becoming aware of the economic realities behind their troubles and they are beginning to fight. What has this to do with writing? So far as I am concerned, it has everything. It is impossible for me to stop myself from writing about anything so real. It is a subject matter that inspires. It would be a very dark world to-day were it not for the hope reposing in the working class. This is a marvelous time in which to be alive. It is immeasurably better than 1890, when literature was devoted to *trivia*. To-day we have everything *but* triviality to write about."

The same thought was expressed in another way, and from

another point of view, by Hays Jones, the editor of *Marine Workers' Voice,* whose blunt, sincere vitality elicited abundant applause. Mr. Jones said:

"First I want to dispel any ideas of my acceptance of the title of writer. I may be a propagandist after a fashion, but a writer, no. I want, however, in the name of the workers of New York, and especially of the marine workers, to issue an invitation and an ultimatum.

"These writers are all professionals. They make their living by writing, and I am just wondering whether they want to starve today or not. Because if they don't want to starve, they have got to do certain things, and that is to come down to the place where they have a market. You have heard that story about the poet who starves to death writing beautiful poems in a garret. There just is nothing to it. As professionals they ought to aspire to white tile bathrooms and things of that kind, and I don't blame them because we workers also aspire to those things. I rather imagine these writers are also losing hope of finding them in capitalism unless they go in for some decidedly unpleasant things.

"For a long time it has been regarded that in the working class there is no life, no interest, just a dead, sodden mass that the writer has no need to look to as a source of material. But I say that to-day the only thing that's alive in capitalist society is the working class. The day in the life of a man who spends nine hours in front of a punch press or on a ship has more reality, more beauty and more harmony than you will find in all of Park Avenue with its boredom, its waste of time and its quest for joy that doesn't exist. Therefore we want to issue an invitation to these writers assembled to-night, to come down among the workers to find that life and to create a synthesis for it with their tools as writers. Well, that is a big job. Some of us are a little skeptical about it. If the writers accept our invitation, we will furnish the market for their works and that is what they are looking for.

"On the other hand, if they don't take the invitation, we'll give them an ultimatum. They can go on writing about the dead until finally we have to shove them into the grave and cover them up with the dirt."

The last speaker, Michael Gold, was introduced as "the best loved American revolutionary writer"; he spoke on "The Workers as an Audience for Writers." He alluded to the huge audiences which the Theater Union and the Group Theater have commanded; to the huge editions of non-fiction pamphlets and books published by International Publishers; to the huge editions of novels, plays and poems published in the Soviet Union.

"Our writers must learn that the working class," he said, "which has created a great civilization in the Soviet Union, is capable of creating a similar civilization in this country. It has heroism, intelligence, courage. We must never forget that a class which has such depths of creative power deserves only the best literature we can give.

"The charge has been made that writers who ally themselves with the workers are artists in uniform. This charge is made by intellectuals who believe they do not wear a uniform—the uniform of the bourgeoisie. Well, we are proud of our role. This great meeting to-night, attended by more than four thousand people, many of whom are workers, could not have been convoked by any bourgeois audience or any group of bourgeois writers. This meeting, and the Congress which it opens, is a demonstration of the creative depths that are in the working masses.

"May this Congress be the beginning of a great new literature which will reflect, truthfully, the struggles of the workers, the soul of the workers, the soul of the basic American human being. May this Congress be another of the landmarks in American history by which our happier descendants will discern the steps in our progress toward a richer and more social life and a more intelligent America."

There were six sessions of the Congress—the public one on Friday evening, morning and afternoon sessions on Saturday and Sunday for the delegates and guests, and a group of small craft meetings on Saturday night. I have prepared a running account of these sessions which will be found in an appendix, entitled "Discussion and Proceedings."

The arrangement of the papers which compose this volume does not follow the sequence of their delivery before the Congress. An attempt has been made to place them in an order which will make it easier for the reader to discern the general purpose and scope of the Congress—the position of the writer in the contemporary world, the dangers which assail him and make his alliance with the 0 one revolutionary class imperative; the fruits of such alliance in the lary Soviet Union; the craft and general problems of the revolutionary writer, and their solution. Several papers arrived too late to be read before and to be discussed by the Congress—notably Louis Aragon's and John Dos Passos'.

Editing the proceedings of this first American Writers' Congress has not been easy, for it entailed some more or less arbitrary decisions uncongenial to a temperament such as my own. The labor of bringing so much material into publishable form was considerable, and I would like to thank Joseph Freeman, who wrote some of the sentences at the opening of this introduction and who reduced much of the discussion (retrieved from stenographic notes taken during the Congress sessions) to usable proportions; also Kenneth Burke and Edwin Seaver, who edited many of the papers in order that their individual length might not exceed the exigencies of space.

HAKI R. MADHUBUTI

Gwendolyn Brooks (1969)

she doesn't wear
costume jewelry
& she knew that walt disney
was/is making a fortune off
false-eyelashes and that time magazine is the
authority of the knee/grow.
her makeup is total-real.

a negro english instructor called her:
        "a fine negro poet."
a white critic said:
        "she's a credit to the negro race."
somebody else called her:
        "a pure negro writer."
johnnie mae, who's a senior in high school said:
        "she & langston are the only negro poets we've
        read in school and i understand her."
pee wee used to carry one of her poems around in his
        back pocket;
        the one about being cool. that was befo pee wee
        was cooled by a cop's warning shot.

into the sixties
a word was born .... BLACK

& with black came poets
& from the poet's ball points came:
black doubleblack purpleblack blueblack beenblack was
black daybeforeyesterday blackerthan ultrablack super
black blackblack yellowblack niggerblack blackwhite-man
blackerthanyoueverbes ¼ black unblack coldblack clear
black my momma's blackerthanyourmomma pimpleblack fall
black so black we can't even see you black on black in
black by black technically black mantanblack winter
black coolblack 360degreesblack coalblack midnight
black black when it's convenient rustyblack moonblack
black starblack summerblack electronblack spaceman
black shoeshineblack jimshoeblack underwearblack ugly
black auntjimammablack, uncleben'srice black
      williebest
black blackisbeautifulblack i just discoveredblack negro
black unsubstanceblack.

and everywhere the
lady "negro poet"
appeared the poets were there.
they listened & questioned
& went home feeling uncomfortable/unsound & so-untogether
they read/re-read/wrote & re-wrote
& came back the next time to tell the
lady "negro poet"
how beautiful she was/is & how she had helped them
& she came back with:
      how necessary they were and how they've helped her.

the poets walked & as space filled the vacuum between
        them & the
lady "negro poet"
u could hear one of the blackpoets say:
        "bro, they been callin that sister by the wrong name."

Frank Chin, Jeffery Paul Chan, Lawson Fusai Inada, and Shawn Wong

An Introduction to Chinese- and Japanese-American Literature (1975)

In the 140-year history of Asian America, fewer than ten works of fiction and poetry have been published by American-born Chinese, Japanese, and Filipino writers. This fact suggests that in six generations of Asian-Americans there was no impulse to literary or artistic self-expression. The truth is that Asian-Americans have been writing seriously since the nineteenth century, and writing well.

Sui Sin Fah, an English-born Eurasian, wrote and published short fiction in the nineteenth century. She was one of the first to speak for an Asian-American sensibility that was neither Asian nor white American. And, interestingly enough, in her work, there is no cultural conflict between East and West. That is a modern invention of whites and their yellow goons—writers who need white overseers to give them a license to use the English language. In 1896 the California magazine *Land of Sunshine* said her stories' characters ". . . are all of Chinese characters in California or on the Pacific Coast; and they have an insight and sympathy which are probably unique. To others the alien Clestial is at best mere 'literary material': in these stories he (or she) is a human being." Working within the terms of the stereotype of the Chinese as laundryman, prostitute, smuggler, coolie, she presents "John Chinaman" as little more than a comic caricature, giving him a sensibility that was her own.

Americans' stereotypes of "Orientals" were sacrosanct and no one, especially a "Chink" or a "Jap," was going to tell them that America, not Asia, was their home, that English was their language, and that the stereotype of the Oriental, good or bad, was offensive. What America published was, with rare exception, not only offensive to Chinese and Japanese America but was *actively inoffensive* to white sensibilities.

World War II signaled the suppression of a Japanese-American writing movement that had been active since the late twenties and the sudden popularity of Chinese-Americans' writing to encourage America to "assimilate her loyal minorities," as the dust jacket of Pardee Lowe's *Father and Glorious Descendant* states. The implied worth of these first Chinese-Americans to reach mass print and enjoy a degree of popularity was that they mostly had patriotic virtues rather than literary ones. They were more manipulable. The autobiographies of Pardee Lowe and later Jade Snow Wong were treated less as works of art than as anthropological discoveries. Indeed, the dust jacket of Lowe's book said that he "enlisted in the U.S. Army shortly after delivering the manuscript of this book," as if this patriotic gesture affected its literary worth.

Much of Asian-American literary history is a history of a small minority being cast into the role of the good guy in order to make another American minority look bad. In World War II the Chinese were used against the Japanese. Today, Chinese- and Japanese-Americans are used to mouth the white racist cliches of the fifties, as evidenced by a recent *Newsweek* magazine article (June 21, 1971) entitled "The Japanese-American Success Story: Outwhiting the Whites," and the favorable reception of Daniel I. Okimoto's *American in Disguise* and Betty Lee Sung's *Mountain of Gold: The Story of the Chinese in America.*

Betty Lee Sung's *Mountain of Gold* (1967) went through two printings of 7,500 and in 1971 was issued in a paperback edition under the title *The Story of the Chinese in America.* Hers is the only book by a Chinese-American still in print, and further enjoys the distinction of being cited by scholars in *Forgotten Pages of American*

Literature, edited by Gerald Haslam as an authoritative source, supporting the age-old stereotype of Chinese-Americans being culturally Chinese and only monetarily white.

"There is nothing wrong with autobiography," writes Kai-yu Hsu in his introduction to *Asian-American Authors* (1972), "except when one realizes that the perceptions of reality revealed through these works seem to continue to confirm rather than to modify a stereotyped image of the Chinese and their culture." Part One of Virginia Lee's novel *The House that Tai Ming Built* consists mostly of the retelling of the legend of "the house that Tai Ming built." This narration is supposed to be from the Chinese point of view, but we find that the point of view is surprisingly Western:

> Grandfather Kwong continued: "To know why Tai Ming wore a queue we must go back in Chinese history, to the time when the Mongol Emperor Kublai Khan and his successors ruled China for nearly a century in the Yuan Dynasty from the year 1230 until 1368 A.D., when they were driven out of power by the Chinese."

Virginia Lee is the victim, so completely brainwashed that she sees no discrepancy between an old man from China talking about China in reference to the white Christian calendar. Yet she would be the first to protest if John Wayne were to speak about Abraham Lincoln freeing the slaves in the Year of the Pig. In the early novels, confirming the education of the white reading audience became an obsession, to the point where writers such as Virginia Lee obviously had to do a lot of research into such things as Chinese history, Chinese-American history, Chinese art, and Chinese opera—all from the white point of view. And the white point of view was that Chinese were "culturally superior." That the cultural superiority of the Chinese served white supremacy by keeping Chinese in their place is clear in the work of Jade Snow Wong and Virginia Lee. They both respond to racism silently and privately, not with action but with an attitude of a noncommunicative cultural superiority that as a response is ineffectual. Virginia Lee in *The House that Tai Ming Built* illustrates this concept:

> The first thing Lin noticed as she stepped into the house of Mrs. Hayes was the wallpaper in the foyer. It was a lovely medallion design in pale yellow. She wondered if Mrs. Hayes knew that the ancient Chinese had invented wallpaper and that it was not until the fourteenth century that wallpaper was introduced into Europe.

This was not a firsthand knowledge of Chinese culture, but it was being passed off as such. Virginia Lee paraphrases Chinese history as written by white and Chinese scholars.

Kai-yu Hsu correctly states that "These largely autobiographical works tend to present the stereotype of Chinese culture as described in the connoisseur's manual of Chinese jade or oolong tea, and the stereotype of the Chinese immigrant who is, or should be, either withdrawn and stays totally Chinese, or quietly assimilated and has become unobtrusively American, exhibiting a model of the American ideal of the melting pot process."

An American-born Asian, writing from the world as Asian-American who does not reverberate to gongs struck hundreds of years ago or snuggle into the doughy clutches of an America hot to coddle something ching chong, is looked upon as a freak, an imitator, a liar. The myth is that Asian-Americans have maintained cultural integrity as Asians, that there is some strange continuity between the great high culture of a China that hasn't existed for five hundred years and the American-born Asian. Gerald Haslam in *Forgotten Pages of American Literature* perpetuates this idea:

. . . the average Chinese-American at least knows that
China has produced "great philosophies," and with that
knowledge has come a greater sense of ethnic pride.
Contrasted, for example, with the abject cultural dep-
rivation long foisted upon Afro-Americans, Asian-
Americans have an inner resource: The knowledge
that their ancestors had created a great and complex
civilization when the inhabitants of the British Isles
still painted their fannies blue.

Thus, fourth-, fifth-, and sixth-generation Asian-Americans are still
looked upon as foreigners because of this dual heritage, or the con-
cept of dual personality which suggests that the Asian-American
can be broken down into his American part and his Asian part.
This view explains Asian assimilation, adaptability, and lack of
presence in American culture. This sustaining inner resource keeps
the Asian-American a stranger in the country in which he was
born. He is supposed to feel better off than the blacks, whose
American achievement is the invention of their own American cul-
ture. American language, fashions, music, literature, cuisine,
graphics, body language, morals, and politics have been strongly
influenced by Black culture. They have been cultural achievers, in
spite of white supremacist culture, whereas Asian America's repu-
tation is an achievement of that white culture—a work of racist art.

The overthrow of the Manchus, the Sino-Japanese War, World
War II, the success of the Communist Revolution, and the Cultural
Revolution are five major events resulting in a China the Chinese
of a hundred years ago, the ancestors of fourth-, fifth-, and sixth-
generation Chinese-Americans, never saw and wouldn't under-
stand. These new Chinese are emigrating to America. The assertion
of distinctions between Chinese and Chinese-Americans is neither
a rejection of Chinese culture nor an expression of contempt for
things Chinese, as the whites and the Chinatown Establishment

would make them out to be. It is calling things by their right names. Change has taken place in China, in American Chinatowns, and in the world generally—changes that have been ignored and suppressed to preserve the popular racist "truths" that make up the Oriental stereotype.

It is the racist truth that some nonwhite minorities, notably the Asians, have suffered less and are better off than the other colored minorities. It is generally accepted as fact that Asians are well liked and accepted in American society, that they have been assimilated and acculturated and have contributed to the mainstream of American culture. There is racist hate and racist love. That is, if the system works, the stereotypes assigned to the various races are accepted by the races themselves as reality, as fact, and racist love reigns. The minority's reaction to racist policy is acceptance and apparent satisfaction. Order is kept, the world turns without a peep from any non-white. One measure of the success of white racism is the silence of the minority race and the amount of white energy necessary to maintain or increase that silence. The Chinese-American is told that it is not a matter of being ignored and excluded but of being quiet and foreign. It is only recently that we have come to appreciate the consequences of that awful quiet and set out collecting Chinese-American oral history on tape. There is no recorded Chinese-American history from the Chinese-American point of view. Silence has been a part of the price of the Chinese-American's survival in a country that hated him. That was the trouble with the language. It was full of hate. Silence was love.

The failure of white racism can be measured by the amount and kind of noise of resistance generated by the race. The truth is that all of the country's attention has been drawn to white racism's failures. Everything that has been done by whites in politics, government, and education in response to the failure of white racism, while supposedly antiracist, can be seen as an effort to correct the flaws, redesign the instruments, and make racism work. White racism has failed to convince the blacks that they are animals and failed to convince the Indians that they are living fossils. Nightriders, soldier boys on horseback, fat sheriffs, and all the clowns of racism did destroy a lot of bodies, and leave among these minorities a legacy of suffering that continues to this day. But they did not destroy their impulse to cultural integrity, stamp out their literary sensibility, and produce races of people who would work to enforce white supremacy without having to be supervised or watchdogged.

In terms of the utter lack of cultural distinction in America, the destruction of an organic sense of identity, the complete psychological and cultural subjugation of the Asian-American, the people of Chinese and Japanese ancestry stands out as white racism's only success. The secret lies in the construction of the modern stereotype and the development of new policies of white racism.

The general function of any racial stereotype is to establish and preserve order between different elements of society, maintain the continuity and growth of Western civilization, and enforce white supremacy with a minimum of effort, attention, and expense. The ideal racial stereotype is a low-maintenance engine of white supremacy whose efficiency increases with age, as it becomes authenticated and historically verified. The stereotype operates as a model of behavior. It conditions the mass society's perceptions and expectations. Society is conditioned to accept the given minority only within the bounds of the stereotype. The subject minority is conditioned to reciprocate by becoming the stereotype, live it, talk it, believe it, and measure group and individual worth in its terms. The stereotype operates most efficiently and economically when the vehicle of the stereotype, the medium of its perpetuation, and the subject race to be controlled are all one. When the operation of the stereotype has reached this point, at which the subject race itself embodies and perpetuates the white supremacist vision of reality, indifference to the subject race sets in among mass society. The successful operation of the stereotype results in the neutralization of the subject race as a social, creative, and cultural force. The race poses no threat to white supremacy. It is now a guardian of white supremacy, dependent on it and grateful to it. In Monica Sone's *Nisei Daughter* the operation of the stereotype in the Japanese-American is clearly evident:

> Although I had opinions, I was so overcome with self-consciousness I could not bring myself to speak. Some people would have explained this as an acute case of adolescence, but I knew it was also because I was Japanese. Almost all the students of Japanese blood sat like rocks during discussion period. Something compellingly Japanese made us feel it was better to seem stupid in a quiet way rather than to make a boner out loud. I began to think of the Japanese as the Silent People, and I envied my fellow students who clamored to be heard. What they said was not always profound or even relevant, but they didn't seem worried about it. Only after a long, agonizing struggle was I able to deliver the simplest statement in class without flaming like a red tomato.

For the subject to operate efficiently as an instrument of white supremacy, he is conditioned to accept and live in a state of euphemized self-contempt. This self-contempt itself is nothing more than the subject's acceptance of white standards of objectivity, beauty, behavior, and achievement as being morally absolute, and his acknowledgement that, because he is not white, he can never fully measure up to white standards. In *American in Disguise* (1971), this self-contempt is implicit in Daniel I. Okimoto's assessment of Japanese-American literary potential:

. . . it appears unlikely that literary figures of comparable stature to those minorities like the Jews and Blacks will emerge to articulate the nisei soul. Japanese-Americans will be forced to borrow the voices of James Michener, Jerome Charyn, and other sympathetic novelists to distill their own experience. Even if a nisei of Bernard Malamud's or James Baldwin's talent did appear, he would no doubt have little to say that John O'Hara has not already said.

The stereotype within the minority group itself, then, is enforced by individual and collective self-contempt. This gesture of self-contempt and self-destruction, in terms of the stereotype, is euphemized as being successful assimilation, adaptation, and acculturation.

If the source of this self-contempt is obviously generated from outside the minority, interracial hostility will inevitably result, as history has shown us in the cases of the blacks, Indians, and Chicanos. The best self-contempt has its sources seemingly within the minority group itself. The vehicles of this illusion are education and the publishing establishment. Only five American-born Chinese have published what can be called serious attempts at literature. We have already mentioned Pardee Lowe, Jade Snow Wong, Virginia Lee, and Betty Lee Sung. The fifth, Diana Chang, is the only Chinese-American writer to publish more than one book-length creative work to date. She has published four novels and is a well-known poetess. Of these five, Pardee Lowe, Jade Snow Wong, Virginia Lee, and Betty Lee Sung believe the popular stereotypes of Chinese-Americans to be true and find Chinese America repulsive and do not identify with it. They are "exceptions that prove the rule." In an interview taped by Frank Chin in 1970, Virginia Lee said, "so in other words, you want the white population to start thinking of Chinese other than being quiet, unassuming, passive, et cetera, right? That's what you want, huh?"

"I don't want to be measured against the stereotype anymore," answered Frank Chin.

"But," she said, "you've got to admit that what you call the stereotype does make up for the larger majority of Chinese-Americans, now I've seen that in school. [Virginia Lee is a schoolteacher.] I think it behooves all minorities, Blacks, Chinese, what not, not to feel so insulted so fast. It's almost a reflex action."

Frank asked her if she would continue to write about Chinese America. She said, "I wouldn't want to go on a Chinese, you know, American conflict like that again. I don't want to do another one."

"Why?" he asked. "Was it difficult?"

"It wasn't difficult," she said, "but very candidly now, this might not even . . ." She took a deep breath. "I just don't think it's that interesting."

And Jade Snow Wong on Chinese America as it exists here: "The American-Chinese I grew up with, in high school, out of forty or fifty . . . none of them went to college. We're not friends now." Jade Snow Wong, Virginia Lee, Pardee Lowe, and Betty Lee Sung are all of the first generation to go completely through the public school system. The preceding generations were barred, by law, from attending public schools. Their parents went to segregrated mission schools if they went to school at all. Diana Chang lived from infancy to her early twenties in China.

Of these five, four were obviously manipulated by white publishers to write to and from the stereotype. Of these four, three do not consider themselves to be serious writers and welcomed the aid of editors, as Jade Snow Wong describes in this interview:

"Elizabeth Lawrence was the one who asked me to write it. And the other one was Alice Cooper, who's dead now. She was my English teacher at City College."

Frank Chin asked her, "What did their help consist of?"

"Oh, Elizabeth Lawrence, you know, she said, 'I want a story,' or something. Then I wrote up maybe three times as long as what finally came out in the book. I sent it to her and she went through it and said, 'ten, twenty, thirty pages, this may be necessary for the writer to write, but it's not necessary for the reader to read.' So then she took parts out. And then I took what was left of the manuscript and went to Los Angeles to see Alice Cooper who helped me bind it together again."

"You think this is right? Are you happy with the book?"

"I finally got to read it the second time about two or three years ago. It reads all right. Some of the things are missing that I would have wanted in, then, you know, it's like selling to Gumps or sending to a museum. Everybody has a purpose in mind, in what they're carrying out. So, you know, you kind of have to work with them. If this is what they want to print, and it's the real thing. I mean they didn't fabricate anything that wasn't so."

This was the talk of a good businesswoman, not a serious or very sensitive writer. Chin asked, "But you feel things were left out?"

She matter of factly expressed an acceptance of her inferior status as if it were a virtue. "Oh, maybe they were too personal, you see. I was what? Twenty-six then. And, you know, it takes maturity to be objective about one's self."

The construction of the stereotype began long before Jade Snow Wong, Pardee Lowe, Virginia Lee, and Betty Lee Sung were born within it and educated to fulfill it. It began with a basic difference between it and the stereotypes of other races. The white stereotype of the acceptable and unacceptable Asian is utterly without manhood. Good or bad, the stereotypical Asian is nothing as a man. At worst, the Asian-American is contemptible because he is womanly, effeminate, devoid of all the traditionally masculine qualities of originality, daring, physical courage, and creativity. The mere fact that four out of five American-born Chinese-American writers are women reinforces this aspect of the stereotype, as does the fact that four of these writers, the four autobiographers, completely submerge and all but eradicate all traces of their characters in their books. Sung, by writing almost exclusively about "cases I beard of" and what happened to "an acquaintance of mine," and Wong by writing about herself in the third person, further reinforce the stereotypical unmanly nature of Chinese-Americans. Virginia Lee's novel *The House that Tai Ming Built* depicts a Chinese-American girl, for instance, who is just too much for the wishy-washy boys of Chinatown and falls in love with an "American," meaning "white," man.

The Chinatowns of Jade Snow Wong and Virginia Lee and Pardee Lowe differ starkly from the drab, even boring Chinatown described in Louis Chu's novel *Eat a Bowl of Tea*. In *Eat a Bowl of Tea* you have the first Chinese-American novel set against an unexoticized Chinatown—the kind of Chinatown that has been duplicated wherever large numbers of Chinese emigrants settle. It was basically a bachelor society, replete with prostitutes and gambling, existing as a foreign enclave where the white world stands at an officially described distance, where Chinatown and its inhabitants are tributaries to a faceless and apathetic authority. Published in 1961, one can imagine the reception of such a work by a public so fully grounded in the machinations of family associations, picture brides, and a reminiscence for a China that no longer exists. From Lin Yutang's euphemized portrait of Chinatown to C. Y. Lee's imported apothecary of ginseng and tuberculosis, the white reading audience has been steeped in the saccharine patronage of Chinatown culture.

Chu's portrayal of Chinatown is an irritating one for white audiences. The characters in this book are not reassured by the pervasive influence of the kind of Chinatown that we see in the autobiographies and pseudo-novellas of Wong, Lee, and Lin. The kind of Chinatown that the characters are secure in is a Chinatown devoid of whites. It is a Chinatown that we are familiar with—filled with vulgarity and white whores, who make up for the scarcity of Chinese women. In the same way that Chu's Chinatown holds the white reader at a distance, his characters speak a language that is offendingly neither English nor the idealized conception that whites have of a "Chinaman's tongue"—the pseudo-poetry of a Master Wang in *Flower Drum Song* or a Charlie Chan. Witness:

> "Go sell your ass, you stinky dead snake," Chong Loo tore into the barber furiously. "Don't say anything like that! If you want to make laughs, talk about something else, you troublemaker. You many-mouthed bird."

The manner and ritual of address and repartee is authentic Chinatown. Chu translates idioms from the Sze Yup dialect, and the effect of such expressions on his Chinese-American readers is delight and recognition. Chu's unerring eye and ear avoids the cliché, the superficial veneer and curio-shop expressions. He knows Chinatown people, their foibles and anxieties, and at once can capture their insularity as well as their humanity.

This picture of a predominately male Chinatown is not unique in Chinese-American literature. As early as 1896, Sui Sin Fah wrote about the Chinese on the Pacific Coast. Like Louis Chu, she accurately portrayed Chinatown's bachelor society. In the story "A Chinese Feud," she wrote:

> He saw therein the most beautiful little woman in the world moving about his home, pouring out his tea and preparing his rice. He saw a cot; and kicking and crowing therein a baby—a boy baby with a round, shaven head and Fantze's eyes. He saw himself receiving the congratulations of all the wifeless, motherless, sisterless, childless American Chinamen.

Historically, Chinatowns were predominately male. Chinese families like those described in Jade Snow Wong, Virginia Lee, and

Pardee Lowe's books were rare. In these better known works, the frustrated bachelors of Chinatown, making up the majority of the Chinatown population, are symbolically rejected or totally ignored.

Unlike Chinese-American literature, Japanese-American writing has only recently accepted the concept of the dual personality. Daniel Okimoto's *American in Disguise,* of all the Japanese-American book length works, unquestioningly accepts the concept of the dual personality and makes it central to the work. Significantly, though Lawson Inada, who ignores the concept, also published a book in 1971, Okimoto's book has been favorably reviewed by the nation's press, while Inada's book of poetry *Before the War,* the first book of poetry published by an American-born Japanese-American, has been ignored, as is most poetry, and the reviews of his work submitted to metropolitan newspapers have been rejected. The works of Japanese-American writers Toshio Mori (1949), John Okada (1957), Mine Okubo (1946), and Lawson Inada (1971) all see through the phoniness of the concept of the dual personality and reject it. Even Monica Sone's *Nisei Daughter* (1953) rejects this concept in spite of the publisher's blatant attempt to emulate Jade Snow Wong's *Fifth Chinese Daughter* (1950) and capitalize on that book's success.

"Although a 'first person singular' book, this story is written in the third person from Chinese habit." Thus Jade Snow Wong, in her author's note, immediately gives herself to the concept of the dual personality. George Sessions Perry, on the book's dust jacket, both accepts the concept of the dual personality and accidentally hints at its debilitating effect on the individual, if not its phoniness:

> Here is the curious dissonance of a largely Americanized young lady seeing her purely Chinese family life from both her and their points of view.

The suggestion is that the "dissonance" arises from her being a "largely" but not completely Americanized "young Chinese girl." The "dissonance" that thrills, bewilders, and charms Perry is built into the concept of the dual personality that controls his perception of Asian America. That the concept does not arise naturally from the Asian-American experience is dramatized clearly in Monica Sone's account of attending public school in the daytime and Japanese school (Nihon Gakko) in the afternoon:

> Gradually I yielded to my double dose of schooling. Nihon Gakko was so different from grammar school I found myself switching my personality back and forth daily like a chameleon. At Bailey Gatzert School I was a jumping, screaming, roustabout Yankee, but at the stroke of three when the school bell rang and the doors burst open everywhere, spewing out pupils like jelly beans from a broken bag, I suddenly became a modest, faltering, earnest little Japanese girl with a small, timid voice.

This concept of the dual personality was forced on her from without. Social pressure and education make her both Japanese and American. From her own experience, she is neither:

> Mr. Ohashi and Mrs. Matsui thought they could work on me and gradually mold me into an ideal Japanese ojoh-san, a refined young maiden who is quiet, pure in thought, polite, serene, self-controlled. They made little headway, for I was too much the child of Skidrow.

She declares herself a "child of Skidrow" and a "blending of East and West." For the Nisei authoress this was a fatal mistake, in terms of sales and popularity. The concept of the dual personality and conflict between the two incompatible parts are central to

Wong's work, as it is with the work of all Chinese-Americans except Diana Chang. *Fifth Chinese Daughter* has gone through several paperback editions in the United States and England. It has been published in several languages and is critically and financially the most successful book ever produced by a Chinese-American.

Unlike Chinese America, Japanese America produced serious writers who came together to form literary-intellectual communities. As early as the twenties, Japanese-American writers were rejecting the concept of the dual identity and asserting a Nisei identity that was neither Japanese nor white European American (according to a 1934 essay by Toyo Suyemoto in "Hokubei Asahi").

Through the thirties and forties Japanese-American writers produced their own literary magazines. Even in the internment period, Japanese-American literary journals sprang up in the relocation centers. During this, one of the most trying and confusing periods of Japanese-American history, their writing flourished. In the pages of *Trek* and *All Aboard* and the magazines and newspapers of camps around the country, Japanese-American English was developed and the symbols of the Japanese-American experience codified by writers like Toshio Mori, Globularius Schraubi, poet Toyo Suyemoto, artist Mine Okubo, and Asian-America's most accomplished short story writer, as of this writing, Hisaye Yamamoto. In spite of the more highly developed literary skills of Japanese-American publications, much of it commissioned by Japanese-American community organizations, more books by Chinese-Americans have been published than by Japanese-Americans.

No-No Boy (1957) is the first and, unfortunately, the last novel by John Okada. At the time of his death in 1971, he was planning a new novel on the Issei and their immigration from Japan to America. As it stands, this novel is the first Japanese-American novel in the history of American letters and the second book to be produced by a Seattle Nisei in the fifties (the other was Monica

Sone's *Nisei Daughter*). Some scholars of Asian-American literature have said that *No-No Boy* has no literary value, but is worth reading as a fairly accurate representation of the emotional and psychological climate of Japanese-Americans at a certain period in history. Okada is worth reading as a social history, not as literature, these critics say. The distinction between social history and literature is a tricky one, especially when dealing with the literature of an emerging sensibility. The subject matter of minority literature is social history, not necessarily by design but by definition. There is no reference, no standard of measure, no criterion. So, by its own terms, Okada's novel invented Japanese-American fiction full-blown, was self-begotten, arrogantly inventing its own criteria.

The minority writer works in a literary environment of which the white writer has no knowledge or understanding. The white writer can get away with writing for himself, knowing full well he lives in a world run by people like himself. At some point the minority writer is asked for whom he is writing, and in answering that question must decide who he is. In Okada's case, being Japanese or American would seem the only options, but he rejects both and works on defining Nisei in terms of an experience that is neither Japanese nor American. Okada's hero, embodying his vision of the Japanese-American, cannot be defined by the concept of the dual personality that would make a whole from two incompatible parts. The hero of the double and hyphenated "No" is both a restatement of and a rejection of the term "Japanese-American"—"No" to Japanese and "No" to American.

The question of point of view is only partially stylistic in the case of minority writing. It has immediate and dramatic social and moral implications. As social history, the mere gesture of Japanese-American writing is significant. Then the question of control follows, that is, what forces are operating and influencing the writer and how aware of them is he? Specifically, how does he cope with and reflect prevalent white and nonwhite attitudes of the period? How is he affected by the concept of the dual personality? By Christianity? How does he define the relationship between his own race, the other minorities, and the white race? How seriously committed to writing and his point of view is this writer? And if, as is too often the case, the writer is no writer at all, by his own admission, the question of white publisher and editor manipulation is raised, usually after the answer has become obvious.

So the serious Asian-American writer, like any other minority writer, who works with the imperatives and universals of minority experience and applies them to his work, is treated as a quack, a witch doctor, a bughouse prophet, an entertaining fellow, dancing the heebie-jeebies in the street for dimes. Okada wrote his novel in a period all but devoid of a Japanese-American literary tradition above ground. There were only three predecessors, a book of short stories, Toshio Mori's *Yokohama, California,* an autobiography, *Nisei Daughter,* and the short stories of Hisaye Yamamoto. Okada's novel was an act of immaculate conception, it seemed, producing from nowhere a novel that was by any known criterion of literature so bad that Japanese-American literary critics ignored the book or dumped heavily on it, loaded up again and dumped on it again. *No-No Boy* became an instantly forgotten work, evidenced by the fact that fifteen years after its publication the first edition of 1,500 copies had not sold out.

The critics have forgotten that the vitality of literature stems from its ability to codify and legitimize common experience in the terms of that experience and to celebrate life as it is lived. In reading Okada or any other Asian-American writer, the literary establishment has never considered the fact that a new folk in a strange land would experience the land and develop new language out of old words. Strangely, the critics accept this change in science-fiction stories of new planets in the future. Even the notion that the cultural clash produced by future overdoses of mass media will make new folks and new languages is accepted as shown by the critical success of Anthony Burgess' *A Clockwork Orange* in the sixties, funny-talking Flash Gordon in the fifties, Buck Rogers, and *The Wizard of Oz* in the thirties.

The critics were wrong in calling Toshio Mori's language "bad English," as William Saroyan did in his introduction to Mori's book *Yokohama, California*:

> Of the thousands of unpublished writers in America there are probably no more than three who cannot write better English than Toshio Mori. His stories are full of grammatical errors. His use of English, especially when he is most eager to say something very good, is very bad. Any high school teacher of English would flunk him in grammar and punctuation.

The critics were also wrong in ignoring or being too embarrassed by Okada's use of language and punctuation to deal with his book at all. The assumption that an ethnic minority writer thinks in, believes he writes in, or has ambitions toward writing beautiful, correct, and well-punctuated English sentences is an expression of white supremacy. The universality of the belief that correct English is the only language of American truth has made language an instrument of cultural imperialism. The minority experience does not yield itself to accurate or complete expression in the white man's language. Yet, the minority writer, specifically the Asian-American writer, is made to feel morally obligated to write in a language produced by an alien and hostile sensibility. His task, in terms of language alone, is to legitimize his, and by implication his people's, orientation as white, to codify his experience in the form of prior symbols, clichés, linguistic mannerisms, and a sense of humor that appeals to whites because it celebrates Asian-American self-contempt. Or his task is the opposite—to legitimize the language, style, and syntax, of his people's experience, to codify the experiences common to his people into symbols, clichés, linguistic mannerisms, and a sense of humor that emerges from an organic familiarity with the experience.

The tyranny of language continues even in the instruments designed to inject the minority into the mainstream. Virtually every anthology of Third World writing containing Asian-American sections confuses Chinese from China with Chinese-Americans, conveniently ignoring the obvious cultural differences. C. Y. Lee and Lin Yutang, born and raised in China, are secure in their Chinese culture, and unlike Chinese-Americans, are Chinese who have merely adapted to American ways and write about Chinese America as foreigners. Their work inevitably authenticates the concept of the dual personality. However, their being Chinese precludes their ability to communicate the Chinese-American sensibility. The other Chinese-American writers collected in this new splash of anthologies most often include Jade Snow Wong and Pardee Lowe, who also reinforce the stereotype. Lowe's book, *Father and Glorious Descendant,* came out in 1943. The dust jacket revealed the racist function of the book, saying that *Father and Glorious Descendant* "is a timely document at a moment when America must learn how to assimilate its loyal minorities."

The deprivation of language in a verbal society like this country's has contributed to the lack of a recognized Asian-American cultural integrity (at most, native-born Asian-Americans are "Americanized" Chinese or Japanese) and the lack of a recognized style of Asian-American manhood. These two conditions have produced "the house nigger mentality," under which Chinese- and Japanese-Americans accept responsibility for, rather than authority over the language and accept dependency. A state of dependency is encouraged by the teaching of English and the publishing establishment. This state of dependency characterizes the self-consciously grammatical language of Jon Shirota's first two novels, *Lucky Come Hawaii* (1966) and *Pineapple White* (1970). Shirota's communication of his Nisei orientation is handicapped by a language he seems to feel is not his own, unlike Toshio Mori and John Okada, who write strong in a language that comes from home. Mori and Okada demonstrate, as did Claude McKay, Mark Twain, and N. Scott Momaday, that new experience breeds new language.

John Okada writes from an oral tradition he hears all the time, and talks his writing onto the page. To judge Okada's writing by the white criterion of silent reading of the printed word is wrong. Listen as you read Okada or any other Asian-American writer. Okada changes voices and characters inside his sentences, running off free form but shaping all the time. These voice changes grate against the white tradition of tonal uniformity and character consistency, but more accurately duplicate the way people talk: "a bunch of Negroes were horsing around raucously in front of a pool parlor." There is a quick-change act here among "horsing around" and "raucously" and "pool parlor." The style itself is an expression of the multivoiced schizophrenia of the Japanese-American compressed into an organic whole. It's crazy, but it's not madness.

John Okada's work is new only because whites aren't literate in the Japanese-American experience, not because Okada has been up late nights inventing Japanese-American culture in his dark laboratory. And though he presents an ugly vision of America in which Japanese-Americans wander stupefied with self-contempt, then overcompensate with despairing wails of superpatriotism, his book cannot honestly be dismissed as an operatic cry of self-pity or a blast of polemic. Yet the book has been ignored, if not by whites, then by Japanese-Americans fearful of being identified with Okada's work. Charles Tuttle, the publisher of *No-No Boy*, writes in a letter, "At the time we published it, the very people whom we thought would be enthusiastic about it, mainly the Japanese-American community in the United States, were not only disinterested but actually rejected the book."

Depression, despair, death, suicide, listless anger, and a general tone of low-key hysteria closed inside the gray of a constantly overcast and drizzling Seattle pervade the book. Definitely not the stuff of a musical. There is at the same time something genuinely uplifting and inspiring about this book—at least for Asian-American readers. The book makes a narrative style of the Japanese-American talk, gives the talk the status of a language, makes it work and styles it, deftly and crudely, and uses it to bring the unglamorous but more commonly lived aspects of Japanese-American experience into the celebration of life. The style and structure of the book alone suggest the Japanese-American way of life of a specific period in history. All in all, there is nothing arcane or mysterious about why this book satisfies and, through all its melodramatic gloom, cheers the blood to running warm. This is new literature, one for which the experience and the people have already been tried and want nothing but the writing and the reading. This isn't an attempt to appeal to old values, translate life into a dead language, or drive whites into paroxysms of limpid guilt, or an effort to destroy the English language.

Ichiro, the *No-No Boy* of the title, is a Nisei who refused to be inducted into the armed forces during the war and chose prison instead. The novel opens with Ichiro's arrival in Seattle, home from two years in prison. He has come home to a mother who is so convinced that Japan has won the war that she refuses to send money or goods from the family store to relatives writing from Japan, begging for help. Ichiro's father is an alcoholic; his younger brother, Taro, drops out of high school to join the army to make up for the shame of Ichiro's being a "no-no boy." Other "no-no boys" fade into easy booze and easy women and out of Ichiro's life. His best friend turns out to be Kenji, a war hero with a medal and without a leg, whose heroism has cost him his leg, and by the end of the book his life. Kenji, the admirable war hero, dying of a progressive creeping crud that repeated amputations of his leg have failed to check, seems to have the divinity of the suffering. He gives Ichiro an understanding woman, an abandoned wife whose husband, rather than coming home, re-enlists and stays in Europe. Kenji makes Ichiro himself a symbol of goodness and strength.

Ichiro has come home to a world in which everything he touches and loves dies, is killed, or goes mad. All offers of life, the love of a woman, a job by an understanding Mr. Carrick, are refused because he is unworthy, because he must somehow prove himself worthy by himself. He has been spat on, rejected by his brother, lost his good and his bad friends and his parents. Ichiro seems to be a pathological loser. What he does is wrong, and what he doesn't do is wrong. He is full of self-contempt, self-pity, and yet is governed by an innate sense of dignity, if not a coherent sense of humor. He is not Stephen Dedalus out to "forge the unformed conscience of his race in the smithy of his soul," but he is searching for something more than his identity. It is the nature of the language itself, this embryonic Japanese-American English language that can only define the Japanese-American who is neither Japanese nor American, in anything but negative terms, that makes every attempt at positive expression an exercise in futility and despair. "Think more deeply and your doubts will disappear," Ichiro's mother says. "You are my son," she says, triggering a spinning, running internal monologue and one of the most powerfully moving passages in the book:

> No, he said to himself as he watched her part the curtains and start into the store. There was a time when I

was your son. There was a time that I no longer remember when you used to smile a mother's smile and tell me stories about gallant and fierce warriors who protected their lords with blades of shining steel and about the old woman who found a peach in the stream and took it home, and, when her husband split it in half, a husky little boy tumbled out to fill their hearts with boundless joy. I was that lad in the peach and you were the old woman and we were Japanese with Japanese feelings and Japanese pride and Japanese thoughts because it was all right then to be Japanese and feel and think all the things that Japanese do even if we lived in America. Then there came a time when I was only half Japanese because one is not born in America and raised in America and taught in America and one does not speak and swear and drink and smoke and play and fight and see and hear in America among Americans in American streets and houses without becoming American and loving it. But I did not love enough for you were still half my mother and I was thereby still half Japanese and when the war came and they told me to fight for America, I was not strong enough to fight you and I was not strong enough to fight the bitterness which made the half of me which was bigger than the half of me which was America and really the whole of me that I could not see or feel. Now that I know the truth when it is late and the half of me and the half that remains is enough to know why it was that I could not fight for America and did not strip me of my birthright. But it is not enough to be only half an American and know that it is an empty half. I am not your son and I am not Japanese and I am not American. I can go someplace and tell people that I've got an inverted stomach and that I am an American, true and blue and Hail Columbia, but the army wouldn't have me because of the stomach. That's easy and I would do it, only I've got to convince myself first and that I cannot do. I wish with all my heart that I were Japanese or that I were American. I am neither and I blame you and I blame myself and I blame the world which is made up of many countries which fight with each other and kill and hate and destroy again and again and again. It is so easy and simple that I cannot understand it at all. And the reason I do not understand it is because I do not understand you who were the half of me that is no more and because I do not understand what it was about the half of me which was American and the half which might have become the whole of me if I had said yes I will go and fight in your army because that is what I believe and want and cherish and love.

This passage is central to the book in suggesting the wholeness that Ichiro contains and is searching for. His whole life is contained in the paragraph, beginning with childhood and Japan in the form of his family moving from the first "no" through the samurai defending their lords to Ichiro refusing to defend America and ending on a hypothetical positive chord ringing with "yes" and "cherish and love."

A sign of Ichiro's strength, and his sense of despair, and the truth of his being neither Japanese nor American is the fluid movement into the sick joke about the inverted stomach that simultaneously recalls the stereotype of Japanese being slant-eyed, sideways, doing things backwards, and draft-dodger humor. His being not Japanese is subtly underscored by his avoidance of Japanese terms: "gallant and fierce warriors" instead of "samurai."

Okada's *No-No Boy* is an exploration of the universe of racial self-contempt. At one point, through Ichiro, Okada suggests that self-contempt based on your physical and cultural difference from other more favored races produces a contempt for all who are like you:

> . . .I got to thinking that the Japs were wising up, that they had learned that living in big bunches and talking Jap and feeling Jap and doing Jap was just inviting trouble, but my dad came back . . . I hear there's almost as many in Seattle now as there were before the war. It's a shame, a dirty rotten shame. Pretty soon it'll be just like it was before the war. A bunch of Japs with a fence around them, not the kind you can see, but it'll hurt them just as much. They bitched and hollered when the government put them in camps and put real fences around them, but now they're doing the same damn thing to themselves. They screamed because the government said they were Japs and when they finally got out, they couldn't wait to rush together and prove that they were.

The literature of Japanese America flourished through the thirties, into the war years and the camp experience. These were years of tremendous literary and journalistic output. The question of Japanese-American identity, the conflicts between Issei and Nisei, yellow and white relations, black, white, and yellow relations, and the war were all examined and re-examined in camp newspapers, literary magazines, diaries, and journals. The result of the camp experience was a literate Japanese America that had encompassed broad areas of American experience. Highly skilled writers came from camps, like Bill Hosokawa and Larry Tajiri who became editors of the Denver *Post,* and fiction writers and poets like Iwao Kawakami, Hiroshi Kashiwagi, Paul Itaya, Jack Matsuye, Toshio

Mori, Toyo Suyemoto, and Hisaye Yamamoto. The journalists got recognition, but the writers of fiction and poetry, all native to their brand of English, with rare exceptions remain confined to the pages of the Japanese-American Citizens League paper, the *Pacific Citizen*. To preserve the illusion of our absence, many Asian-American writers have been asked to write under white pseudonyms. C. Y. Lee was told a white pseudonym would enhance his chances for publication. To his credit, he kept his name.

The first novel published about the camp experience was predictably written by a white, non-Japanese woman, Karen Kehoe. The appearance of *City in the Sun* in 1947 led the *Pacific Citizen* to wonder why a Japanese-American had not written a work of fiction or nonfiction about the camp experience. The editors then went on to speculate that perhaps the experience had been too traumatic. The truth is that the camp experience stimulated rather than depressed artistic output. The Japanese-Americans did write of the camp experience, but were not published outside the confines.

Blacks and Chicanos often write in unconventional English. Their particular vernacular is recognized as being their own legitimate mother tongue. Only Asian-Americans are driven out of their tongues and expected to be at home in a language they never use and a culture they encounter only in books written in English. This piracy of our native tongues by white culture amounts to the eradication of a recognizable Asian-American culture here. It is ridiculous that a non-Japanese woman should be the one and only novelist of the Japanese-American camp experience. And it is a lie.

As in the work of John Okada, there is nothing quaint about Lawson Inada's poetry, no phony continuity between sign-inspiring Oriental art and his tough, sometimes vicious language. No one, not even William Saroyan trying hard, can make Inada out to be quaint or treat his work as a high-school English paper.

"Inada's poem is lean, hard, muscular, and yet for all that it has gentility, humor and love," Saroyan says on the jacket of Inada's first book, *Before the War.* Inada is a monster poet from the mul-tiracial ghetto of West Fresno, California, where he ran with blacks, grew up speaking their language, playing their music. But his voice is his own, a Japanese-American, Sansei voice afraid of nothing. It is as distinct from the blacks now as country-western is from soul.

In an anthology of Fresno poets, *Down at the Santa Fe Depot,* Inada wrote of hatreds and fears no Asian-American ever wrote of before. Inada is tough enough to write about self-contempt. He took the names white folks called Chinese and Japanese and used them to violate the holy word of the English language. The result is not death but magic and a new American truth:

> CHINKS
> Ching Chong Chinaman
> sitting on a fence
> trying to make a dollar
> chop-chop all day.
>
> "Eju-kei-shung! Eju-kei-shung!"
> that's what they say.
> When the War came
> they said, "We Chinese!"
>
> When we went away,
> they made sukiyaki,
> saying, "Yellow all same."
>
> When the war closed,
> they stoned the Jap's homes.

Grandma would say:
"Marry a Mexican,
a Nigger, just don't
marry no Chinese."

The Chinese were contemptible for being actively "not Japanese." In *No-No Boy*, Kenji tells Ichiro, essentially, to be not Japanese. "Go someplace where there isn't another Jap within a thousand miles. Marry a white girl or a Negro or an Italian or even a Chinese. Anything but a Japanese. After a few generations of that, you've got the thing beat."

Inada echoes *No-No Boy*. The similarity is and is not accidental. Inada is bound to Okada by a common sensibility and not by any real knowledge of his predecessor. Inada did not learn of the existence of Okada's work until ten years after he had written "West Side Songs." Both articulated the belief common among Japanese-Americans that one remedy for being a contemptible, self-hating Japanese-American is to leave that society, associate oneself with whiteness of some kind and rise in the world.

As in "Chinks," "Japs" ends with the formal name of the race, and it, not Chinks or Japs, is the dirty word.

JAPS
are great imitators
they stole
the Greek's
skewers,
used them
on themselves.
Their sutras
are Face
and Hide.
They hate

      everyone else

      on the sly.

      They play

      Dr. Charley's

      games—bowling,

      raking,

      growing forks

      on lapels.

      Their tongues

      are yellow

      with "r's"

      with "l's."

      They hate

      themselves

      on the sly. I

      used to be

      Japanese.

Inada confronts his own experience. Everything in his life is in his deceptively simple and humorous poems that have the feel of having been written in the guts of a juke box. He tears himself apart exposing all the symbols of Asian assimilation—education, the preservation of Oriental culture—as acts of desperation, terrific efforts to buy a little place in the country. It is the fear of America that causes this, not assimilation.

A constant theme in Asian-American literature, from Pardee Lowe's *Father and Glorious Descendant* through *No-No Boy* to Frank Chin's play *The Chickencoop Chinaman* (1972), is the failure of Asian-American manhood to express itself in its simplest form: fathers and sons.

"There is nothing good about being a son," says the unnamed narrator in Wallace Lin's "Rough Notes For Mantos." "I know; I am a son. When you have to admit that you have a father, allowing people to think that you are a father and son, as if any relation existed between those two terms, when there is really nothing to say."

What exists in these works is that mutual self-contempt. In Pardee Lowe's *Father and Glorious Descendant,* Father names his "Glorious Descendant" after Governor Pardee of California not to inspire his son with an American identity but to offer his son up as a sacrifice to white supremacy. Inspired by his American name, young Pardee has childhood visions of becoming the first Chinese-American President of the United States. The true meaning of his name comes home when his father tells him to forget his dream, not only because it is impossible, but because it is, by implication, immoral. The book seems to celebrate a healthy relationship between father and son. Set in the context of Asian-American literature and history, this relationship is thinly disguised mutual contempt. In *No-No Boy,* the most sympathetic emotion Ichiro can muster for his father is pity. The dominant emotion is contempt. The perpetuation of self-contempt between father and son is an underlying current in virtually every Asian-American work. "Chinamans do make lousey fathers. I know. I have one," says Tam Lum, the main character of *The Chickencoop Chinaman.* He suggests that he is "a lousey father" himself when he says, "I want my kids to forget me." As the comic embodiment of Asian-American manhood, rooted in neither Asia nor white America, Tam is forced to invent a past, mythology, and traditions from the antiques and curios of his immediate experience. In an effort to link himself with the first known Chinese-Americans, he states, "Chinamen are made, not born, my dear. Out of junk-imports, lies, railroad scrap iron, dirty jokes, broken bottles, cigar smoke, Cosquilla Indian blood, wino spit, and lots of milk of amnesia."

In white writing there is a tradition of communication breaking down between father and son. The son rebels against the accepted past, strikes out for the future to dare the unknown. In *The Chick-encoop Chinaman* the past is the unknown. Tam breaks with the past by trying to find it, define it, and identify with it. At the end of the play he links himself with the railroad, Chinese restaurants, and the future:

> Now and then, I feel them old days, children, the way I feel the prowl of the dogs in the night and the bugs in the leaves and the thunder in the Sierra Nevadas how-ever far they are. The way my grandmother had an ear for trains. Listen, children. I gotta go. Ride Buck Buck Bagaw with me . . . Listen in the kitchen for the Chick-encoop Chinaman slowin on home.

Chin, if not Tam Lum, is saying that an Asian-American sensibility is not a recent invention.

Language is the medium of culture and the people's sensibility, including the style of manhood. Language coheres the people into a community by organizing and codifying the symbols of the people's common experience. Stunt the tongue and you have lopped off the culture and sensibility. On the simplest level, a man in any culture speaks for himself. Without a language of his own, he no longer is a man. The concept of the dual personality deprives the Chinese-American and Japanese-American of the means to develop their own terms. The tyranny of language has been used by white culture the to suppress Asian-American culture and exclude it from operating in the mainstream of American consciousness. The first Asian-American writers worked alone within a sense of rejection and isolation to the extent that it encouraged Asian America to reject its own literature. John Okada and Louis Chu died in obscurity, and Toshio Mori lives in obscurity. In the past, being an Asian-American writer meant that you did not associate with other Asian-American writers. Emulating the whites, we ignored ourselves. Now we seek each other out.

Recently in San Francisco twenty Asian-American writers, representing three generations of writers, gathered together for the first time as Asian-American writers. Attending were Kai-yu Hsu, editor of the first Asian-American anthology of writing, Toshio Mori, one of the first Asian-Americans to publish a book-length creative work, Lawson Inada, the first Asian-American to publish a book of poetry, Frank Chin, author of the first Asian-American play produced in the history of the American legitimate theater, Victor and Brett Nee, authors of the first Chinese-American history from the Chinese-American point of view, and young Asian-American writers, many of whom are included in this book and who represent the first generation of Asian-Americans to be aware of writing within an Asian-American tradition. We know each other now. It should never have been otherwise.

LAWRENCE FERLINGHETTI

Adieu à Charlot
(Second Populist Manifesto) (1975–1978)

Sons of Whitman sons of Poe
sons of Lorca & Rimbaud
or their dark daughters
poets of another breath
poets of another vision
Who among you still speaks of revolution
Who among you still unscrews
the locks from the doors
in this revisionist decade?
'You are President of your own body, America'
Thus spoke Kush in Tepotzlan
youngblood wildhaired angel poet
one of a spawn of wild poets
in the image of Allen Ginsberg
wandering the wilds of America
'You Rimbauds of another breath'
sang Kush
and wandered off with his own particular paranoias
maddened like most poets
for one mad reason or another
in the unmade bed of the world
Sons of Whitman
in your 'public solitude'

bound by blood-duende
'President of your own body America'
Take it back from those who have maddened you
back from those who stole it
and steal it daily
The subjective must take back the world
from the objective gorillas & guerrillas of the world
We must rejoin somehow
the animals in the fields
in their steady-state meditation
'Your life is in your own hands still
Make it flower make it sing'
(so sang mad Kush in Tepotzlan)
'a constitutional congress of the body'
still to be convened to seize control
of the State
the subjective state
from those who have subverted it
The arab telephone of the avant-garde
has broken down
And I speak to you now
from another country
Do not turn away
in your public solitudes
you poets of other visions
of the separate lonesome visions
untamed uncornered visions
fierce recalcitrant visions
you Whitmans of another breath

which is not the too-cool breath of modern poetry
which is not the halitosis of industrial civilization
Listen now Listen again
to the song in the blood the dark duende a dark singing
between the tickings of civilization
between the lines of its headlines
in the silences between cars
driven like weapons
In two hundred years of freedom
we have invented
the permanent alienation of the subjective
almost every truly creative being
alienated & expatriated
in his own country
in Middle America or San Francisco
the death of the dream in your birth
o meltingpot America
I speak to you
from another country
another kind of blood-letting land
from Tepotzlan the poets' lan'
Land of the Lord of the Dawn

                              Quetzalcoatl

Land of the Plumed Serpent
I signal to you
as Artaud signaled
through the flames
I signal to you
over the heads of the land

the hard heads that stand like menhirs
above the land in every country
the short-haired hyenas
who still rule everything
I signal to you from Poets' Land
you poets of the alienated breath
to take back your land again
and the deep sea of the subjective
Have you heard the sound of the ocean lately
the sound by which daily
the stars still are driven
the sound by which nightly
the stars retake their sky
The sea thunders still to remind you
of the thunder in the blood
to remind you of your selves
Think now of your self
as of a distant ship
Think now of your beloved
of the eyes of your beloved
whoever is most beloved
he who held you hard in the dark
or she who washed her hair by the waterfall
whoever makes the heart pound
the blood pound
Listen says the river
Listen says the sea Within you
you with your private visions
of another reality a separate reality

Listen and study the charts of time
Read the sanskrit of ants in the sand
You Whitmans of another breath
there is no one else to tell
how the alienated generations
have lived out their expatriate visions
here and everywhere
The old generations have lived them out
Lived out the bohemian myth in Greenwich Villages
Lived out the Hemingway myth
in *The Sun Also Rises*
at the Dôme in Paris
or with the bulls at Pamplona
Lived out the Henry Miller myth
in the *Tropics* of Paris
and the great Greek dream
of *The Colossus of Maroussi*
and the tropic dream of Gauguin
Lived out the D. H. Lawrence myth
in *The Plumed Serpent*
in Mexico Lake Chapala
And the Malcolm Lowry myth
Under the Volcano at Cuernavaca
And then the saga of *On the Road*
and the Bob Dylan myth Blowing in the Wind
How many roads must a man walk down
How many Neal Cassadys on lost railroad tracks
How many replicas of Woody Guthrie with cracked guitars
How many photocopies of longhaired Joan

How many Ginsberg facsimiles and carbon-copy Keseys

still wandering the streets of America

in old tennis shoes and backpacks

or driving beat-up school buses

with destination-signs reading 'Further'

How many Buddhist Catholics how many cantors

chanting the Great Paramita Sutra

on the Lower Last Side

How many Whole Earth Catalogs

lost in out-houses on New Mexico communes

How many Punk Rockers waving swastikas

Franco is dead but so is Picasso

Chaplin is dead but I'd wear his bowler

having outlived all our myths but his

the myth of the pure subjective

the collective subjective

the Little Man in each of us

waiting with Charlot or Pozzo

On every corner I see them

hidden inside their tight clean clothes

Their hats are not derbys they have no canes

but we know them

we have always

waited with them

They turn and hitch their pants

and walk away from us

down the darkening road

in the great American night

GEARY HOBSON

The Rise of the White Shaman as a New Version of Cultural Imperialism

It seems redundant to write a brief preface to this particular essay, since the last essay in this section is a revisiting of it, more than twenty years later. Therefore, with merely the observation that White Shamanism still exists, I commend the reader to the essay at hand and the one at the end of the section, while keeping this preface short.

Recently, at a poetry reading at one of the universities in the southern part of a southwestern state, a middle-aged, Anglo poet, after referring to himself as a "shaman," began reading poems in which he identified himself with several historical Indian personae. He had made it clear at the outset that he wasn't merely a poet—as if that weren't enough in itself—but he was a "shaman," a man who was going to re-create the world through the power of his words. I wasn't present at this reading, though a friend of mine, a well-known Chicano poet, was there, and it was he who later told me about it. The "shaman," at midpoint in his reading, began another sequence of poems by suddenly inveighing the audience with the salutation "I AM GERONIMO!" in a squeaky falsetto, causing the handful of Indians among the listeners to laugh out loud. I am told that the "shaman" appeared perplexed for a moment, as though at a loss to understand why someone should rudely laugh at such a dramatic moment.

   I have seen variations of this moment repeated many times in the past several years. Sometimes it occurs in art galleries, when little old ladies from Boston or Kansas City interrupt the Indian artist, there also on exhibit along with his works, to tell whoever happens to be listening what Indian art—and perhaps even that particular artist's work—is all about. Or, when the visitor to Acoma Pueblo or Taos Pueblo begins to tell the residents there of his or her grandmother back in Syracuse who was a Cherokee, or Sioux, or Blackfoot (it's surprising how popular Blackfoot is becoming these days) princess—(always *Princess,* not merely an Indian *woman*—and certainly *never,* a *squaw,* although they will refer to other Indian women as squaws, but not their own mythical Indian grandmothers). Or, the Junior Chamber of Commerce–types who explain the new housing project designed for a low-rent district as being "simply constructed" like an "Indian pueblo," and, one assumes, with all the comforts of the reservation. Or, in certain university departments whose liberal members sit dreaming up new grant proposals and programs for Indian students without even bothering to consult the Indians themselves; of course, the grant money is available: big corporate industry wants not just to absolve its part in the national guilt, but, more importantly, is slobbering for the tax write-offs that are involved in their Santa Claus-like gestures. In short, it is still the same old ballgame: Indians are still being exploited, both materially and culturally, but the forms now employed are much more subtle than the forms used a century ago by the mountain men and the Seventh Cavalry.

So, in the same spirit as Leslie Silko's two-part old-time Indian attack, I would like to examine some things that are happening on the literary scene today—things that I feel are detrimental to both Indian people, not only of the past but of the present as well, and to non-Indians, whose knowledge of Indian cultures has, unfortunately, been formed too often by the romantic (and now the neo-romantic) writers/artists/ethnologists who have avidly and imperiously staked out their claims as unequivocal experts on our Indian cultures.

It seems a foregone conclusion of non-Indians that the great store of wisdom "collected" from Indian cultures by these same "friends" is *their* property and no longer that of the Indians—that this body of knowledge and consciousness, like the land and water and the sky itself, now belongs to them by dint of appropriation. Leslie has already touched on this, but it bears repeating that the same attitudes implicit in the bullying "guests" of this continent in the past—the Captain John Smiths, the Custers, and other Great White Fathers—are equally as prevalent today as they were then; and they are even present when such well-meaning hot-shots as Elsie Clews Parsons, D. H. Lawrence, and Mabel Dodge invaded Taos Pueblo in the 1920's (to cite only one tribe and its own particular set of "friends") and claimed it as their own. The assumption seems to be that one's "interest" in an Indian culture makes it okay for the invader to collect "data" from Indian people, when, in effect, this taking of the essentials of cultural lifeways, even if in the name of Truth or Scholarship or whatever, is as imperialistic as those simpler forms of theft, such as the theft of homeland by treaty.

I find it amusing that hippies who are now glutting the market with tons of bogus "Indian" jewelry get uptight when an Indian asks them why *they* are making jewelry copied after the Indian forms and designs. One has only to spend a day or so here in Albuquerque or in Gallup to see the extent to which this form of Indian art has been cheapened and bastardized and taken over by non-Indians. In fact, it has recently been reported that the increase of non-Indian exploitation of the silver, turquoise, and heishi market here in New Mexico has raised serious speculation concerning the future survival of these ancient crafts. The Santo Domingo smith, for example, who spends weeks working on a single silver bracelet, can't compete with the assembly-line, machine-produced, or non-Indian-made, or even foreign-made, *junk* that is marketed here and in the East as "authentic" Indian-made. The rationale of the non-Indian who makes Indian jewelry even when he calls it "imitation"

Indian jewelry, is a 20th-century counterpart of the buffalo hunters of the last century, the Buffalo Bills and the Billy Dixons, who, even as they killed off the great herds for economic reasons, were aware of the immensity of their exploitation. When the non-Indian jewelry maker is confronted with questions of why he is selling his silver gimcracks and gee-gaws on the mall of the University of New Mexico campus, becomes defensive and usually answers with "I've got a *right* to do it; besides, *my* jewelry is not Indian-imitated!" or "*Everybody* else is doing it, so why pick on just me?" or "I've got to make a living, *too,* haven't I?" He knows what he is doing, but he continues doing it anyway. And so the rip-off continues.

The current fad in some small magazines of poets calling themselves "poet-shamans," or even "shamans," is another counterpart of the Indian crafts exploiters, the imperious anthropologists, and the buffalo hunters. Writing from what they generally assume to be an Indian point of view, calling their poems "shaman songs," posturing as "shamans," and pontificating about their roles as remakers of the world through the power of their words, they seem to have no particular qualms about appropriating the transliterated forms of American Indian songs and poetry and then passing off their own poems, based on those transliterations, as the pronouncements of "shamans." Thus, they "become" Indian by equating their poems with what they feel to be the intentions of the original singers. Anyone who has the slightest familiarity with an American Indian language, and is aware of the wide gap between the original work and the transliterations, can readily perceive the differences. But, unfortunately, non-Indian readers, who are used to seeing the transliterations, accord these newer productions as works of an authentic Indian consciousness.

What do I mean by a "white shaman"? These are the apparently growing number of small-press poets of generally white, Euro-Christian American background, who in their poems assume the persona of the shaman, usually in the guise of an American Indian medicine man. To be a poet is simply not enough; they must claim a power from higher sources. As Gene Fowler says in a "shaman song" from his book *Fires* (Thorp Springs Press, 1972):

> My ancestors were shamans.
> But I am not my ancestors.
> I am shaman
> to a tribe recently come.
>
> A tribe with fear of the Other.
> I wear animal skins
> and cast huge shadows on the wall.

Despite the remonstrations of several of the white "shamans" (including Fowler) that their usage of "shaman" is Siberian and not American Indian, the implication that they are modeling themselves after Indians seems clear in the excerpt from the above poem. I doubt very seriously if there is anything in their own cultural environments that really affords them such power, or even the access to such power, to say nothing of the spuriousness of their ancestors being shamans. Even the various dictionary definitions concerning the shaman or shamanism illustrates that there is little in the Euro-Christian American traditions to lend them ready access to shamanistic power. Yet the second-rate efforts continue to pour forth:

1

Come

2

People of this place

3

Come

4

People of this place

5

To the River

6

To the place of the Bear

7

To the place of the Snake

etc., etc., for another tedious forty-eight "stanzas."

Non-Indian readers with little knowledge of American Indian cultures reading the foregoing poem are left with the impression that Indians, as they have always heard, are a people with a "simplistic" way of life. Such readers look at the "simple" phraseology and are further confirmed in that particular stereotype of the Indian—that of the Native American as a "childlike savage." The "white shaman," like other romanticists of the past, quite clearly sees the Indian as something exotic, and he oversimplifies in his efforts to extoll and imitate; unfortunately, when he views the Indian more closely, seeing the everyday occurrences, the prosaic and undramatic elements of small things conducted in almost unnoticeable ritual, he then refurbishes it all into more vivid productions. Pretty soon he has rewritten *Hiawatha* all over again, calling it now perhaps *Seven Arrows* or *Winterhawk* or one of the godawful Billy Jack movies—or "white shaman" poetry. Thus the resurrection of Romanticism, or the beginnings of Neo-Romanticism.

A serious problem involved here for Indian writers, as I see it, is the stone wall of public knowledge confronting them when they begin to put forth their own works based on what they know of their own particular tribal and cultural matrix. Since the American public has already become accustomed to seeing Jerome Rothenberg "translations," the poetry of the "white shamans" such as Gary

Snyder, Gene Fowler, Norman Moser, Barry Gifford, David Cloutier, to name a few, and other neo-romantic writers posing as Indians and/or Indian experts/spokesmen, such as Carlos Castaneda, Hyemeyohsts Storm, Tony Shearer, Doug Boyd, the Baha'i influenced "Indian" works of Naturegraph Publications, contemporary Indian writers are often discounted or ignored since they are not following or conforming to the molds created by these "experts." Just as the "experts" at the turn of the century—the Bureau of American Ethnology writers (Boas, Swanton, Densmore, etc.), Clark Wissler, Theodore Roosevelt, Edward S. Curtis, Oliver LaFarge, etc.—were genuinely concerned with the "Vanishing American," as the American Indian was called then, so too, I believe, are these modern writers likewise concerned. But what is distressing is the fact that these contemporary writers, like the turn-of-the-century people, are often blind to actuality—that Indian cultures *still* exist, and most often, are in far different forms than those which they project in their writings and preachments. Strangely, the contemporary writers, especially the "white shamans," too often perceive Indian cultures through not only the rose-colored glasses of a white, Anglo-Saxon Protestant viewpoint, but the Day-Glo spectacles of a hastily assumed Oriental (Buddhist, Taoist, etc.) outlook. My concern is not merely the cultural borrowing from Oriental cultures, which I suspect has been as imperialistically bowdlerized as the American Indian conscience (but I'll leave this to Alex Kuo, Frank Chin, and Lawson Inada to examine), but the manner in which outsiders presume to define Indian people and lifeways in an authoritative way. My concern, also, is for the great need which Indian people have of being the ones to speak for themselves, of being the ones to define themselves and their cultures. Quite simply, I believe Indian people are growing tired of the Oliver LaFarges and Jerome Rothenbergs speaking for them—and making reputations and money at their expense—however honorable and sensitively felt the original intentions of these outsiders may have been.

Part of the "white shaman" thing is due largely, it seems, to the traditional American way of viewing Indians. Ten to fifteen years ago, white Americans, concerned about the rise of the Black Power movement, were asking the question, sometimes quite earnestly— "What do you people *want,* anyway?" or "Why all this rebellion and dissatisfaction?" Very few non-Indian Americans have bothered to ask these questions of Indian people today—if they have had occasion to reflect on our particular discontent at all. The reason for not asking us these questions, or at least comparable ones, seems to be that since Indians continue to exist almost totally in the minds of most Americans as an *idea* rather than a reality, it is therefore not essential to deal with Indians as people. As *idea,* everyone from early childhood, thanks to elementary school and Hollywood, has known about Indians, and thus all Americans are "experts" about Indians. The fact that these ideas are merely stereotypes is beside the point: nobody has to be told about Indians; everyone knows everything about them already! Indeed, it would be "un-American" not to know about Indians!

When Indian writers/scholars have sought to answer and correct the misconceptions about their people, they have often been smiled at rather patronizingly and then ignored. After all, most of them don't have Ph.D.'s or other academic credentials, and some, Heaven forbid, have only the barest elementary grade schooling. But the condescension hasn't come only from the academics and the Ph.D.'s. The self-appointed "white shamans," who incidentally make it part of their posture to sneer at Academia in their "return to the earth" nostalgia, also condescend in their recognition of "things Indian." In various letters and public readings, "white shaman" poets have scorned the bookishness and pedantry of the university-trained scholars—people for the most part, for good and for bad, who have at least gone into the field for their researches. These modern poets tend to scoff at this, using instead the arcane, exotic, half-baked works by non-Indian people published by other small presses. In reality, since the "white shaman" attains his knowledge totally from books, he is probably more "academic" than the BAE people at any rate.

An example of the imperious way of discounting what Indians relate about themselves and their cultures can be seen in how various non-Indian writers reacted to Rupert Costo's negative review of *Seven Arrows* (in *The Indian Historian*, Vol. 5, No. 2; Summer 1972), and to what the Northern Cheyenne people themselves had to say about how they were offended by the book (*Wassaja*, Vol. 2, No. 4; April–May 1974, and in *Wassaja*, Vol. 2, No. 7; August 1974). Many non-Indians were so eager to defend *Seven Arrows* that what Costo and the Cheyennes had to say somehow became lost in all the noise. Since *Seven Arrows* seems to be so very much what the counter-culture wants to hear about Indians—full of peppermint and saccharine, Tantra-like Day-Glo art superimposed on traditional Plains Indian shield designs, and almost Kahlil Gibran in its message and tone—it is natural to expect the New Age hippies to yell loudly in its behalf, and to hell with how Indians feel about it.

It is interesting to note that two people who are allied with the "white shaman" fad—Gene Fowler and Jim Cody—have discounted the Cheyennes' complaints about the book. Cody, in particular, shrugged off Cheyennes as being "typical" of a Plains Indian tribe, "whose members generally don't agree on anything anyway." Fowler, in a section of *Fires*, entitled "Shaman Songs", seems to be the most vociferous in his claim to be a "shaman", but he is by no means the only one. In a series of incoherent letters in *Wood Ibis* and *Greenfield Review*, Fowler has proclaimed his "shamanism." In fact, he even begins one of his letters rather chummily by saying "Everyone of us is part Indian, yeh know. Some can trace that through a grandmother or grandfather to the Amerindian. Others across Europe to the Phoenicians (red men). In my case, it goes back to the owl in FOWLer. Magician in the workshop, as it were, hidden there, the skeleton of the shop." Which does nothing to endear him to Indians, and certainly creates no sense of relationship with Indian people whatsoever.

The "white shaman" fad seems to have begun inadvertently with Gary Snyder in his "Shaman Songs" sections of *Myths and Texts,* in which the poet speaks through the persona of an Indian shaman, and his words become calls to power, of a sort, which in and of itself is innocuous enough, since poetry of this kind does seek to transcend the mundane in such a way that people's lives are revivified. The poems contain great vitality and are, I believe, sincere efforts on Snyder's behalf to incorporate an essential part of American Indian philosophy into his work. Importantly, nowhere does Snyder refer to himself as a "shaman." But, along came the bastard children of Snyder who began to imitate him, especially in the Shaman Songs section, and not being content with that, began to call themselves shamans—which, as I understand it, Snyder still refuses to do. Not so with Fowler, Cody, Norman Moser, and Barry Gifford—these are only a few with whose posturings I am familiar.

There have been various other literary fads which exploited Indians. Just as white liberals have their "dilemmas," and Blacks have their "problems," Indians have their "plight"—not the least of which has been the white American writer. Most of the stereotyping of Indians has been perpetuated by well-meaning writers in every century since America's "discovery." One of the silliest fads, before the current one, was the "death song" fad of the Romantic period in the early days of the American Republic. People such as Philip Freneau, Mrs. John Hunter, and Royall Tyler, in the period between 1780 and 1810, wrote gobs of these embarrassingly sentimental poems written from the viewpoint of a "dying" Indian chief or "maiden." That these poems had more in common with Greek and Latin orations and 18th-century English drama, than the actual speeches of genuine Indians, is not surprising; nor is it surprising that few of these poems possess any literary merit at all. The fatuousness and pretentiousness of these lofty elegies have, I feel, much in common with the "white shaman" songs that are oozing onto the literary scene today—and have nothing in common with the actual Indian conscience.

The southwestern and western tribes' most prevalent trickster persona—the coyote—has become a favorite guise for white writers to assume. These writers, like the hippie movement of which they are an unacknowledgeable part, are obsessed with Coyote now—writing "Tantras" about him, renaming him "Charlie Kiot" in cutesy misspelling, finding him in every shadow of their lives. I'd be willing to bet that most of these guys, growing up in the 1950's, were once walking around, bored and sulking and pissed because they couldn't go to a Saturday matinee, carrying their .22's and taking potshots at coyotes—this their only association with coyotes—if they had any association with them at all. Nowadays, though, they are deifying Him, and, like with their understanding of Indian things, are calling themselves Coyote, just as some call themselves "Indians"—as though the greatest compliment that can be paid to Indians is to become Indians or Coyotes. I understand that the New Mexico poet John Brandi and fellow hippie communards up around Guadalupita are now calling themselves the "Coyote Tribe." It is also significant to note, as Lawrence Evers has, that Gary Snyder, in his "Incredible Survival of Coyote," totally ignores what modern Indian writers such as Simon Ortiz, Leslie Silko, and L. Scott Momaday have done with Coyote in their works, and instead praises certain "white shamans" who have suddenly discovered Coyote.

Shamanism, at least in the Indian way of using and making medicine, is a much larger thing than the poet who all of a sudden *decides* he is one. To be a medicine-maker in the tribes of my parents, the Cherokee and the Chickasaw, one—both men and women—has to be something of an apprentice for twenty years or more. Obviously, one can't simply and suddenly decide to be a shaman or a medicine-maker. He or she must have confirmation of the community, a great sense of the community, a profound knowledge of animals and plants, a knowledge of pain and suffering, and a sense of power that can be found only in an adherence to the old things. I know I do not have these powers, and I am Indian. Nor do most of the younger Indian writers that I know, nor would we call ourselves "shamans." For Leslie Silko, Joy Harjo, Simon Ortiz, Bill Oandasan, Joseph L. Concha, Ron Rogers, Goweitduweetza (Veronica Riley), Luci Cadzow, Larry Emerson, Gerald Wilkinson—any number of other Indian writers in the Southwest today—to suddenly declare themselves to be shamans would constitute an embarrassment both to themselves and to their friends and family. When an Indian is learning the medicine of his or her tribe, he or she is darned well not going to prance around spilling his or her guts about it, since (or at least in the Indian way that I know about) to tell about something to outsiders while it is in the process of being made, lessens both its value and its potential power, and cheapens it for the maker. White men seem to have a hard time understanding this.

The desire of "white shaman" poets to remake themselves into new personae seems to be an aspect of the "New Age" philosophy which posits that one can re-create one's karma, that one can assume a totally new consciousness. Missionaries such as Baba Ram Dass and Maharaji-Ji gleefully exhort the true believer–types to accept such a philosophy, but, I think it is absurd to think that if one has grown up in Oakland, California, or Topeka, Kansas, of

Euro-Christian American heritage, has been weaned on and inured to *American Bandstand* and the Mickey Mouse Club, that one can, all of a sudden, through enlightenment, become Hindu boddhisatvas, Zen masters, or even American Indian shamans. Thus, the shaman-singing of these poets becomes the cries of the culturally crippled. They are drowning men clutching at the straws of convenient cultures, as though to save themselves from their history. And I don't think it can be done. Such efforts to become new personae, replete with new racial or cultural backgrounds, not only cheapens the cultures which these true believers seek to join, but cheapens as well the culture from which they are fleeing. It should go without saying that the evasion of a culture's history and destiny, by those within it, is not a realistic way of understanding the past—or even the world. As Santayana said (with a bit of paraphrasing), those who do not know their history, acknowledging and accepting it for what it is, are then doomed to repeat it—all good intentions to the contrary.

What, then, should be the roles for "white shamans"? Or for non-Indians who continue to have a genuine and sincere regard for Indian peoples and Indian cultures? First, obviously, is the need for them to restore themselves to their own houses—by learning and accepting their own history and culture. If it has become a tired stereotype to depict the Indian variously as a "red devil" or a "noble savage," it is likewise tedious for Indians to constantly lay guilt-instilling trips on whites. I am not suggesting that we, whites and Indians alike, turn our backs on history, pretending that that which happened did not happen, but I am hoping that we can all learn to accept our histories—and our ancestors—for what they are and were.

Secondly, white men writing as Indian medicine-makers, whether as shamans or coyotes, must not continually denigrate their own cultural traditions. If one, then, is not a shaman, but nonetheless feels deeply the dictates of his calling as a poet—he should content himself with being a poet. (Anyway, I've yet to see the various shenanigans of "white shamans" at poetry readings or on the printed page do the things that Indian medicine-makers can do.) Or, if one is not content to be called a poet, if he is from the white Euro-Christian American tradition, he might consider calling himself a bard, or a skald, or a scop, or a troubadour, or even a minstrel. These terms were in usage in the early centuries of the emerging European nations; they were used to describe the poet or singer in ways which the continual impoverishment of modern English makes difficult for us to understand today. As a matter of fact, Bob Dylan has been referred to recently as a bard— and I, for one, would certainly accord him that title. Shakespeare, Blake, Ronsard, Villon, Dylan Thomas, Keats—all have been called bards, or troubadours, or even singers. To me, Gary Snyder—one of the finest poets in America today when is not pontificating about Indian things—is a bard. Shaman, he is not. Nor are Fowler and Moser and company. But, I suppose as long as second-raters continue to name themselves "shamans," to bless themselves mightily through their efforts to become something they are not and can never hope to be, then Indians will still have a "white problem" to deal with—another aspect of our "plight."

CAROLYN KIZER

from *Pro Femina (1973)*

Three

I will speak about women of letters, for I'm in the racket.
Our biggest successes to date? Old maids to a woman.
And our saddest conspicuous failures? The married spinsters
On loan to the husbands they treated like surrogate fathers.
Think of that crew of self-pitiers, not-very-distant,
Who carried the torch for themselves and got first-degree
   burns.
Or the sad sonneteers, toast-and-teasdales we loved at
   thirteen;
Middle-aged virgins seducing the puerile anthologists
Through lust-of-the-mind; barbiturate-drenched Camilles
With continuous periods, murmuring softly on sofas
When poetry wasn't a craft but a sickly effluvium,
The air thick with incense, musk, and emotional blackmail.

I suppose they reacted from an earlier womanly modesty
When too many girls were scabs to their stricken
   sisterhood,
Impugning our sex to stay in good with the men,
Commencing their insecure bluster. How they must have
   swaggered
When women themselves indorsed their own inferiority!

Vestals, vassals and vessels, rolled into several,

They took notes in rolling syllabics, in careful journals,

Aiming to please a posterity that despises them.

But we'll always have traitors who swear that a woman

    surrenders

Her Supreme Function, by equating Art with aggression

And failure with Femininity. Still, it's just as unfair

To equate Art with Femininity, like a prettily-packaged

    commodity

When we are the custodians of the world's best-kept

    secret:

Merely the private lives of one-half of humanity.

But even with masculine dominance, we mares and

    mistresses

Produced some sleek saboteuses, making their cracks

Which the porridge-brained males of the day were too

    thick to perceive.

Mistaking young hornets for perfectly harmless

    bumblebees.

Being thought innocuous rouses some women to frenzy;

They try to be ugly by aping the ways of the men

And succeed. Swearing, sucking cigars and scorching the

    bedspread,

Slopping straight shots, eyes blotted, vanity-blown

In the expectation of glory: *she writes like a man!*

This drives other women mad in a mist of chiffon

(one poetess draped her gauze over red flannels, a practical

    feminist).

But we're emerging from all that, more or less,

Except for some lady-like laggards and Quarterly
    priestesses

Who flog men for fun, and kick women to maim
    competition.

Now, if we struggle abnormally, we may almost seem
    normal;

If we submerge our self-pity in disciplined industry;

If we stand up and be hated, and swear not to sleep with
    editors;

If we regard ourselves formally, respecting our true
    limitations

Without making an unseemly show of trying to unfreeze
    our assets;

Keeping our heads and our pride while remaining
    unmarried;

And if wedded, kill guilt in its tracks when we stack up the
    dishes

And defect to the typewriter. And if mothers, believe in the
    luck of our children,

Whom we forbid to devour us, whom we shall not devour,

And the luck of our husbands and lovers, who keep
    free women.

ALICIA SUSKIN OSTRIKER

The Introduction to *Stealing the Language, the Emergence of Women's Poetry in America (1986)*

I am obnoxious to each carping tongue
Who says my hand a needle better fits.

Thus briskly wrote the pilgrim mother Anne Bradstreet in the "Prologue" to her book of poems, first published in 1650, adding, "If what I do prove well it won't advance, / They'll say it's stolen, or else it was by chance." Two stanzas later the first woman poet in America apologized:

Men have precedency and still excel . . .
Men can do best and women know it well.
Preeminence in each and all is yours;
Yet grant some small acknowledgment of ours.

A fraction over three centuries later, Erica Jong observed in "Bitter Pills for the Dark Ladies" (1968) just how small the acknowledgment could be:

If they let you out   it's as Supermansaint
& the ultimate praise is always a question of nots:
    viz. not like a woman
    viz. "certainly not another poetess"

meanin'
    she got a cunt but she don't talk funny
    & he's a nigger but he don't smell funny
& the only good poetess is a dead.

The "certainly not another poetess" remark was Robert Lowell's at the advent of Sylvia Plath's *Ariel*, and Plath, who certainly did not want to be another poetess, might well have been pleased by it. She was not the first woman to be praised in this fashion, for it has always been customary when praising women writers to say that they do not write like most other women. The commendatory couplets written by Bradstreet's brother-in-law began, "If women, I with women may compare, / Your works are solid, others weak as air." T. S. Eliot concluded an essay on Marianne Moore with "one final, and 'magnificent' compliment" on her work: "one never forgets that it is written by a woman; but . . . one never thinks of this particularly as anything but a positive virtue." Theodore Roethke declared Louise Bogan an exception to the run of women poets, whose typical deficiencies included a set of "esthetic and moral shortcomings":

> the spinning out; the embroidering of trivial themes; a concern with the mere surfaces of life—that special province of the feminine talent in prose—hiding from the real agonies of the spirit; refusing to face up to what existence is; lyric or religious posturing; running between the boudoir and the altar; stamping a tiny foot against God or lapsing into a sententiousness that implies the author has re-invented integrity; carrying on excessively against Fate, about time; lamenting the lot of the woman; caterwauling; writing the same poem about fifty times, and so on.

We may note that Roethke disparages in women poets characteristics which would be commended in men. As Sandra Gilbert and Susan Gubar observe, "shaking a Promethean male fist 'against God' is one perfectly reasonable male strategy, apparently, but stamping a 'tiny' feminine foot is quite another."

   All of us know, or think we know, what a poetess is, and, to paraphrase Marianne Moore, we too dislike her. But what has been the impact of this dislike—on the reputations of women already producing and on the ambitions of those who hope to produce good poetry?

Like many of the poets I discuss in this book, I received my literary education in the 1950s and early 1960s. My opinions on poetry were therefore formed predominantly by reading male poets and by the dicta of professors and critics who eloquently and reverently represented what Matthew Arnold called "the best that has been thought and said" in western culture. That their eloquence veiled gender bias, and that what they believed to be "universal" was only partial, did not occur to me. Subsequently I have come to believe that we cannot measure the work of women poets, past or present, without a thorough—and if possible demystified—awareness of the critical context in which they have composed and continue to compose their work. We need to recognize that our customary literary language is systematically gendered in ways that influence what we approve and disapprove of, making it extremely difficult for us to acknowledge certain kinds of originality—of difference—in women poets.

Like poetic argument, critical argument often conducts itself through metaphor. We need first of all, therefore, to become aware that some of our most compelling terms of critical discourse imply that serious poetry is more or less identical with potent masculinity. Emerson toward the close of his essay "The Poet" hears with his mind's ear "these throbs and heart-beatings at the door of the assembly, to the end namely that thought may be ejaculated as Logos, or Word." Elsewhere he cries, "give me initiative, spermatic, prophesying, man-making words." The metaphor of the pen as the penis has a long literary history. In our own time we are impressed by the heroic notion of literary succession as a "battle among strong equals, father and son as mighty opposites, Laius and Oedipus at the crossroads." Sometimes the metaphor may involve size rather than force, as when we admire "greatness" or "stature" or "high" achievement, or when a critic asks:

> Who are the major and crucial American poets, both in literary excellence and in the difference they make to their successors? Two American poets pre-eminently answer this description: Whitman and Pound. The other nineteenth century poets pass through Whitman's legs like Lilliputians.

Has the critic been reading Bradstreet on the subject of "preeminence" (itself a metaphor; "eminence" means elevation or protuberance)? Obviously we cannot fancy any poets passing between Emily Dickinson's legs; consequently she is not a major and crucial American poet.

We seldom encounter, in praise of women poets, terms like *great, powerful, forceful, masterly, violent, large,* or *true.* The language used to express literary admiration in general presumes the masculinity of the author, the work, and the act of creation— but not if the author is a woman. Complimentary adjectives of choice then shift toward the diminutives: *graceful, subtle, elegant, delicate, cryptic,* and, above all, *modest;* for the most continuous term of approbation for a woman poet from the early nineteenth century to the day before yesterday has been *modesty.* We are perhaps not surprised that an anthologist of American female poets in 1849 says that "the most worthy are the most modest," since we think of the Victorian period as a nadir in women's history. But in our own emancipated time Roy Harvey Pearce approves of Marianne Moore because her "insights are as modest" as the scale of the world she examines. Elizabeth Bishop "is modest and she is dignified." Louise Bogan is "elegant and remarkably self-effacing" and stands "for public reticence." Adrienne

Rich's first poems "are neatly and modestly dressed, speak quietly but do not mumble, respect their elders but are not cowed by them, and do not tell fibs," according to W. H. Auden. Most curiously, in the preface to *Ariel* already quoted, Lowell also commends Plath for "her hand of metal with its modest, womanish touch." Was any male poet, even a young one, ever praised for being modest? Is it possible to be both "modest" and "great"?

One role of the critic is to discover the individual talent which alters the shape of literature. Yet originality has never protected the woman poet from the condescension of critics, and the terms of depreciation remain remarkably fixed despite changes in literary fashions. To take the most obvious example in American literature, the few poems Emily Dickinson published in her lifetime were editorially emended, their odd prosody normalized, their quirky metaphors conventionalized. To her mentor and posthumous editor T. W. Higginson, Dickinson was "my half-cracked poetess," and the neurotic-spinster motif has remained a staple of Dickinson criticism; in 1971 her psychiatrist-biographer John Cody concluded that the frustration of Dickinson's romantic life was responsible for the emergence of her genius:

> If in spite of her wifely and motherly duties, she had still felt the need to express herself in verse, what would her subject matter have been? Would art have sprung from fulfillment, gratification, and completeness as abundantly as it did from longing, frustration, and deprivation?

A writer who in 1971 could believe that "wifely and motherly duties" could constitute "fulfillment, gratification, and completeness" for a woman was not reading many women writers; but the belief that what is convenient for men is fulfilling to women dies hard. It is difficult to imagine a writer speaking in this vein of Shelley, Keats, or even D. H. Lawrence, for we do not reduce male creativity to the presence or absence of a love life. Another staple notion has been the idea that Dickinson wrote good poetry not as other poets do, by marrying genius to effort, but—in Anne Bradstreet's phrase—"by chance." To R. P. Blackmur,

> she was neither a professional poet nor an amateur; she was a private poet who wrote indefatigably as some women cook or knit. Her gift for words and the cultural predicament of her time drove her to poetry instead of antimacassars.

This is to say: women do busywork, Dickinson was a woman, therefore her poetry is busywork. But it would be as reasonable to remark that Ezra Pound wrote the *Cantos* indefatigably as some men work on an assembly line, and that his gift for words and his cultural predicament drove him to poetry instead of bowling. Similarly, when John Crowe Ransom comments on the first edition of Dickinson's poems, which attempts to reproduce the poet's idiosyncratic grammar, punctuation, lineation—an edition made feasible by the literary public's familiarity with the far more idiosyncratic habits of E. E. Cummings, Eliot, and Pound—he finds her "a little home-keeping person" who never learned the concessions poets must make to printers, publishers, and the public. Of her nature poems he observes that "the woman poet as a type . . . makes flights into nature rather too easily and upon errands which do not have metaphysical importance enough to justify so radical a strategy." Male poets engage in quests; women poets run errands. What we may call the "accident" theory of female creativity persists in, among others, David Porter, whose *Dickinson: The Modern Idiom* argues that

Dickinson's evasions of "reality" inadvertently anticipate the radical gestures of postmodernism.

Accusations of "privacy" and "escapism" have pursued other women poets besides Dickinson. From Douglas Bush's massive *Mythology and the Romantic Tradition in English Poetry* comes the pronouncement that "H. D. is a poet of escape" whose Greece "has no connection with the Greece of historic actuality," although this is not a complaint Bush registers about the Greece of Keats, Matthew Arnold, or Edgar Allan Poe. From Hugh Kenner's *The Pound Era* we learn that H. D.'s Imagism was a pebble in the great Pound stream and that her first published poem "is 'about' her taut state of mind, a wried stasis like a sterile homecoming, and a homecoming not to a person but to a mute numinous ikon. That was to be, over and over, the story of her life. Ahead lay marriage, childbirth, desertion, bisexual miseries, and Freud's couch." *The Pound Era* appeared years after the publication of H. D.'s major works, *Trilogy* and *Helen in Egypt*, yet Kenner implies that H. D. expired in neurosis after composing a few enigmatic lyrics. Similarly, there are the Freudian critics who discover that H. D.'s epic structures were substitutes for her missing penis, and Dennis Donaghue, who scolds her for "resorting" to images of dream and myth.

The discomfort provoked by original women is half-articulated by Yvor Winters writing on Dickinson. Commenting on "I like to see it lap the miles," Winters dislikes "the quality of silly playfulness which renders it abominable" and which he finds diffused throughout her writing so that "her best poems . . . can never be isolated certainly and defensibly from her defects; yet she is a poetic genius of the highest order, and this ambiguity in one's feeling about her is profoundly disturbing." Winters' essay is entitled "The Limits of Criticism," and his confusion is evidently genuine, yet it does not lead him to guess that an ostensibly objective critical methodology may itself be defective, or that Dickinson's

playfulness may not be merely offensive and accidental but sub-
versive and strategic: a means of registering feminine powerless-
ness and of attempting to overcome it.

While few critics are as perspicacious or as honest as Yvor Win-
ters, it is not difficult to multiply examples of gender-linked criti-
cism inexorably diminishing the accomplishment of women poets
under the authoritative guise of aesthetic standards. Originality in
a woman poet is censured by the commentator or is invisible to
him because it does not resemble masculine originalities with
which he is already familiar. The woman poet who writes prob-
lematically on religious, political, or social issues is irrelevant, sen-
tentious, or silly. The feminist poet is strident. The emotionally
intense poet is neurotic. Above all, the poet who attempts to
explore female experience is dismissed as self-absorbed, private,
escapist, nonuniversal—although, as Carolyn Kizer puts it, women
writers "are the custodians of the world's best-kept secret: / Merely
the private lives of one-half of humanity."

As several major studies of women's writing have demon-
strated, the woman writer throughout most of our history has
had to state her self-definitions in code, disguising passion as
piety, rebellion as obedience. "Tell all the truth but tell it slant"
speaks for writers who in every century have been inhibited both
by economic and legal dependence and by the awareness that
true writer signifies assertion while *true woman* signifies submis-
sion. Insofar as poetry ranks above fiction in our hierarchies of
genre, women poets have been discouraged from literary ambi-
tion even more than women novelists. Occasionally a critic
expresses some slight hesitation over his capacity to judge a
woman poet adequately, a hint of a sense that his mode of criti-
cism may, in Winters' phrase, have limits beyond which it cannot
successfully be applied. That an individual woman poet might
achieve greatness not because she can be fitted into existing lit-
erary strictures but because she violates them—just as great male

poets often violate them—is a disturbing notion. That a sub-merged tradition of women's poetry should exist, following certain rules of its own, is more disturbing. Most disturbing of all is the moment when the submerged tradition surfaces and when much of what we think we know about "women" and "poetry" is called into question.

LESLIE SCALAPINO

from *The Public World/Syntactically Impermanence*

The Cannon (1999)
Political/Social Demonstration of the Time of Writing

The role of poetry in society is a secret doctrine—One is the visitor, yet the man reading first takes up most of the time. At a reception following the reading, a student engaging one, says, "It seems to me your work is like Gertrude Stein." The man, one's reading partner, immediately inserts himself and says, "Gertrude Stein. Certainly not! Gertrude Stein is the human mind—*she* [oneself] is merely human nature. [Reading of] someone dying of AIDS!" he scoffs. "*Her* writing is human nature, not the human mind," he instructs the student. At a reading with him a few days later, he insists that he will go first and "read for a very long time!"

Any interpretation or reference to this instance is merely experience/anecdotal, it is of human nature-therefore impermanent.

"As, one example, Godard's 'The immediate is chance. At the same time it is definitive. What I want is definitive by chance."[1]

> the man's death—from
> being sick at a young age—as not a
> senseless point—not to—
> by desire—reach such a thing in
> that way[2]

This segment is from a long poem, *way*, in which each line and poem-segment is qualified (changed from within) by, and in, the entire structure of the extended writing. Yet the unplanned, forward structure is at once entirely changed by the minute, present-time unit. Real-time events 'recorded' (as only events as written, fragments that are sound patterns) were frequently so minute (with the exception of a friend dying of AIDS) that in passing they could not be remembered later, had existence only as writing. Any event is qualified by the future even—in the writing itself.

One feels a sense of despair-trying to unravel a dichotomy that is despair. It's impossible to undo it because it is similar to the conventions that exist.

I have to unravel it as that is (one's) existing at all—interior instruction.

Yet someone else thinks that maintaining the dichotomy hierarchical is existing—*for them.*

Seated in the audience, much of which is volatile—two men are to arise—yet a destitute man is lying on the floor (he's come in because it's cold outside), he's stinking, only a few teeth, drunk raving, lying he has no arms

drunk he can't hear their asking him to be quiet.

The armless is dragged raving from the room by a crowd of men and put outside on the street. A young woman in the crowd comments that some people, disturbed by this, are voicing "sentimentality."

When one of the two men arises—an outsider, strong, frisky, who *has* arms, also drunk, rises voluble and is dragged from the room and thrown into the street—he returns with a huge lionish cat in its arms and says "Look at this *big* cat" and is hurled through the door again— *One of these men later says to oneself "And to think that you noticed this—there at a time" (one had written it in a segment—he hears it being read): as if one did not exist—as if only their existing occurred then.*

He is no more responsible for that occurrence than oneself, although he was regarded as 'in charge' of that context in which one was an outsider. *One as the outsider sees oneself as observing actively and at the same time being inactive in the past event and the insider as active yet unobservant there. The event itself occurs 'between' these.*

(My) intention—in poetry—is to get complete observing at the same instant (space) as it being the action.

There's no relation between events and events. Any. They are separate. Events that occur—(regardless of their interpretation—). (But also that they are at once *only* their interpretation and *only* their occurrence.)

Radicals in the sixties and seventies used to speak at the same time when authorities were speaking to change *what* the officials were saying.

Outside(-events) is bounced to be occurrence. itself.

Paul Celan was described (I can't remember the source of this interpretation) as being essentially conflicted (just in written—or in spoken word also?) in his own language, German being the language of the nation (his own) that had exterminated his people. (His written language was) articulation within the language that is seen to be oppression/to be separation from that which one loves.

The dichotomy is impermanence/separation; a distinction made, for example, by Bob Perelman, between writing based in the "experiential" (thus without authority or as the 'authority' of the bogus self only)—

and writing that is articulation of/and *as* social polemic (the writing of which is then regarded as not being "narrative"—the word "narrative" used as if that were anecdotal *per se*). Yet in the distinction there is an equivalence drawn between 'anecdotal' and formal innovation itself.

Two sentences from Bob Perelman's talk at the Assembling Alternatives conference at the University of New Hampshire: "This equation of social power, or say social intelligibility—the familiar—and poetic value challenges much of our poetics." "The equation is less clear in any positive sense, i.e., that social marginality produces good poetry.'

The conception of a normative language as being dominant perspective (conception that there is such a dominant perspective; and that such is or should be determining) is hierarchical conception *per se*. I think that power is the poetic issue or narrative of this period. An aspect of the conflict broached in that narrative is: the continual transmogrification of gesture, making something into an intellectual concept that can't simply exist there, only the concept of the gesture respected.

In academic terminology, for example, there is now a category spoken of as "other," the assumption being that *we* are not that and therefore this area cannot be rendered, or even broached except from a distance. As if 'we' are of the world that articulates. The implication even is that if one is "other"—while a recipient of sympathy and elucidation, or lip-service—one being outside (as minorities, or lower class, at any rate experientially) has no repute or credibility, cannot speak. The assumption is that language be polemical or discursive exposition as it/one has no (or exposes there being no) intrinsic relation to the subject "other."

Yet that is one.

Distinction as 'doctrine' and 'experience' is the conventional social separation here; that is, it is the way our experience is culturally described. The other side of this coin (the camp of "emotion") bolsters the same view of reality but with an opposing allegiance: that is the 'opposite' view (opposite from: ideology as basis) is that emotion/narrative/experience are aspects of "self" that, being viewed 'inherently,' appear not to be the same as (appear not to have any relation to) outside events. The personal, the confessional, is an "expression" of an inherent self as if that self were the *cause* (of events, of cognition), thus (in my view, and in that also of Perelman presumably) mistaking the nature of self in reality.

Yet either causal agent (self-scrutinizing 'conceptualization' or

'concept of personal self') are inaccurate as revelation of events—
events' natures and relation to each other. "Stillness of that order,
perhaps a node peculiar to the mind alone."[3] They are aspects of
hierarchical categorization that merely duplicate that categorization.

Giving a reading from *As: All Occurrence in Structure, Unseen—(Deer
Night)*, which is an intricate interweave, I included a passage, an overlay
itself of seeing an impression (image) of blue dye on the surface of the
eye only, dye: that in fact in the circumstance is infused within the left
side of the body of the person who thrashes being turned on a table.

A man speaking to me afterward referred only to the reference,
in the writing, to the dye: *"that sounds like something that happened
to you,"* *with the implication tonally as well as in mentioning only that
point in the writing, it is thus inferior*

or that its happening explains the whole away.

it invalidates it by being experience

Bob Perelman argued (in his talk at the Assembling Alternatives
symposium—attended by poets and professors from United
Kingdom, United States, Canada, Australia, China, and elsewhere—
at the University of New Hampshire, 1996) that contemporary
poets working in 'experimentalist' modes have failed because their
writing, by being its formal medium—(that is, cognition being
changed by its articulation)—does not have "social power" (in that
poetry does not communicate with large numbers of the public).

His argument and his own writing practice imply a writing
based on the use of social stereotype as a polemical device—which
thus eschews one's 'interior' thought/shape/motions articulated as
motions/shape in syntax.

"Life opens into conceptless perspectives. Language surrounds
chaos."[4]

In an exchange in the *Los Angeles Times* between John Ashbery and reviewer Alexander Theroux, Theroux declares:

> I am unaware of shooting at any *bêtes noires* in my review of his [Ashbery's] books other than those [Pound, Stein, Olson, Zukofsky] who practice the crapulous and farcically self-defeating act of offering bad or half-made work under the guise of serious poetry to be pondered, when it remains in fact impossible to be understood . . . Obscurantism is morally wrong precisely for the lie it tells in the pretense of coming forward with the truth it simultaneously—and always posturingly—refuses to divulge . . . How can a poet of such byzantine contrivances miss my homely truth? Who should know better than he the moral and aesthetic bankruptcy of calling gibberish "poetry" or nonsense "modernist"? We have evidence he is able to write a simple line. What kind of modernish mind do we need to understand "Once I let a guy blow me . . . "

The notion of "communication," articulated as synonymous with power and as if a product with a normative format, is a slogan now at the same time that the schools and education are being contracted/denuded, to offer—to those who are not wealthy—curricula limited in informative, let alone exploratory, investigative content (such as history), that which is subject to conjecture.

Poetry in this time and nation is doing the work of philosophy—it is writing that is conjecture.

'Obscurantism' is related to the market notion of 'current history' (the effect—the 'social'—has already occurred supposedly) as cost-effective; the effect (of social power, or lack thereof) being assessed in present-time unrelated to the substance of occurrence.

Thought or apprehension—in this conception of utility—is not (to be) in relation to action which occurs (or as it occurs) outside.

All demonstrations as writing or speaking) are sidetracked by being defined as a category. There's no answer to one as that would admit of something other into the conversation.

At a time when bookstores are closing, the market argument is that books are not needed because they won't sell. Barnes & Noble is receiving manuscripts from publishers to guide editors as to which manuscripts should be published based on projected sales. Big chains crush other bookstores, as well as publishing companies (Barnes & Nobles market advantages, and its selection against non-format books). "And the diluted formalism of the academy (the formal culture of the U.S.) is anemic & fraught with incompetence & unreality."[5]

The notion of defining 'the life' narrative as inferior is also defining what 'the life' *is*.

Defining is conceptualizing that separation of the public and 'interior' as power.

Writing may be discursive connections or stream-series of distillation of apprehension, the acknowledgment of its narrative being its scrutiny. The contemporary poetic-polemics association of "narrative" as being only convention—'experience' thus denigrated, not regarded as exploratory—in fact does not allow scrutiny of one's own polemic.

There is a conflation in leftist thought with conservative thought in devaluing writing/experience as demonstration/process (rather than doctrine-based). "Procedure" or formalism as modes of writing are embraced by both.

A characteristic of conservative thought is iteration of tradition for its own sake, valuable in that it *is* that. Social conditioning is transcended—there is no "other"—rather than perspective itself being seen being created. Without the conception of the social as phenomenological, actions that are rebellious in response to whatever conditions, are seen as 'personal' merely. Articulating outside's warp imitated as being one—is interpreted as one's being unable to comprehend, couldn't put things together.[6] A syntax that is this dismemberment will be incomprehensible in the framework of conservative thought (one characteristic of which: conception of the past as entity to be preserved as being the present). In terms of a conservative framework, 'dis-location' is seen as merely personal aberration or failure to comprehend the whole, rather than strategic and phenomenological.

Phenomenological 'dis-location' in writing is strategic and specific, detail arising from or noting social conditions or background; which conservative ideology regards without transcendence, transient. Yet such transience is change as writing's subject (in avant garde or radical practices).

The view of aberration as failure is an exclusion that is an action, rendering what it defines as minor to the condition of non-existent or irrelevant 'over-time.' (As if there were an 'objective' cultural basis that becomes or *is* 'history.')

Polemics was to be demonstration (that was the intention)—yet now poetry is society's secret interior—thought's demonstration is scrutiny (there is no 'history', because that is merely a description of an overview)—in that polemics-based writing merely imposes a point of view and suppresses demonstration.

Right-wing Republicans castigate labor on the radio by asking "how can 'our' society's labor compete while wearing combat boots?" That is, they should not have labor demands in order to compete in the world market.

One should dismantle protection of oneself in laboring *for* others in order to compete with outsiders—who can underbid one if employed *by* those others.

• • •

The attitude that the writing is invalidated by it being experience has its corollary—in the objection to there being in writing 'thought' which is at one in the same time as 'occurrence.' *Is* that occurrence.

This is what makes the present-time troubling, as Gertrude Stein said.

That 'one' is separate in occurrence (as if occurrence were collective) is particularly heinous to Americans.

Perelman (in that articulation of 'social power') is taking both of these positions (critique of and authority) at once, deftly enshrining authority—seemingly in the 'outside' as if *that* were causal. The illusion of 'occurrence' and that it is 'collective'.

'Social power' is the formation ('I') am trying to ('*must*') dispel.

(The delineated cultural dichotomy itself 'makes' the reverberation in this last above sentience only 'extreme' defined as such [categorical terms such a "lyrical" "personal"—negatives from a radical perspective].

One can reverberate that ridicule itself [as echo of social] on oneself effectively *as* the writing-syntax—to 'bounce' it to be a separated *occurrence* also.

This can reveal something about 'one' in relation to social occurrence. And also the intention is to see what *occurrence* is.

Polemical device as a writing process isn't to investigate shape and motion to find out what the event is—it is to instruct what one is to think about the event.

But the event (any) isn't even there (as that formation):

One/events can only exist outside of formation there.

People in this culture are ('described as' being) 'given' the view (as if view and description were an action, and as if it were causal) that they like that which is liked—if something appears *not liked* (by others) it can't have value. 'Separation' therefore is to be 'ridicule' itself.

As successful current poetic-critical 'theory'—a description of *itself* as radical (left), which is at once sign and definition of status, is dependent on reproducing the conventional distinctions (as categories of thought).

The closing of bookstores and the utter commercialization of publishing and distribution indicate there will be few reading anywhere.

My sense is 'subjectivity'—rendered at all-is separation *per se* simply as observation of phenomena.

Poetically, this separation itself (delineated *as* writing *as* its shape/syntax) is also a shadow (evocation) of that which is 'exterior,' the public.

Much of contemporary writing practice (of the 'experimentalist' mode) now is delineation (*in its syntax—i.e. it is gestural, an action*) of this separation of one. Writing now is being the 'interior' *and* the 'exterior.' To make these occur, *and* to see them 'real'-ly.

"We're not going to go on playing games, even if the rules are downright fascinating. We require a situation more like it really is—no rules at all. Only when we make them do it in our labs do crystals win our games. Do they then? I wonder."[7]

—*in one's conflict—in surveillance*—is at once interior and exterior. The 'directions' (as in a text of a play, in italics), which is the same as the rendering (as reading) of public context/scene, are the same as interior-speaking to oneself. *Writing to engage the interior of the writing itself, (which are then) as exterior events, for anything to occur—its motions change events.*

The discovery that poetry *has no relation to society*—I'd been struggling to maintain a relation. Yet writing is an interiorization (*not*/of that relation?). That is a separate action.

In a critical reading group where, in one meeting, writers were discussing dreams they had had, a man, having recounted (or read)

his dream, whose connections and process were its activity said—
yet how could this (dream) be translated into a thought that was not
personal, that was not the dream? (to be made useful—in that it is
not from oneself, not a mind action.)

Articulated only *as experience—an intense separation where there's no*
translation. If one speaks his language one can't be in friendship with
him. Friendship having to do with extending across the social line or
interior division where one has no power. Or it is that, one articulates
relation to him that is not related to power.

My sense of relief that 'poetry has no relation to society'—is that
one has despair in 'experiencing' that people have no connection to
actions (outside, on their own)-even though these actions as if
taking place 'secretly' change everything.

That 'poetry' (interior) 'has no relation' occurs as its being
extended, as it is not determined actions by being 'those' (initiating
in that space)—it has to be *continual* motions.

In a footnote to his book *The Marginization of Poetry*, Perelman
quotes a passage from my exchange with Ron Silliman, "What/
Person: From an Exchange." In this complex exchange, (published
in the *Poetics Journal*)[8], I was answering Silliman's position that
women, gays, and minorities tend to write "conventional narrative"
in that they have to "tell their stories," arising from their social con-
ditions; whereas white heterosexual male writers (he says) are in a
position to experiment formally.

The passage that Perelman quoted from my response to Sil-
liman implies that I simply 'favor' "narrative" (whatever that is);
that is, it reverses, erases the argument I was making by quoting a
tiny passage out of context.

A person describing a creationist view that all minute events
and phenomena are in God's eye or plan beforehand—so evolution
cannot exist or occur—nothing is *occurring* first or apart from the

plan—no actions are later events; astonished, I made the remark, "This is completely alien to poetry." Alien to observation, and also to action.

There is no cause or effect—the moment of occurrence doesn't exist either—in that the present moment is disjunction *per se* only (Nāgājurnian login, which is early Zen, rendering modern physics?). All times (past, present, and future) are occurring at the same time separately *as that* disjunctive space or moment (rendition of Dōgen's and Einstein's sense of being as time). So occurrence is not hierarchically ordered. (These views of time and being are also [elsewhere] articulated as socially shared experiences.)

The language that is 'experimentally' based corresponds to people's *experience;* as the act of 'one's' experiencing; and (though not widely disseminated, thus not part of 'communal' experience) it is not an 'elite' language.

Doctrine doesn't reflect 'our'/their experience; is alien to it.

The' contradictory, problematic factor is in divorcing 'experience' from 'non-referential' writing (originally with radical intention); a separation that sometimes simply stems from an attitude that 'experience' is lowly (that is, from snobbery and also regard for authority as opposed to demonstration).

One point I made to Silliman in the exchange was that the form of one's articulation may be a reconstituting of the general social narrative, may be a radical change in expression arising from one's *separation* from social convention.

Silliman's position was negating the factor of the individual's articulation as motion/shape in syntax *being* a radical change in thought.

In the early eighties, Silliman, in conversation and talks in San Francisco, urged poets to write syntax that was paragraphs without line breaks, paratactic, described as a communal, non-individualistic expression. The syntax has a recognizable sound pattern which is what poetic syntaxes are, as from other periods, say languages called Beat or New York School). In the same spirit in that period, Bob Perelman stated, during a talk given by Michael Palmer on autobiography, that the erotic was not to enter into writing, the erotic was a form of ego to be stricken or omitted from writing. (At the time, this was related to a Marxist-based conception of writing that should be egoless: 'non-narrative' is *not* self-expression'—that's an action.)[9]

Roughly, paratactic syntax is juxtaposition to each other of 'unrelated,' which itself beomes a form of relation, statements or questions in one paragraph—a series of such leaps in continuing paragraphs or lines. A single statement is potentially examined or refuted by being in a series of such single 'unrelated' statements. This is a form of 'not holding onto a thought.' However, I think in order for the structure not to be deterministic, one would have to transgress the entirety— (as reader or writer) not be 'inside' the statements or questions having to respond to them. Either power or critique of it occurring as poetic syntax (of the time), 'one' must continually instigate—that is, one will write outside a 'given' syntax; not being defined by social articulation in any instant as syntactically.

There is no way in which women can apprehend conservative social articulation if they write uniform syntax (dictated by men) that excises the erotic.

One could not be separating the event—from/as thought (or apprehension).

Recently a man giving a (literary) talk showed slides of a 'pin-up girl' interpreting the past to make the point that he thought she had a lot of "autonomy." The subject (pin-up girl[10]) has no writing 'as poetry'/*expression that's its writing*—and she's 'in' the past. *Granting those in the past, in their erotic being, "autonomy."*

Present as disjunct *per se* only—*that* space/time can't be his narrative—or one's. *Event is between*. One has to modify one's tone if one is a woman to be heard as saying anything.

"To change without belief is anarchistic as instinct pricks from the Latin (stinguere), no law but that the absence of law is the resistance of love instinct with tact like the expression of this thought."[11]

Assessing relation of power between people—such as that say based in gender—merely becomes the articulating of those relations, as oneself having power. One would have to disrupt in writing one's own articulation of power at all.

A communal syntax being community could have occurred in an instant. When it occurs again, it isn't in the same syntax?

Format (when experiment becomes format) is not articulating occurrence (events/thoughts). It cannot, inherently. That is, those experimenting formally (as per Silliman's description) by accepting polemic directive are *per se* not practicing experiment—in that they are divorced from the live gesture?

The very nature of descriptive language is 'other' than the subject. What Giorgio Agamben identifies (locating it in infancy) is a silent pre-language state is going on at all times in one simultaneously 'alongside' one's language apprehension?[12]

('Experiment"—not as itself a brand of writing or as 'unfinished' 'attempts' rather than the 'finished products'—but as 'scientific experiment to find out what something is, or to find out what's happening.)

In the view (such as in Anne Waldman's statements[13]) that (which is the real) poetry is "speech," there's a sense of "speech" (spoken is social, convention of 'conversation'?)—that is not "thought" [interior], is not 'felt spatially / such a correspondences in the limbs.' Tonal is considered thus as ranges of speaking voice or breath.

Yet poets have been writing other tones—that are in the written text only—tones not occurring as speaking. These are 'sounded' silently, spatially—a separation; between 'one' and 'social'? Or separation between 'one' and 'correspondences in the limbs'—and night. (As if a butterfly and the butterfly motion of a swimmer.)

We've mutated and become ventriloquists who speak 'inner' unspoken 'movements' and various types of speech at the same time.

I was interested in a syntax whose very mode of observation was to reveal its structure; that is its subject and its mode are subjectivity being observation. Since it is itself subjective the viewpoint is 'without basis.' It removes its own basis, that of exterior authority, as a critique of itself.

As an example, sentences that are single, dual, or multiple clauses are only intonation, dislocating their 'interior' and 'exterior' subject-by one's 'interior' intonation and 'exterior' reference being the same (being a clause of the sentence, dissonant notes played at the same time) and as such also mutually exclusive, separately critiquing each other.

Statements of definition (that perceived as 'givens' 'in-coming' from the outside society, which 'determine' social reality) are apprehended as bogus. Because they are revealed as subjective, without basis. One is only constructing a reflection of these as one's reorientation of apprehension. The syntax itself reorients one's apprehension (by continual dis-location) and enables that which is exterior to be included in a process of its examination, necessarily self-examination.

My argument to Silliman was that no one can conceive within the 'given' language—and articulate reality, as that. It can't be 'there' because it *isn't* that.

This may or may not be a different concern from that of women and imported minorities working here as illegal indentured servants who are slaves, for example.

That is, individuals in writing or speaking may create a different syntax to articulate experience, as that is the only way experience occurs. Or they may describe their circumstances and contexts, as if from the outside, using normative language.

The dichotomy is in anyone as a function of the world? *Language as interior and entirely from the outside at once—which is a series, starting up throughout.*

"Holding to a course with the forbidden sublime, love of beauty originally obfuscates or sublimates to refine what is unclear to be scrambled later from its perception of perfection by that continuing. Which is to change the world. As it does which is why, nothing individually lost, there's a difference to be told."[14]

Notes

1. Clark Coolidge, quoted in *Postmodern American Poetry*, ed. Paul Hoover (New York: Norton, 1994), 652. My intention in taking all the written quotes from one source was to indicate the similarity of direction articulated by poets with widely varying aesthetics collected in one text. I was pointing to the existence of a commonality, which is 'public' even if not numbered in millions. However, Joan Retallack accurately pointed out to me that I didn't comment on the role in the canon of anthologizing: "A surface illusion of comprehensiveness gives these compendiums the power to conceptually blot out the possible presence of multitudes of other interesting writers and (in the case of the Hoover and Messerli anthologies) the small presses that publish them. I.e., they become a substitute (for teachers and writers) for going to the individual books of individual poets. That there are

many anthologies of contemporary work coming out right now seems to me the only good sign. . . . Since the essay is entitled 'The Cannon' I immediately assumed you would be commenting on the way in which anthologies take over the reference market so to speak."

2. Leslie Scalapino, *way* (San Francisco: North Point Press, 1988), p. 105.

3. Clark Coolidge, in *Postmodern American Poetry*, p. 651.

4. Susan Howe, quoted in *Postmodern American Poetry*, p. 648.

5. Amiri Baraka, quoted in *Postmodern American Poetry*, p. 645.

6. "Everything is in the poems, but at the risk of sounding like the poor wealthy man's Allen Ginsberg I will write to you because I just heard that one of my fellow poets thinks that a poem of mine that can't be got at one reading is because I was confused too. Now, come on." Frank O'Hara, quoted in *Postmodern American Poetry*, p. 633.

7. John Cage, quoted in *Postmodern American Poetry*, p. 652.

8. Ron Silliman and Leslie Scalapino, "What / Person: From an Exchange," *Poetics Journal 9* "The Person," pp. 51-68, ed. Lyn Hejinian and Barrett Watten, Berkeley, Calif., June 1991.

9. Bob Perelman doesn't remember making this remark and states he would not make such a comment as it is puritanical and offensive. It was not recorded (the tape ended). His words were only *part* of an exchange in which a number of men spoke, then agreed with his statement. No women spoke to this. He replied to this essay: "So I look at the picture of my literary position in your paper and see an inflexible anti-erotic commissar insisting that people write conventionally." His point or remark to me here is well-taken: I do not mean to characterize his writing or thought in that manner, but rather to demonstrate occurrence in public expression of ideology.

10. Betty Page, referred to in a talk by Barrett Watten at the University of Maine.

11. Bernadette Mayer, quoted in *Postmodern American Poetry*, p. 659.

12. *Infancy & History / Essays on the Destruction of Experience*, Giorgio Agamben, Verso, 1993.

13. Talk given at Philip Whalen's Birthday Reading at the San Francisco Art Institute, October 20, 1996; and talk given at Allen Ginsberg's memorial in San Francisco.

14. Bernadette Mayer, quoted in *Postmodern American Poetry*, p. 659.

DEAD PREZ

Police State

[Chairman Omali Yeshitela]
You have the emergence in human society
of this thing that's called the State
What is the State? The State is this organized bureaucracy
It is the po-lice department. It is the Army, the Navy
It is the prison system, the courts, and what have you
This is the State—it is a repressive organization
But the state—and gee, well, you know,
you've got to have the police, cause. . .
if there were no police, look at what you'd be doing to yourselves!
You'd be killing each other if there were no police! But the reality is..
the police become necessary in human society
only at that junction in human society
where it is split between those who have and those who ain't got

[Dead Prez]
I throw a Molotov cocktail at the precinct, you know how we
   think
Organize the hood under I Ching banners
Red, Black and Green instead of gang bandanas
F.B.I. spyin on us through the radio antennas
And them hidden cameras in the streetlight watchin society
With no respect for the people's right to privacy
I'll take a slug for the cause like Huey P.

while all you fake niggaz {*UNNNGH*} try to copy Master P

I want to be free to live, able to have what I need to live

Bring the power back to the street, where the people live

We sick of workin for crumbs and fillin up the prisons

Dyin over money and relyin on religion for help

We do for self like ants in a colony

Organize the wealth into a socialist economy

A way of life based off the common need

And all my comrades is ready, we just spreadin the seed

(Chorus: Dead Prez)

The average Black male

Live a third of his life in a jail cell

Cause the world is controlled by the white male

And the people don't never get justice

And the women don't never get respected

And the problems don't never get solved

And the jobs don't never pay enough

So the rent always be late; can you relate?

We livin in a police state

[Dead Prez]

No more bondage, no more political monsters

No more secret space launchers

Government departments started it in the projects

Material objects, thousands up in the closets

Could've been invested in a future for my comrades

Battle contacts, primitive weapons out in combat

Many never come back

Pretty niggaz be runnin with gats

Rather get shot in they back than fire back

We tired of that—corporations hirin blacks

Denyin the facts, exploitin us all over the map

That's why I write the shit I write in my raps

It's documented, I meant it

Every day of the week, I live in it; breathin it

It's more than just fuckin believin it

I'm holdin them ones, rollin up my sleeves an' shit

It's cee-lo for push-ups now, many headed for one conclusion

Niggaz ain't ready for revolution

(Chorus: Dead Prez)

{*police siren wails*}

[Fred Hampton]

I am . . . a revolutionary

and you're gonna have to keep on sayin that

You're gonna have to say that I am a proletariat

I am the people, I'm not the pig

[another speaker]

Guiliani you are full of shit!

And anybody that's down with you!

You could man-make things better for us

and you cuttin the welfare

Knowin damn well when you cut the welfare,

a person gon' do crime.

CONTRIBUTORS

MIGUEL ALGARÍN (b. 1941) was born in Santurce, Puerto Rico, emigrated to New York City with his family in the early 1950s, and grew up in Spanish Harlem and Queens. He wrote his first poem on April 27, 1967, "to cure a terrible headache." Since then he has published five collections of poetry, including *Mongo Affair* (1978), *On Call* (1980), *Body Bee Calling from the 21st Century* (1982), *Time's Now/Ya Es Tiempo* (Arte Publico Press, 1985), which received the 1986 American Book Award; and *Love Is Hard Work*. He is a founder of the Nuyorican Poets Cafe and has won an Obie for his work in theater. He also has written plays and short stories and is a translator, publishing his translations of the poetry of Pablo Neruda in *Cancion de gesta/A Song of Protest* in 1976. He has coedited various anthologies of writers associated with the Nuyorican Poets Cafe, including *Nuyorican Poets: An Anthology of Puerto Rican Words and Feelings* (1985), edited with Miguel Piñero; *Aloud! Voices from the Nuyorican Poets Cafe* (Henry Holt, 1994), a poetry anthology edited with Bob Holman; and *Action!*, a collection of plays produced at the Nuyorican that was edited with Lois Griffith. Algarin, also a Shakespearean scholar, recently retired from teaching at Rutgers University, where he was a professor of English.

AGHA SHAHID ALI (1949–2001), was born into a Muslim family in New Delhi and grew up in Kashmir. He earned a Ph.D. in English from Pennsylvania State University in 1984 and an M.F.A. from the University of Arizona in 1985. His poetry volumes include *Bone Sculpture* (1972), *In Memory of Begum Akhtar and Other Poems* (1979), *The Half-Inch Himalayas* (1987), *A Nostalgist's Map of America* (Wesleyan New Poets, 1991), *The Beloved Witness: Selected Poems* (1992), *The Country without a Post Office* (1997), and *Rooms Are Never Finished* (Norton, 2001), a 2001 National Book Award finalist. He taught at various universities, including the University of Delhi, Penn State, SUNY Binghamton, Princeton University, Hamilton College, the University of Massachusetts at Amherst, and the University of Utah. He was translator of Faiz Ahmed Faiz's *The Rebel's Silhouette: Selected Poems* (1992) and editor of *Ravishing Disunities: Real Ghazals in English* (2001). A posthumous collection of his poetry, *Call Me Ishmael Tonight,* is forthcoming in 2003.

JIMMY SANTIAGO BACA (b. 1952), of Chicano-Indio ancestry, was born in Santa Fe, New Mexico. Abandoned as a child, he became a poet while incarcerated in an Arizona prison, publishing poems about his prison experiences in his first major collection, *Immigrants in Our Own Land* (1979). New Directions has published three books of his poetry: *Immigrants in Our Own Land and Selected Earlier Poems* (1991), *Black Mesa Poems* (1989), and *Martin & Meditations on the South Valley* (1987), which won the 1988 American Book Award. Recipient of the 1989 International Hispanic Heritage Award, he was World Champion Poetry Bout winner at Taos in 1996 and 1997. Grove Atlantic published two of his books in 2001: a memoir, *A Place to Stand*, and a poetry collection, *Healing Earthquakes*. Baca has also published essays and novels and produced film scripts, including the critically acclaimed *Bound by Honor*. His essay collection, *Working in the Dark: Reflections of a Poet of the Barrio* (1992), won a 1993 Southwest Book Award. He currently lives with his family on a small farm outside Albuquerque, New Mexico.

DAVID BARAZA attended Ishmael Reed's spring 1994 poetry class at the University of California, Berkeley.

ELIZABETH BISHOP (1911–1979) was born in Worcester, Massachusetts. She was raised by various relatives in the Boston area and in Nova Scotia after her father died in 1911 and her mother became permanently institutionalized for mental illness in 1916. A writer of poetry, essays, and short stories, Bishop traveled widely, living in Key West, Florida; Brazil; New York City; and Washington, D.C., where she worked a term as consultant in poetry at the Library of Congress. She later settled in Cambridge, Massachusetts, and taught at Harvard University from 1969 until her retirement in 1977. Bishop, who started writing poetry in college with her mentor, Marianne Moore, was friends with the poets Robert Lowell, Pablo Neruda, and Frank Bidart. Her poems were frequently published in *Poetry* and the *Partisan Review*, and her collected volumes include *Poems: North & South—A Cold Spring* (1946), winner of the 1955 Pulitzer Prize; *Questions of Travel* (1965); *The Complete Poems* (1969), winner of a 1969 National Book Award; and *Geography III* (1976). *The Complete Poems of Elizabeth Bishop, 1927–1979* was published in 1983 and *The Collected Prose* in 1984.

PETER BLUE CLOUD (ARONIAWENRATE) (b. 1933) was born into the Kanawake (Caughnawaga) Mohawk Nation, on the south side of the St. Lawrence River in Quebec. He has worked as a steelworker, carpenter, logger, brush-clearer, and editor—of the Native journals *Akwesasne Notes* and *Indian Magazine*—and has lived for many years in the Sierra Nevada foothills of California. His books include *Alcatraz Is Not an Island* (1973); *Bear & Wolf* (1976); *Back Then Tomorrow* (Blackberry Press, 1978, 1980), which won the 1981 American Book Award; *With Crows* (1981), *the Other Side of Nowhere* (1991); and *Clans of Many Nations: Selected Poems, 1969–1994* (White Pine Press, 1995).

WILLIE BORUM (AKA MEMPHIS WILLIE B.) (1911–late 1960s), a singer, guitarist, and harmonica player, was a lifelong resident of the city of Memphis, although his sound resembled country blues. A player with Jack Kelly's Jug Busters and the Memphis Jug Band during the 1920s and 1930s, he also performed with bluesmen Sonny Boy Williamson II (Rice Miller), Robert Johnson, Willie Brown, Will Shade, and Joe Hill Louis. He continued playing until World War II, when he served in the army. After the war he earned his living mostly as a laborer, although in the 1940s he appeared on the *King Biscuit Time* radio show. In the 1950s he was redis-covered by folklorist Sam Charters, who recorded him. These sessions are available on the Prestige/Bluesville label on the albums *Introducing Memphis Will B.* and *Memphis Willie B., Hard-Working Man Blues.*

EVAN BRAUNSTEIN was a student in Ishmael Reed's spring 1994 poetry class at the University of California, Berkeley.

CECIL BROWN (b. 1943), the son of a sharecropping farmer, was born in Bolton, North Carolina, a rural world he documents in his memoir, *Coming Up Down Home* (The Ecco Press, 1993). Resolved to leave the agrarian world of his ancestors, he received degrees in literature at Columbia University and the University of Chicago, and a Ph.D. in folk-lore at the University of California, Berkeley. A writer of fiction, poetry, plays, essays, and screenplays, Brown also wrote two novels published by Farrar, Straus & Giroux: *The Life and Loves of Mr. Jiveass Nigger* (1969) and *Days Without Weather* (1983). Script writer for the film *Which Way Is Up?*, he has taught at various colleges and universities, among them the University of Illinois, the University of California, Davis, and the University of California at Berkeley.

LAURA SOUL BROWN is a writer, artist, and cultural critic from Boston. Her poems and essays have appeared in the *Boston Globe, artsMedia, Sojourner Women's Forum, Birthrights*, and various journals. She has contributed poetry and narration to the Blackside Productions film *This Far by Faith,* which aired on PBS in February 2002. She has performed her poetry in various venues, from Boston to San Francisco to Havana. A recipient of writing fellowships from the Voices of Our Nation Arts foundation (VONA), the Atlantic Center for the Arts, and the Massachusetts Cultural Council, Brown has been cited by the City of Cambridge and the Cambridge Peace Commission for her work as a cultural activist. She presently works as an arts director, curator, and media producer.

GWENDOLYN BROOKS (1917–2000), one of two daughters of a schoolteacher mother and a janitor father, was born in Topeka, Kansas, and raised in Chicago. She wrote poetry as a child and was first published in a magazine when she was thirteen. After marrying fellow writer Henry Blakely in 1939 and having two children, she published *A Street in Bronzeville* (1945), the first of more than twenty poetry books that include *The Bean Eaters* (1960), *In the Mecca* (1968), *Family Pictures* (1970), *The World of Gwendolyn Brooks* (1971), *Primer for Blacks* (1981), *Near-Johannesburg Boy* (1986), and *Children Coming Home* (1991). In 1949 she came out with *Annie Allen*, winning the Eunice Tietjens prize and becoming the first African American to receive a Pulitzer. Among her other writings are anthologies, children's books, her autobiography, *Report from Part One* (1972), *A Capsule Course in Black Poetry Writing* (1975), and a novel, *Maud Martha* (1953). Brooks taught writing workshops at community venues and in colleges, hosted literary conferences, and graciously supported the work of black writers, both young and established. She was named poet laureate of Illinois in 1968 and honorary consultant in American literature to the Library of Congress in 1985 and 1986. She made her home in Chicago and remained active in her community up to the time of her death.

CHEZIA THOMPSON CAGER is a St. Louis native whose grandmother was Mississippi poet–playwright Mary Ellen Gideon. Based in Baltimore, she teaches at the Maryland Institute College of Art, where she administrates the arts presenting series and serves on the board of the Baltimore Writers' Alliance. Besides contributing to various literary journals, she collected ten years of her poetry in *The Presence of Things Unseen: Giant Talk* (Maisonneuve Press, 1996) and edited *When Divas Laugh: The Diva Poetry Squad Poetry Collective* (Black Classic Press, 2001). A recipient of the Maryland State Arts Council Individual Award in Poetry and an Artscape Poetry Award winner, Cager was an associate artist in Ishmael Reed's summer 2002 workshop at the Atlantic Center for the Arts.

CORDELIA CANDELARIA, a New Mexico native, is a scholar, teacher, critic, and author who has been a leading advocate and mentor for Chicana literature. The editor-author of eight books and numerous articles, her publications include a collection of poetry, *Ojo de la Cueva/ Cave Springs* (Maize Press, 1984), and two critical books published by Greenwood Press, *Chicano Poetry: A Critical Introduction* (1986) and *Seeking the Perfect Game: Baseball in American Literature*. She is presently chair of the department of Chicana and Chicano studies at Arizona State University.

ANA CASTILLO (b. 1953) was born and raised in Chicago. She is a Chicana activist and writer of Mestiza heritage and the author of six books of poetry, five novels, one book of essays, and numerous short stories. In 1977 she received the Before Columbus Foundation's American Book Award for her novel *The Mixquiahuala Letters* (Bilingual Review Press, 1986; Doubleday, 1992). Her nonfiction work *Massacre of the Dreamers: Reflections on Mexican-Indian Women in the United States 500 Years after the Conquest* (University of New Mexico, 1992) received the 1993 Carl Sandburg Literary Award in fiction and the 1994 Mountains and Plains Bookseller Award. She first published her poetry in the chapbooks *Otro Canto* (1977) and *The Invitation* (1979), followed by the volumes *Women Are Not Roses* (Arte Publico, 1984), *My Father Was a Toltec* (West End Press, 1988), *My Father Was a Toltec and Selected Poems 1973–1988* (1995), and *I Ask the Impossible* (2001). The cofounder and contributing editor of the literary magazine *Third Woman*, Castillo has also edited several anthologies, most recently *La Diosa de las Americas/Goddess of the Americas* (Riverside/Putnam, 1996), which focuses on la Virgen de Guadalupe. She has also taught feminist journal writing, women's studies, creative writing, and Chicano/Latina literature at various colleges and universities.

ROSEMARY CATACALOS is of Mexican and Greek descent. Raised in San Antonio, she has worked as a newspaper reporter and arts columnist and has published two volumes of poetry, a chapbook, *As Long As It Takes* (Iguana Press, 1984), and *Again for the First Time* (Tooth of Time Books, 1984), which received the Texas Institute of Letters Prize in Poetry. Former director of the Guadalupe Cultural Arts Center's literature program and poetry center, she oversees the American Poetry Archives at San Francisco State University.

LORNA DEE CERVANTES (b. 1954), born in San Francisco to a fifth-generation California family of Mexican and Chumash Indian ancestry, grew up in California, where she began writing poetry at a very young age. Her first published book of poetry, *Emplumada* (University of Pittsburgh Press, 1981), won the 1982 American Book Award. *From the Cables of Genocide: Poems on Love and Hunger* (Arte Publico Press, 1991) won a 1992 Paterson Poetry Prize and Latin American Writers Institute Award. In 1976 Cervantes founded Mango Publications, a small press that focuses on Chicano and multicultural literature. It also publishes *Red Dirt*, a journal of multicultural literature that she edits. Cervantes teaches creative writing at the University of Colorado, Boulder.

JEFFERY PAUL CHAN (b. 1942) is one of the four coeditors of two major anthologies of Asian-American literature: *Aiiieeeee! An Anthology of Asian American Writers* (Howard University Press, 1974), which was reprinted in four different editions by three different publishers in the twenty-five-year history of the book; and *The Big Aiiieeeee! An Anthology of Chinese American and Japanese American Literature* (Meridian/NAL, 1991). He is a professor of Asian-American studies and English at San Francisco State University.

FRANK CHIN (b. 1940), a fifth-generation Chinese-American, was born in Berkeley, California, and now lives in Los Angeles. He has written numerous plays, novels, and essays, and is an editor, political activist, freelance consultant, and lecturer who has focused on Chinese-Americans and racism. In the sixties and seventies he was a film consultant and taught creative writing at San Francisco State College, the University of California at Berkeley, and Western Washington University. With coeditors Jeffery Paul Chan, Lawson Inada, and Shawn Wong, Chin documented the development of Asian-American writing in the anthology *Aiiieeeee! An Anthology of Asian American Writers* (1974) and its successor, *The Big Aiiieeeee! An Anthology of Chinese American and Japanese American Literature* (1991). These groundbreaking books, as strongly criticized as they have been praised, helped establish and define the Asian-American literary tradition. From 1974 to 1986, Chin worked with Lawson Inada to collect what is now the Frank Chin Oral History Collection, a library of audiotape interviews and transcripts that documents the lives of Japanese Americans. In addition to his ongoing efforts to document the lives of Asian Americans, Chin has published several plays, including *The Chickencoop Chinaman* (1972), the first Asian-American play performed in a legitimate New York City theater. His play *The Year of the Dragon* (1974) appeared on the PBS series Theater in America. Other works are the novels *Donald Duk* (1991) and *Gunga Din Highway* (Coffee House Press, 1994), and a short-story collection, *The Chinaman Pacific & Frisco R.R. Co.* (1988), which won the Before Columbus Foundation American Book Award. His most recent essay collection is *The Bulletproof Buddhist*.

LUCILLE CLIFTON (b. 1936) was born in Depew, a suburb of Buffalo, and is the author of ten poetry books and more than twenty children's books. Her first poetry collection, *Good Times* (1969), was followed by *Good News About the Earth* (Random House, 1972); *An Ordinary Woman Poems* (Random House, 1974); *two-headed woman* (University of Massachusetts Press, 1980), winner of the 1980 Juniper Prize for Poetry; *The Book of Light* (Copper Canyon Press, 1993); *The Terrible Stories* (1996); and *Blessing the Boats, New and Selected Poems 1988–2000* (BOA Editions, Limited, 2000), which won the National Book Award. Recipient of numerous other honors—including an Emmy Award from the American Academy of Television Arts & Sciences—she became the only poet to have two books chosen as finalists for a Pulitzer Prize in the same year (1988): *Good Woman: Poems and a Memoir 1969–1980* (BOA) and *Next: New Poems* (BOA). She was also a National Book Award finalist that year. Employed in state and federal government jobs until 1971, Clifton began the first of three writer-in-residency appointments at the historically black school Coppin State College in Baltimore, followed by Columbia University School of the Arts and George Washington University. In 1979 she was appointed poet laureate of the state of Maryland. In 1999 she was appointed chancellor of the Academy of American Poets and was elected to be a fellow in literature of the American Academy of Arts and Sciences. Presently she is a distinguished professor of humanities at St. Mary's College in Columbia, Maryland.

BILLY COLLINS (b. 1941) was born in New York City and is a professor of English at Lehman College, City University of New York. He is author of several books of poetry, including *Poker Face* (1977), *Video Poems* (1980), *The Apple that Astonished* (University of Arkansas Press, 1988), *Questions About Angels* (William Morrow, 1991), *The Art of Drowning* (1995), *Sailing Alone Around the Room: New and Selected Poems* (2001), and *Nine Horses* (Random House, 2002). He can be heard reading thirty-three of his poems on a recording, *The Best Cigarette*. As the eleventh poet laureate of the United States (his term started fall 2001), he read "The Names" before a special joint session of Congress that convened in New York City on September 11, 2002.

DAVID COLOSI is a writer and an artist who lives in Brooklyn. He received his M.F.A. from CalArts in 1991. He has read, performed, collaborated, and exhibited work at various venues, including the KGB Bar and Tonic in New York City, Highways in Los Angeles, and the Proto Theater in Tokyo. He is currently at work on two novels and a collection of poetry.

WILLIAM COOK is a poet, critic, teacher, actor, and director who has worked in theater, film, and television. He is currently chair of the National Black Theatre Summit. Both his criticism and poetry have appeared in various journals and publications. His first book of poetry was *Hudson Hornet* (Ishmael Reed Publishing, 1989) and his second was *Spiritual* (Ishmael Reed Publishing, 1999). A professor of English, African, and Afro-American studies at Dartmouth College, he also chairs the Department of English and is the Israel Evans Professor of Oratory and Belles Lettres.

INA COOLBRITH (1841–1928) was born in Illinois, a niece of Joseph Smith, the founder of the Mormons. In 1851 her widowed and remarried mother decided to leave the Mormon church and go west. Coolbrith became the first white child to enter California after noted black and Crow Indian scout Jim Beckwourth placed her at the front of his saddle as they crossed the border at Beckwourth Pass. Her poetry was published in three volumes: *A Perfect Day* (1881), *The Singer of the Sea* (1894), and *Songs from the Golden Gate* (1895). Coolbrith's friends included the California-based writers Samuel Clemens, Bret Hare, Joaquin Miller, Charles Warren Stoddard, and later, Jack London. She lost everything in the fires that consumed her home after the 1906 earthquake, including her notes for an autobiography that were to chronicle her experiences at the center of California's literary movement. After that tragedy, she focused her energies on helping promote literature and other arts, offering her various Bay Area homes as salons and becoming the first librarian of the Oakland Public Library and the first woman Bohemian Club member. The state legislature named her the first poet laureate of California in 1915.

JAYNE CORTEZ (b. 1936) was born in Fort Huachuca, Arizona, where her father's army base was located. She began writing and performing in Los Angeles, where she cofounded the Watts Repertory Theater and served as its artistic director from 1964 to 1970. She is a performance poet whose influential performance style—a mix of African rhythms, avant-garde jazz, blues, and black speech—is heard both in collaborations with jazz musicians and solo. Her performances are featured on the 1982 films *Poetry in Motion* and *War on War*, and recorded on *There It Is* (1982), *Maintain Control* (1986), *Everywhere Drums* (1990), and *Taking the Blues Back Home: Poetry & Music* (with the Firespotters, 1996). She has also published many poetry books, including *Pisstained Stairs and the Monkey Man's Wares* (1969); *Festivals and Funerals* (1971); *Scarifications* (1973); *Mouth on Paper* (1977), which received the 1980 American Book Award; *Merveilleux Coup de Foundre: Poetry of Jayne Cortez and Ted Joans* (1982); *Coagulations: New and Selected Poems* (Thunder's Mouth, 1984); and *Somewhere in Advance of Nowhere* (1996). Published widely in journals and anthologies, her work has been translated into twenty-eight languages, and she has lectured and read her poetry on four continents.

VICTOR HERNANDEZ CRUZ (b. 1949) was born in Aguas Buenas, Puerto Rico, and moved with his family to Spanish Harlem when he was five. During the mid-1960s, while at Benjamin Franklin High School in New York City, he started writing and publishing his poetry. Called the "Nuyorican poet most recognized and acclaimed by the mainstream" by Nicolas Kanellos, Arte Publico's publisher, Cruz paid for his first chapbook, *Papo Got His Gun* (1966), with donations from neighbors. His first poetry book, *Snaps* (Random House, 1969), was followed by *Mainland* (Random House, 1973), *Tropicalization* (Reed, Cannon & Johnson, 1976), *Bilingual Wholes* (Momos Press), *Rhythm, Content, and Flavor* (1989, Arte Publico Ress), and *Red Beans* (Coffee House Press, 1991). He is a winner of the World Heavyweight Poetry Bout at the Taos Poetry Circus, and coeditor of *Paper Dance, 55 Latino Poets* (Persea Books, 1995). Starting in the mid-1970s he lived in the Bay Area, where he worked for the U.S. Postal Service before returning to Puerto Rico in 1989. Today he maintains homes in his birthplace and in Morocco. He is currently working on a novel and writing a collection of poems in Spanish.

FRANK MARSHALL DAVIS (1905–1987) was born in Arkansas City, Kansas, and moved to Chicago in 1927, where he wrote for black newspapers, such as the *Chicago Evening Bulletin*, the *Whip*, and the *Gary American*. He started writing poetry as a freshman majoring in journalism at Kansas State University. His first collection, *Black Man's Verse* (1935), was followed by *I Am the American Negro* (1937), *Through Sepia Eyes* (1938), and *47th Street* (1948). He joined various writers' organizations, including the South Side Writers' Group in Chicago, whose membership also included Richard Wright, Fenton Johnson and Arna Bontemps. In

1948 he moved with his wife and children to Honolulu, where he wrote weekly columns for the *Honolulu Record*. Another poetry collection, *Awakening*, appeared in 1978.

THULANI DAVIS (b. 1949), the daughter of two professors at Hampton Institute (now Hampton University), was born and raised in Hampton, Virginia. A poet, novelist, essayist, journalist, editor, performer, playwright, and librettist, she has written two books of poetry, *All the Renegade Ghosts Rise* (1972) and *Playing the Changes* (1985), and two novels, *1959* (Grove Weidenfeld, 1992) and *Maker of Saints* (Scribners, 1996). Her nonfiction work *Malcolm X: The Color Photographs* was published in 1993. Davis has also written extensively for the theater, presenting various one-woman shows. She collaborated with Ntozake Shange and Jessica Hagedorn in *Where the Mississippi Meets the Amazon*, and with Laurie Carlos in *One Day the Dialogue Will Be Endless*. She collaborated with her husband, musician Joseph Jarman, and his Sunbound Ensemble on *Liberation Suite,* and wrote the librettos for two operas composed by her cousin, Anthony Davis. One opera, *X, the Life and Times of Malcolm X* (1986), a libretto in verse, was nominated for a Grammy, and *Amistad* (1997), which premiered in Chicago in 1997, was directed by George C. Wolfe. Another opera collaboration, *The E & O Line* with Anne LeBaron, premiered in Washington, D.C., in 1996. In 1993 she won a Grammy for penning Aretha Franklin's album notes. In 2001 her play, *Everybody's Ruby: Story of a Murder in Florida*, premiered at the New York Shakespeare Festival. A Brooklyn resident, she teaches at Barnard College and regularly contributes articles to the *Village Voice*.

NORA MARKS DAUENHAUER is Tlingit (Raven, Lukaax.adi Clan, Sockeye Crest) from Alsek and Chilkat, Alaska. A native Tlingit speaker with a degree in anthropology, she is internationally recognized for her work in preserving Tlingit literature. For fourteen years she was principal researcher in language and cultural studies at the Sealaska Heritage Foundation, and she served as contributing editor for the original edition of *Alaska Native Writers, Storytellers and Orators*. She is coeditor of three major volumes on Tlingit oral literature, including *Life Woven with Song* (University of Arizona Press, 2000) and *Haa Tuwunaagu Yis, for Healing Our Spirit: Tlingit Oratory* (University of Washington Press, 1991), which she compiled with her husband, Richard Dauenhauer, and which received the 1991 American Book Award. She is also a poet and her work has been widely anthologized. A recipient of the Alaska Governor's Award for the Arts, she presently lives in Juneau, Alaska.

DIANE DI PRIMA (b. 1934), who was born in Brooklyn, a second-generation Italian-American, began writing at seven years of age. By fourteen, she had decided to be a poet. She has thirty-five books of poetry and prose by 2002 to her name. Also a publisher, editor, performer, theater director, and playwright, she cofounded the New York Poets Theatre, founded Poets Press, and coedited *The Floating Bear* (1961–1969) with Amiri Baraka. *Memoirs of a Beatnik* (Olympia Press, Paris & NY, 1969) chronicles her years as one of the most prominent and respected woman among Beat writers. Her poetry books include *This Kind of Bird Flies Backward* (Totem Press, 1958); *Selected Poems: 1956–1976* (North Atlantic Books, 1977); *Loba*, first published in 1978 and then in an expanded edition by Penguin Poets (1998); and *Pieces of a Song* (City Lights, 1990), which contains "Rant," her often anthologized appeal to the human imagination. This year Tia Chucha Press will publish *The Poetry Deal*, a collection of her poetry from the 1980s and 1990s. Di Prima has lived in the Bay Area since 1968. She recently published an autobiography, *Recollections of My Life as a Woman, the New York Years* (Viking, 2001).

CHITRA BANERJEE DIVAKARUNI (b. 1956) is a native of India who now makes her home in the United States. She has published four collections of poetry: *Dark Like the River* (Writers Workshop, India, 1987), *The Reason for Nasturtiums* (Berkeley Poets Press, 1990), *Black Candle* (Calyx Books, 1991), and *Leaving Yuba City* (Anchor Books/Doubleday, 1997), which won an Allen Ginsberg prize, a Pushcart Prize, and a Gerbode Foundation award. A playwright and editor of anthologies, she is also the author of several highly acclaimed novels and short story collections, such as *Arranged Marriage* (Anchor/Doubleday, 1995), which won an American Book Award, *The Mistress of Spices* (Doubleday, 1997), and *Sister of My Heart* (Doubleday, 1999). While living in the Bay Area, she served as president of MAITRI, a helpline for South Asian women. She currently teaches at the University of Houston in the Department of English.

H. D. (HILDA DOOLITTLE) (1886–1961) was born and raised in Pennsylvania. Her personal spiritual quest for "hermetic definition" was initially inspired by her mother, a member of the Moravian brotherhood and an amateur musician and painter, and her father, a professor of astronomy and mathematics. Her early poems first appeared in Harriet Monroe's *Poetry*. A leading Imagist, H. D. developed a minimalist writing style that exemplified the Imagists' poetic principles, and she became both professionally and personally involved with many writers in that movement. She was briefly engaged to Ezra Pound and married Richard Aldington in 1913. In 1911 she left the States to live as an expatriate in Europe, returning only for visits. On her last trip to the States, in 1960, she received the American Academy of Arts and Letters Award of Merit Medal for Poetry. Her first poetry collections were *Sea Garden* (1916), *Hymen* (1921), *Heliodora and Other Poems* (1924), *Collected Poems* (1925), *Red Roses for Bronze* (1931), *Trilogy* (written 1944-46), *Helen in Egypt* (1961), and *Hermetic Definition* (1972). In addition to poetry, she wrote novels, short stories, and memoirs; translated Greek poetry; and was a filmmaker.

W. E. B. (WILLIAM EDWARD BURGHARDT) DUBOIS (1868–1963) was born in Great Barrington, Massachusetts. An acclaimed essayist, novelist, editor, historian, sociologist, and philosopher, DuBois was called the "founder of black studies in American academic life" by the *Norton Anthology of African American Literature*. His first published work was his doctoral dissertation from Harvard University, titled *The Suppression of the African Slave-Trade to the United States* (1895). His next, and perhaps most influential, publication, was a collection of essays, *The Souls of Black Folk* (1903). Between 1903 and 1910 he published more poetry, including "The Litany of Atlanta," a response to a three-day race riot in 1906 in Atlanta, where members of his family lived. From 1910 to 1934, he served as editor of the official publication of the NAACP, *The Crisis*, where he introduced and provided a major forum for writers, artists, and scholars. He died in Accra, Ghana, while working on a long-planned research project, *Encyclopaedia Africana*. In 1964 his *Selected Poems* was published in Ghana posthumously. *The Autobiography of W.E.B. DuBois* appeared in 1968.

T. S. ELIOT (1888–1965) was born and raised in St. Louis as Thomas Stearns Eliot, the seventh child of poet Charlotte Chauncy Stearns Eliot and Henry Ware. While at Harvard University, he joined the staff of the *Advocate*, which published his first poetry. In 1911 he wrote "The Love Song of J. Alfred Prufrock," which was published in *Poetry* magazine in 1915 and later in his first collection *Prufrock and Other Observations* (1917). *The Wasteland* first appeared in the first issue of *The Criterion*, a journal he founded in 1922. Other poetry collections include *Poems 1909–1925* (1925) and *Four Quartets* (1943). Eliot wrote the verse plays *Murder in the Cathedral* (1935), *The Family Reunion* (1939), and *Old Possum's Book of Practical Cats* (1939)—the inspiration for the libretto of one of Broadway's longest running musicals, *Cats*—in addition to the later plays *The Cocktail Party* (1950), *The Confidential Clerk* (1954), and *The Elder Statesman* (1954).He became a British citizen in 1927, the same year he was baptized into the Anglican Church. In 1948 he was awarded both the Nobel Prize for Literature and England's Order of Merit.

MARI EVANS (b. 1923) was born and raised in Toledo, Ohio. A writer, musician, and educator, she taught literature at various universities in the Midwest and East, including Indiana University, Cornell University, Spellman College, Northwestern University, and Purdue University. She has published four collections of poetry, including *I Am a Black Woman* (1970), *Nightstar: 1973–1978* (1981) and *A Dark and Splendid Mass* (1992) and her work has been widely anthologized. She has also written various children's books and theater pieces, among them a musical adaptation of *Their Eyes Were Watching God* by Zora Neale Hurston, and has edited several literature collections, including *Black Women Writers, 1950–1980*. In 1975 she received the Black Academy of Arts and Letters' first annual poetry award.

SARAH WEBSTER FABIO (1928–1979) was born in Nashville, Tennessee, and was educated at Fisk University and San Francisco State University. A poet, political activist, and teacher, she was a seminal figure in developing educational curriculum for black studies programs and promoting the Black Arts movement in the Bay Area. When she taught at Merritt Junior College in Oakland, the birthplace of the Black Panther Party, she organized the first Black Arts Reading Series and invited Ed Bullins, Haki Madhubuti, Sonia Sanchez, and Marvin X to read their work. Huey P. Newton was her student, as were other Panthers. Her writings include *Race Results: U.S.A.* (1966), *Black Is a Panther Caged* (1968), *Saga of a Black Man* (1968), *Black Talk: Soul, Shield, and Sword* (1973), and *A Mirror: A Soul* (1969). She can also be heard on two Folkways recordings made in 1972, *Boss Soul* and *Soul Ain't, Soul Is*. She died of cancer at the age of fifty-one.

KENNETH FEARING (1902–1961) was born in Oak Park, Illinois. After graduating from the University of Wisconsin, he moved to New York City in the 1930s to become part of the city's literary and radical world. A writer of poetry, novels, pulp fiction, and Hollywood psycho-thrillers, Fearing had much of his earliest poetry published in the *New Masses* and other periodicals. His first collection of poetry, *Angel Arms* (1929), was followed by seven others, including *Dead Reckoning* (1938), *Collected*

Poems (1940), *Afternoon of a Pawnbroker* (1943), *Stranger at Coney Island* (1949), and *New and Selected Poems* (1956). When questioned in 1950, under subpoena by the U.S. attorney in Washington, D.C., about whether he was a Communist Party member, he responded, "Not yet." He also is author of eight novels, among them *Dagger of the Mind* (1941), *Loneliest Girl in the World* (1951), and *The Big Clock* (1946), which was made into a film in 1948 and remade as *No Way Out* in 1987.

LAWRENCE FERLINGHETTI (b. 1919), a veteran of World War II, was born in Yonkers, New York. A poet, painter, editor, and publisher, he cofounded the landmark City Lights Bookstore in San Francisco in 1953. It was the first all-paperbound bookstore in the United States. His debut book of poetry, *Pictures of the Gone World* (1955), was the first book published under the City Lights imprint. *A Coney Island of the Mind* (1958) was the first of thirteen Ferlinghetti books published by New Directions. It sold about one million copies, more than another famous City Lights Press 1956 publication, *Howl*, by Allen Ginsburg, which was to forever connect that poet to the Beat Generation through the First Amendment case "that established a legal precedent for the publication of controversial work with redeeming social importance." Among his other poetry collections are *Starting from San Francisco* (1961), *The Secret Meaning of Things* (1969), *Open Eye, Open Heart* (1973), *Who Are We Now?* (1976), and *Landscapes of Living & Dying* (1979). He was named first poet laureate of San Francisco in 1998 and the Before Columbus Foundation honored him with their American Book Award's Lifetime Achievement citation in 1999.

JACK FOLEY is a poet, critic, and presenter who hosts *Cover to Cover*, a weekly show featuring poetry readings and interviews with writers on the Berkeley radio station KPFA. A contributing editor to the Bay Area's *Poetry Flash*, Foley also writes a weekly book review column, "Foley's Books," for the online magazine the *Alsop Review*, which can be found at www.alsopreview.com. From 1990 to 1995 he edited *Poetry USA*, a National Poetry Association magazine that included a 1993 issue presenting examples of new directions in experimental writing. He performs his poetry with his wife, Adelle, and has published numerous collections and chapbooks, including *Letters/Lights—Words for Adelle* (1987); *Gershwin* (1991); *Adrift* (1993); which was nominated for a Bay Area Book Reviewers' Award; and *Exiles* (1996). In 1998 he coauthored *New Poetry from California: Dead/Requiem* with Ivan Arguelles. *O Powerful*

Western Star (Pantograph Press, 2000), a cultural history of poetry, film, and art in California from the 1940s to the end of the 1990s, received the 1998–2000 Artists Embassy International Literary/Cultural Award.

JACK D. FORBES, of Powhatan-Renape and Delaware-Lenape descent, was born in California. He received his Ph.D. in history and anthropology from the University of Southern California, and in 1971 and 1972 helped found D-Q University, a Native American college in Davis, California. He is presently professor emeritus and former chair of Native American studies at the University of California, Davis. He is author of poetry, fiction, and nonfiction books and articles about Native American people, including *Apache, Navaho, and Spaniard* (1960); *Red Book: A Novel* (1997, Theytus); *Columbus and Other Cannibals* (1992, Automedia); and *Africans and Native Americans, the Language of Race and the Evolution of Red-Black Peoples* (1988, 1993, Illinois). He has been a Guggenheim fellow, a recipient of the Before Columbus Foundation's 1997American Book Award for Lifetime Achievement, and a Fulbright visiting professor in comparative American studies at the University of Warwick.

ROBERT FROST (1874–1963) was born in San Francisco and was eleven when he moved to New Hampshire after his father's death. For much of his life he resided in New England, the region his work is most identified with, mostly writing or teaching in Massachusetts and Vermont. After the failure of his New Hampshire farm in 1912, he spent three years in England. His first published poem, "My Butterfly," appeared in 1894 in a New York City newspaper, the *Independent*. His first published collections were *A Boy's Will* (1913) and *North of Boston* (1914). Other collections are *The Lovely Shall Be Choosers* (1929), *The Lone Striker* (1933), *A Further Range* (1936), *A Witness Tree* (1942), *Hard Not to Be King* (1951), *The Road Not Taken* (1951), and *In the Clearing* (1962). By the 1920s, he had become the most familiar and celebrated American poet and had received numerous honors, including four Pulitzer Prizes and the Bollingen Prize, which was awarded shortly before his death.

ALICIA GASPAR DE ALBA is one of three Chicana poets in the anthology *Three Times a Woman: Chicana Poetry* (Bilingual Review Press, 1989). She also published a book of short stories, *The Mystery of Survival and Other Stories* (Bilingual Review Press, 1992), and a novel, *Sor Juana's Second Dream* (University of New Mexico Press, 1999). In *Chicano Art, Inside Outside the Master's House, Cultural Politics and the CARA Exhibition* (University of Texas

Press, 1998), she combines theories from anthropology, popular culture, semiotics, and cultural and gender studies to discuss a Chicano/Chicana exhibition that toured major United States museums in the early 1990s. She presently teaches at the Cesar E. Chavez Center for Chicana and Chicano Studies at the University of California, Los Angeles.

DANIELA GIOSEFFI (b. 1941), an Italian American, is the author of ten books of poetry and prose. Her first book of poetry was *Eggs in the Lake* (Boa Editions, 1979) and her second and third poetry collections, *Word Wounds and Water Flowers* (1995) and *Going On* (2001), were both published by VIA Folios at Purdue University. In 2002 she will publish another poetry collection, *Symbiosis*, an e-book from Rattapallax Press. She is editor-author of the anthology *Women on War: International Voices for the Nuclear Age* (Touchstone Books, 1989), an American Book Award– and National Book Award–winning collection that is being reissued in a new edition by the Feminist Press in 2002. She is also editor-author of *On Prejudice* and *A Global Perspective* (Anchor Doubleday, 1993). Widely published in literary anthologies and in online and print journals, her first novel was a feminist satire, *The Great American Belly* (Doubleday/Dell, 1979), and her first short story collection was *In Bed with the Exotic Enemy* (Avisson Books,1995). She is editor and publisher of www.PoetsUSA.com, formerly Wise Women's Web, which incorporates five web sites of poetry and prose. She has taught creative writing at various institutions around the metropolitan New York City area and currently teaches "Multicultural Literature: Experiencing Race, Class, and Gender in the United States" in the Humanities Department of the College of the School of Visual Arts in Manhattan.

DIANE GLANCY (b. 1941) was born in Kansas City, Missouri to a mother of English and German ancestry and a father of Cherokee descent. A poet, novelist, essayist, and playwright, Glancy titled her first collection of poetry *Brown Wolf Leaves the Res and Other Poems* (Blue Cloud Quarterly Press, 1984). Her other collections include *Offering: Poetry and Prose* (Holy Cow! Press, 1988). She received the 1991 Native American Prose Award and the 1993 American Book Award for her first collection of essays, *Claiming Breath* (University of Nebraska Press, 1992). Glancy has also published two fiction collections. She currently teaches Native American literature and creative writing in the English department at Macalester College in St. Paul, Minnesota.

RAY GONZÀLEZ was born in El Paso, Texas. He has received many awards for his poetry, essays, short stories, and editing. His seven books of poetry include *The Heat of Arrivals* (BOA Editions, 1996); *From the Restless Roots* (Arte Publico Press, 1985); *Twilights and Chants* (James Andrews & Co., 1987), winner of the 1987 Four Corners Book Award; *Turtle Pictures* (University of Arizona Press, 2000), winner of the 2001 Minnesota Book Award for Poetry; and *The Hawk Temple at Tierra Grande* (BOA Edition, Ltd., 2002). In 1993, the Before Columbus Foundation honored his editing work on numerous anthologies with their Award for Excellence in Editing. His anthologies include *Crossing the River: Poets of the Western U.S.* (Permanent Press, 1987); *Mirrors Beneath the Earth, Short Fiction by Chicano Writers* (Curbstone Press, 1992); *Without Discovery: A Native Response to Columbus* (Broken Moon Press, 1992); and *After Aztlan, Latino Poets of the Nineties* (David Godine, 1992). His first fiction collection, *The Ghost of John Wayne and Other Stories* (University of Arizona Press, 2001), won a Western Heritage Award; the same press is publishing his collection of essays, *The Underground Heart, A Return to a Hidden Landscape* (2003). He has taught at various universities, including the University of Illinois and the University of Minnesota.

SISTER GOODWIN (ELIZABETH FREDA HOPE) (1951–1997), was born in Kotzebue, above the Arctic Circle. *A Lagoon Is in My Backyard*, the only collection of her poetry published to date, was printed by I. Reed Books in 1984 under her maiden name, Sister Goodwin. As far as the publisher and her family know, this book is the first poetry publication written by an Inupiaq Inuit. Her Inupiaq name was Taliiraq, and as the wife of writer and community leader Andy Hope III, she was adopted into the Kiks.'adi (Tlingit Raven moiety) of the Sitka Tlingit Tribe, receiving the name Tsanak in 1985. In the mid-1980s she served on the Alaska Native Arts board and was a member of the Alaska Native Sisterhood Camp 2 and the Native American Writers Circle of the Americas. From 1989 to 1997 she taught elementary school in the Mendenhall River Community School of the Juneau School District. She died after a long battle with cancer at the age of forty-five.

VINCE GOTERA (b. 1952) was born in San Francisco, and raised in San Francisco and the Philippines. Widely published in journals and anthologies, in 1994 he published both a poetry book, *Dragonfly* (Pecan Grove Press), and a book of literary criticism, *Radical Visions: Poetry of Vietnam Veterans* (University of Georgia Press). He is coordinator of the creative writing program at the University of Northern Iowa and editor of the oldest literary magazine in the U.S. (since 1815), the *North American Review.*

LINDA M. RODRÌGUEZ GUGLIELMONI, who was born in San Juan, Puerto Rico, has lived in England, Washington, D.C., Michigan, and California. A literary critic, translator, and bilingual writer, her collection of experimental bilingual poetry, *Metropolitan Fantasies—Textos Errantes—* was published in 2001. She is editor of *Enlaces: Transnacionalidad—El Caribe y su Diaspora—Lengua, Literatura y Cultura en los Albores del Siglo XXI* (The Latino Press, 2000), a record of the proceedings of the Seventh International Conference of Caribbean Women Writers and Scholars, a project she directed and for which she received a National Endowment for the Humanities. She is currently teaching at the University of Puerto Rico, Mayagüez campus, and was an associate artist in Ishmael Reed's summer 2002 workshop at the Atlantic Center for the Arts in New Smyrna Beach, Florida.

JIM GUSTAFSON is deceased. He lived in the Detroit area.

JESSICA TARAHATA HAGEDORN, born and raised in the Philippines, became a resident of the Bay Area at thirteen. A poet, playwright, and performance artist, she was also the songwriter and leader of the art rock band the Gangster Choir for ten years. Her multimedia theater works, such as *Holy Food, Teenytown*, and *Mango Tango*, have been performed at various national venues, including the Public Theater, the New Museum, the Dance Theater Workshop, and the Whitney Museum in New York City; the Walker Art Center in Minneapolis; and the Berkeley Repertory Theater and the Intersection in the Bay Area. She has published three collections of her poetry, prose, and short fiction: *Dangerous Music* (Momo Press, 1975); *Pet Food & Tropical Apparitions* (Momo Press, 1981); and *Danger and Beauty* (Penguin, 1993). Her first novel, *The Dogeaters* (Pantheon, 1990), received a 1990 National Book Award nomination; her second novel, *The Gangster of Love*, appeared in 1996. She is editor of *Charlie Chan Is Dead, an Anthology of Contemporary Asian American Fiction* (Penguin Books, 1993), in which an excerpt of her novel-in-progress, *Film Noir,* appears.

SAM HAMOD (b. 1936) is the son of a Muslim imam and immigrant from Lebanon who built a mosque in his family's new home in Gary, Indiana.

Besides being a poet, scriptwriter, essayist, editor, publisher, and scholar, Hamod has served as the director of the Islamic Center in Washington, D.C., from 1983 to 1984; a professor at Princeton, Michigan, Iowa, and Howard universities; and the editor and publisher of *Third World News* in Washington, D.C. His poetry has appeared in numerous journals and anthologies, including *Unsettling America: An Anthology of Contemporary Multicultural Poetry* (Bt Bound, 1999) and *Grapeleaves: 100 Years of Arab American Poetry* (Interlink Books, 2000), He has published ten volumes, among them *The Holding Action* (SeaMark Press, 1969), *The Famous Boating Party* (Cedar Creek Press, 1970), *Dying With the Wrong Name* (Smyrna/Anthe, 1980), and *The Arab Poems, the Muslim Poems, New and Selected Poems* (Cedar Creek Press, 1998).

JOY HARJO (b. 1951), an enrolled member of the Muskogee tribe, was born in Tulsa, Oklahoma. An artist, photographer, poet, musician, and scriptwriter, she studied painting and theater at the Institute of American Indian Arts in Santa Fe, New Mexico. A saxophonist, she frequently reads her poetry with music that blends tribal, jazz, and rock sounds, appearing in concert and on CDs as Joy Harjo and Poetic Justice and more recently as Joy Harjo and the Real Revolution. Her published poetry collections include *The Last Song* (1975), *What Moon Drove Me to This?* (1980), *She Had Some Horses* (Thunder's Mouth Press, 1983), *In Mad Love and War* (Wesleyan University Press, 1990), *The Woman Who Fell from the Sky* (1994), *A Map to the Next World: Poems and Tales* (W.W. Norton, 2000), and *How We Became Human: New and Selected Poems* (W.W. Norton, 2002). She is also editor of an anthology of Native American women writers, *Reinventing the Enemy's Language: Contemporary Native Women's Writings of North America* (W.W. Norton, 1997).

WILL HEFORD was a poet who published in *The Masses*, a legendary radical and cultural magazine mixing avant-garde poetry, fiction, and art with political and social protest. It was "the recording secretary of the Revolution in the making," according to another poet and contributor, Arturo Giovannitti. *The Masses* was first published in Greenwich Village in 1911; it was put out of circulation by the United States Postal Service in 1917.

CALVIN HERNTON (1934–2001), a poet, novelist, essayist, and social scientist was born in Chattanooga, Tennessee. At the time of his death, he was a professor of African-American Studies at Oberlin College, where he taught African, West Indian, and African-American literature. Hernton published numerous essays and nine books, including the poetry collections *The Coming of Chronos to the House of Nightsong: An Epical Narrative of the South* (1963), *Medicine Man* (Reed, Cannon & Johnson, 1976), and *The Red Crab Gang and Black River Poems* (Ishmael Reed Publishing Co., 1999). His non-fiction works include *Sex and Racism in America* (Anchor Books, 1992), which has been in print for more than thirty years and, has been translated into six languages, and *The Sexual Mountain and Black Women Writers* (Anchor Books, 1990).

JUAN FELIPE HERRERA, the child of campesinos, grew up moving with the seasons through rural California. He has published over twenty poetry books, beginning with *Rebozos of Love* (El Centro Cultural de la Raza of San Diego, 1974). His other work includes *Facegames* (AS Is/So and So Press, 1987), *Akrilica* (Alcatraz Editions, 1989), *Loteria Cards and Fortune Poems, Night Train to Tuxtla: New Poems and Stories* (University of Arizona Press, 1994), *A Book of Lives* (City Lights Books, 1999), *Laughing Out Loud: Poems in English and Spanish* (1999), *Border-Crosser with a Lamborghini Dream* (University of Arizona Press, 1999), *Thunderweavers* (University of Arizona Press, 2000), and *CrashBoomLove* (1999), a novel in verse for youth that won the 2001 Libros Latinos Award. He has also published bilingual children's books and founded several bilingual magazines and performing arts groups, among them Teatro Tolteca, Troka, Poet-sumanos, and Teatro Zapata. He teaches in the Chicano studies program at California State University, Fresno, and is a member of the Before Columbus Foundation board of directors.

GEARY HOBSON, of Cherokee-Quapaw and Chickasaw ancestry, has taught Indian literature and writing in various universities, such as the University of New Mexico and the University of Oklahoma, where he is currently an associate professor in the English department. He is the author of *Deer Hunting and Other Poems* (1990) and editor of *The Remembered Earth: An Anthology of Contemporary Native American Literature* (1979). He serves as project historian of the Native Writers Circle of the Americas, also known as Returning the Gift, and is currently compiling a literary and critical history of North and Central American Indian literature.

LINDA HOGAN (b. 1947), born in Denver, Colorado, of Chickasaw ancestry, was raised in Oklahoma. A poet, novelist, playwright, and essayist, she has published four collections of poetry: *Calling Myself Home* (1978); *Daughters, I Love You* (1981); *Eclipse* (1983); *Seeing Through the Sun* (University of Massachusetts Press, 1985), which received a 1986

American Book Award; and *Savings* (1988). Her first published novel, *Mean Spirit* (1990), was followed by *The Book of Medicines, Dwellings: A Spiritual History of the Living World* (Coffee House Press, 1993) and the novel *Solar Storms* (Scribner, 1997).

BOB HOLMAN is a poet, curator, editor, and producer who works to popularize and disseminate spoken-word poetry through poetry slams, live performance festivals, and the media of television, video, Internet sites, and compact disk. His own poetry is collected in five volumes, including *The Collect Call of the Wild* (Henry Holt, 1995), and on the 1998 CD *In with the Out Crowd*. He worked with filmmaker Joshua Blum to produce the 1996 PBS series *The United States of Poetry*, which featured poets from across the country in over sixty short films. Holman, who currently teaches writing and integrated arts at Bard College, has received a NEA grant for preproduction support of the World of Poetry, his new poetry media project (worldofpoetry.org), and is proprietor of the Bowery Poetry Club, a cafe-bar-performance space that is the beginning of his realization of a poetry-technology lab.

GARRETT HONGO (b. 1951), a poet, editor, and teacher, was born in Volcano, Hawaii, of Japanese-American ancestry and grew up on the North Shore of Oahu and in Los Angeles. Widely anthologized, he has published two collections of poetry, *Yellow Light* (Wesleyan, 1982) and *The River of Heaven* (Knopf, 1988), which was the Lamont Poetry Selection of the Academy of American Poets and a Pulitzer Prize finalist. He also edited the anthology *The Open Boat: Poems from Asian America* (Anchor Books, Doubleday, 1993) and *Songs My Mother Taught Me: Stories, Plays, and Memoir by Wakako Yamauchi* (the Feminist Press at the City University of New York, 1994).

ANDREW HOPE III of Xaastanch /Tlingit ancestry, currently resides in Juneau, Alaska. He is a member of the Sitka Tribe of Alaska, a poet, coeditor of *Will the Time Ever Come? A Tlingit Source Book* (University of Washington Press, 2001), and Southeast regional coordinator of the Alaska Rural Systemic Initiative. A member of the Board of Directors of the Before Columbus Foundation, he formerly served as its president.

LANGSTON HUGHES (1902–1967) was born in Joplin, Missouri, and raised in Lawrence, Kansas. He was nineteen when *The Crisis*, the noted NAACP magazine edited by W .E. B. DuBois, printed his first nationally published poem, "The Negro Speaks of Rivers." It was the beginning of a prolific writing career that included novels, short stories, children's books, essays, songs, plays, and translations of the works of various poets such as Federico García Lorca and Nicolas Guillen. With the publication of his first book of poetry, *The Weary Blues* (1926), Hughes was already on his way to becoming one of the most celebrated American writers. His other books of poetry include *Fine Clothes to the Jew* (1927), *Scottsboro Limited* (1932), *Shakespeare in Harlem* (1942), *Montage of a Dream Deferred* (1951), *Ask Your Mama: Twelve Moods for Jazz* (1961), and *The Panther and the Lash: Poems of our Times* (Knopf, 1967), which was assembled shortly before his death. As editor of the influential anthology *The Poetry of the Negro, 1746–1949* (1949), which he coedited with Arna Bontemps, and *New Negro Poets USA* (1964), Hughes introduced the work of many young writers to a wide audience. Other anthologies he edited or coedited include *The Book of Negro Folklore* (1958) and *The Best Short Stories by Negro Writers* (1967). He published his autobiography in two volumes—*The Big Sea* (1940) and *I Wonder As I Wander* (1956). His complete collection of 860 poems can be found in *The Collected Poems of Langston Hughes*, edited by Arnold Rampersad with David Roessel (Alfred A. Knopf, 1994).

CYNTHIA HWANG was a student in the fall 1998 poetry workshop led by Ishmael Reed at the University of California at Berkeley.

LAWSON FUSAO INADA (b. 1938) is a third-generation sansei Japanese-American who was born in Fresno, California. During World War II, he was incarcerated at the Fresno County Fairground, and later was interned in Japanese-American concentration camps in Arkansas and Colorado. His first published collection of poetry, *Before the War: Poems As They Happened* (William Morrow, 1971), was the first poetry collection by an Asian-American writer to be published by a major United States–based publishing house. Other poetry collections are *Legends from Camp* (Coffee House Press, 1992), which won the 1994 American Book Award, and *Drawing the Line* (Coffee House Press, 1997). Besides being widely anthologized, Inada is a coeditor of *Aiiieeee! An Anthology of Asian American Writers* (Howard University Press, 1974) and *The Big Aiiieeeee!* (Meridian/NAL, 1991). He is a professor in the English department at Southern Oregon College in Ashland, Oregon.

TED JOANS (b. 1928) was born in Cairo, Illinois, the child of two riverboat workers. Joans is a poet, visual artist, and performance artist. In a 1980 interview with Michael Zwerin for the *International Herald Tribune*,

Joans emphasized his belief that "jazz and American poetry go together." In the same interview he is quoted as saying, "I'm a living poem. The poem is the life of Ted Joans, born on the Fouth of July, the same birthday as Louis Armstrong—dig it. When my feet touch the floor in the morning the poem begins." Called both a surrealist and a jazz poet, Joans has lived in Greenwich Village, Harlem, Paris, Timbuktu, Mali, London, the Bay Area, Seattle, and Vancouver, and he travels the world giving lectures and readings. Besides being widely published in journals and anthologies, he has published poetry, collages, and prose, including *Beat Poems* (Deretchin, 1957), *Black Pow Wow: Jazz Poems* (Hill & Wang, 1960), *A Black Manifesto in Jazz Poetry and Prose* (Calder & Boyars, 1971), *Sure, Really I Is* (Transformation Books, 1982), and *Okapi Passion Poems* (Ishmael Reed Publishing Co., 1994).

MANDY KAHN was a student in the spring 1998 poetry class taught by Ishmael Reed at the University of California, Berkeley.

BOB KAUFMAN (1925–1986) was born in New Orleans. His mother was a schoolteacher from Martinique, and his father, a railroad porter, was of African-American and Jewish parentage. Before becoming a street poet, Kaufman worked as a merchant seaman and labor organizer. At the forefront of the Beat movement, he was a cult figure who was active in San Francisco's North Beach and in Manhattan's Lower East Side and Greenwich Village from the 1950s through the 1980s. After President John F. Kennedy was shot, Kaufman entered a decade of self-imposed silence that he broke the day the Vietnam War ended. He felt that a Buddhist vow of silence was the only appropriate response to the events of the time. *The San Francisco Chronicle*'s longtime columnist, Herb Caen, coined the term *beatnik* to describe Kaufman because he was in the news all the time for running up and down Grant Avenue, jumping on cars and shouting his poetry. A jazz poet and a major poet of the black consciousness movement, Kaufman was called one of the few American surrealist poets. His first writing was published in *Beatitude*, a San Francisco magazine, in the late 1950s. City Lights Books published his broadsides "The Abomunist Manifesto," "Second April," and "Does the Secret Mind Whisper," which later were included in the first of eight poetry collections, *Solitudes Crowded with Loneliness* (New Directions, 1965). According to French critics and scholars, this book placed him among the greatest of African-American writers, although his work is often excluded from American anthologies. Among his other published collections are *Golden Sardines* (City Lights Books, 1967) and *The Ancient Rain: Poems, 1956–1978* (1981).

MAURICE KENNY (b. 1929) was born of Mohawk ancestry in Watertown, in northern New York state between the St. Lawrence and Black rivers. He has been a poet, publisher, and editor. Kenny has given reading performances of his poetry across the United States, and his poetry and short stories have been widely anthologized. He has published at least twenty-four books, starting with *Dead Letters Sent* in 1959. His later collections include *Blackrobe: Issac Jogues* (North Country Community College Press, 1982); *The Mama Poems* (White Pine Press, 1984), which won the 1984 American Book Award; *Between Two Rivers: Selected Poems* (1987); and *Tekonwatonti/Molly Brant (1735–1795): Poems of War* (White Pine Press, 1992). He has been a major catalyst in the renaissance of recent American-Indian literature, encouraging young Native American writers through his work as an anthology editor and as coeditor of *Contact/II* and Strawberry Press, which publishes Native American writers exclusively. Kenny founded the press in 1976 and now serves as editor. He also sits on the board of directors of CCLM (Comunidad Cristiana de Los Mochis).

CAROLYN KIZER (b. 1925) was born in Spokane, Washington, to a scientist mother and a lawyer father. She helped found *Poetry Northwest* in 1959 and served as its editor in chief until 1965. From 1966 to 1970, she was director of literary programs at the National Endowment for the Arts. Her own poetry volumes include *Poems* (1959), *The Ungrateful Garden* (1961), *Knock upon Silence* (1965), *Midnight Was My Cry* (1971), *Mermaids in the Basement: Poems for Women* (1984), and *The Nearness of You* (1986). Her 1994 book *Yin* (Ecco Press) won the 1985 Pulitzer Prize. Kizer's writing is influenced by her extensive travels abroad, which include trips to China and Japan. A translator of Urdu poetry, Kizer has also translated Chinese poetry by Tu Fu and others, and in 1964 and 1965 she lived in Pakistan, where she taught at Kinnaird College. Her translations in *Carrying Over: Translations from Various Tongues* (1985) reflect these experiences.

YUSEF KOMANYAKAA (b. 1947) was born James Willie Brown Jr. in Bogalusa, Louisiana, and served in Vietnam as a war correspondent and editor of the *Southern Cross*. He has published twelve volumes of poetry, including *Dien Cai Dau* (Wesleyan, 1988), which was based on his experiences in Vietnam; *Magic City* (Wesleyan, 1992); *Thieves of Paradise* (1998); *Talking Dirty to the Gods* (2000); and *Pleasure Dome: New and Collected Poems* (Farrar, Straus & Giroux, 2001), which spans more than twenty years of his writing. *Neon Vernacular* (1993), his fifth volume was awarded the 1994 Pulitzer Prize for Poetry and the Kingsley Tufts Award. Komanyakaa has also coedited two volumes of the *Jazz Poetry Anthology* (Indiana University Press, Vol. I, 1991 and Vol. II, 1996) with Sascha Feinstein. In 2000 he coedited *Blue Notes: Essays, Interviews and Commentaries* (Poets on Poetry) with Radiclani Clytus. Currently a professor of creative writing at Princeton University, he recently was elected chancellor of the Academy of American Poets.

ALEX KUO, Boston born, was raised in China during World War II. His poetry and prose have been widely published in journals and anthologies, and his poetry has been collected in four volumes: *The Window Tree* (1971), *New Letters from Hiroshima and Other Poems* (Greenfield Review Press, 1974), *Changing the River* (I. Reed Books, 1986), and *This Fierce Geography* (1999). He has taught in the Midwest, Rhode Island, and Colorado, and as a Fulbright scholar and Lingnam fellow and lecturer he completed two novels, *Cold War* and *Point Blank*, while spending four winter months in China in 1991–92. His most recent publications include *Chinese Opera* (Weatherhill, 2000) and *Lipstick and Other Stories* (Asia 2000 Ltd., 2002). He currently lives in Moscow, Idaho.

ALAN CHONG LAU (1948), born in Oroville, a small northern California town at the base of the Sierra Nevada foothills and near the Central Valley, he is from the third generation of a Chinese-American family with origins in Szechwan, China; Chieh An, Taiwan; and Kowloon, China. After traveling outside the country, including several trips to Japan, where he met his wife, Lau returned to California and got his B.A. in art from the University of California, Santa Cruz in 1976. During this time he began to publish his poetry in magazines and important anthologies featuring Asian-American writers, and he coauthored *The Buddha Bandits down Highway 99* (1978) with Garrett Hongo and Lawson Fusao Inada. His first poetry collection, *Songs for Jadina* (Greenfield Review Press, 1980), won the King County Arts Commission Publications Project Selection in Poetry for 1980 in Washington state, which continues to be his home, and also received a 1981 American Book Award. In 1983 he received a Japan–U.S. Creative Artists Fellowship, which is cosponsored by the Japan–U.S. Friendship Commission, the NEA, and Japan's Agency for Cultural Affairs. His most recent publication, *Blues and Greens: A Produce Worker's Journal* (Intersections, 2000), is a memoir of his days working in the markets of Seattle's Chinatown. A painter as well as a writer, he has exhibited his paintings in the United States, England, and Japan.

TATO LAVIERA (b. 1950), who was born in Santurce, Puerto Rico, moved with his family to New York's Lower East Side when he was ten years old. He writes poetry and plays in English, Spanish, and Spanglish, a mixture of his first two languages. His four books—a bilingual jazz and salsa poetry collection, *La Carreta Made a U-Turn* (1979), *Enclave* (1981), which won an American Book Award from the Before Columbus Foundation, *AmeRican* (1986), and *Mainstream Ethics* (1988)—were published by Arte Publico, and all remain in print. Nicolas Kanellos, Laviera's publisher, has called him "the best-selling Hispanic poet in the United States."

ROLAND LEGIARDI-LAURA is a filmmaker, poet, and presenter whose award-winning documentary film, *Azul: Poetry in Nicaragua*, studies Nicaragua's people and their history through poetry. He currently chairs the board of directors of the Nuyorican Poets Cafe. He is the founder of the Fifth Night Screenplay Reading and Short Film series that, over the past five years, has produced 190 screenplay readings. He also founded Words To Go and P.O.E.T., billed as America's first traveling troupes of performance poets, and is editor of poetry-in-translation at *Bomb*. He is currently working on a three-part documentary film project entitled *The Fourth Purpose: The Enigma of Public School*.

RUSSELL CHARLES LEONG (b. 1950) was born and raised in San Francisco's Chinatown. Educated in local American and Chinese schools, he was a member of the original Kearny Street Asian-American Writers Workshop and has traveled widely in Asia. His poetry, short fiction, and essays have been widely published in journals and anthologies, appearing in the first *Aiiieeeee!* (Howard University Press, 1974). His debut collection of poems, *The Country of Dreams and Dust* (West End Press, 1993), received the PEN Oakland Josephine Miles award. *Phoenix Eyes and Other Stories* (University of Washington Press, 2000) received a 2001 American Book Award. In addition to his writing, he has made the documentary films *Morning Begins Here* (1985) and *Why Is Preparing Fish a Political Act? The Poetry of Janice Mirikitani* (1990). Leong has served as editor of *Amerasia Journal* at UCLA's Asian American Studies Center since 1977, and he is also the managing editor of the Center's press.

JERRY LEIBER (b. 1933) was born in New York City and formed a songwriting team with Mike Stoller when they were both seventeen years old. He was working in a record shop and Stoller was a jazz pianist. Their 1950s songs were written and sung by young black vocal groups who were initially unknown, but the songwriters, singers, and their songs became major rock and roll hits. They compiled a huge catalogue of songs, including "Love Potion No. Nine," sung by the Clovers; "Searchin'"; "Little Egypt"; "Yakety Yak"; "Charley Brown," sung by the Coasters (initially called the Robins); "On Broadway"; "Spanish Harlem"; "There Goes My Baby"; "Poison Ivy"; "Stand By Me," for the Drifters; "Hound Dog," which Big Mama Thornton recorded in 1953 and Elvis Presley recorded in 1956; and "Jailhouse Rock," "Baby I Don't Care," "Lovin' You," and "Treat Me Nice" for Elvis Presley. They formed their own record labels and contributed to the Atlantic label. In the 1960s they wrote cabaret-style material for Peggy Lee, including "I'm a Woman," and did some work with Perry Como. After the 1970s, they retired from composing but continue to make appearances at awards ceremonies and to advocate for copyright protections for musicians. They were inducted into the Rock and Roll Hall of Fame in 1987. (See entry on Mike Stoller for further information.)

DENISE LEVERTOV (1923–1997) was born and raised in Ilford, England, the daughter of a Welsh mother and Russian Jewish father who became ordained as an Anglican priest. She was schooled at home. After serving as a civilian nurse during World War II, she married the American writer Mitch Goodman, came to the United States in 1948, had a son in 1949, and became a United States citizen in 1955. The first of her many poetry collections, *The Double Image*, was published in England in 1946. Her other poetry collections include *The Jacob's Ladder* (1961), *O Taste and See* (1964), *The Sorrow Dance* (1967), *Relearning the Alphabet* (1970), *The Freeing of the Dust* (1975), *Candles in Babylon* (1982), *Breathing the Water* (1987), and *A Door in the Hive* (New Directions, 1989). She has also published her essays in two collections, *The Poet in the World* (1973) and *Light up the Cave* (1981). Levertov was the poetry editor of *The Nation* magazine and taught at many universities, including Tufts University and Stanford University. At the time of her death, she was living in Seattle.

GENNY LIM is a native San Franciscan poet, performer, playwright, and educator who has published a collection of her poetry, *Winter Place* (1989), and frequently appears in poetry and music collaborations. She has worked with the musicians Jon Jang, Max Roach, Francis Wong, and Herbie Lewis. Lim has been featured on the PBS series *The United States of Poetry*, KQED-TV's San Francisco *Chinatown, Pins and Noodles* and *Genny Lim: The Voice* by David Moragne. Her plays include *Paper Angels,* which aired on American Playhouse on PBS in 1995, *Bitter Cane, XX,* and *La China Poblana.* She is coauthor of *Island: Poetry and History of Chinese Immigrants on Angel Island, 1910–1940.* She teaches at the New College of California in San Francisco and at the Naropa Institute in Oakland.

VACHEL LINDSAY (1879–1931) was born in Springfield, Illinois, where his family members were Disciples of Christ followers, a sect also called the Campbellites. After changing his mind about entering the ministry, he trained as both a poet and painter, and began his walks or "tramps" around the United States, presenting his work through a combination of visual and verbal images. His early style of performance poetry, which he called his "Gospel of Beauty," was influenced by the revivalist tradition of the YMCA, which he experienced through camp meetings and evangel- ical preachers, and which frequently involved audience participation. He is often credited with discovering the poet Langston Hughes, an impor- tant innovator of poetry performance, after Hughes left three poems beside Lindsay's plate in a Washington, D.C., hotel dining room in 1925, where Hughes was working as a "Negro busboy." One of his most cited poems, the ballad *General Booth Enters into Heaven,* became the title poem of his first poetry collection in 1913, followed by *The Congo* (1914), *The Art of the Moving Picture* (1915), *The Chinese Nightingale* (1917), *The Golden Whales of California and Other Rhymes in the Amer- ican Language* (1920), *The Golden Book of Springfield* (1920), and *Col- lected Poems* (1923). Of his later works, *Johnny Appleseed* (1928) became a standard of children's literature.

REGINALD LOCKETT was born and raised in Berkeley, California, and continues to make his home in the Bay Area. He started writing poetry as a young teenager after joining a creative writing class. He has written three volumes of poetry, including his most recently published poetry col- lection, *The Party Crashers of Paradise* (Creative Arts Book Co., 2001). For fifteen years he has performed spoken-word poetry around the Bay Area with the Wordwind Chorus, a collaboration with Q.R. Hand, Brian Auerbach, and saxophonist Lewis Jordan. In 2000 they recorded a CD, *we are of the saying.* Lockett writes in one poem of how, at the age of seven, he was placed in a class that would today be labeled special education. It turned out that all he needed was glasses. He now teaches writing at San Jose City College in San Jose, California.

AMY LOWELL (1874–1925) was a member of a distinguished and wealthy family from Brookline, Massachusetts, near Boston. One brother, Abbott, became president of Harvard University; another brother, Percival, founded the Lowell Observatory at Harvard. Schooled at home, she published her first book of stories, *Dream Drops, or Stories from Fairy Land, by a Dreamer* (1887), when still a teenager, and her first book of poetry *A Dome of Many-Coloured Glass*, in 1912. Inspired by the innovative writing of U.S. and British-born Imagist poets in *Poetry* magazine, especially the January 1913 issue featuring the free verse of H. D., Lowell traveled to England. There she met Ezra Pound and other Imagists—D. H. Lawrence and Robert Frost among them—and formed lasting professional and personal bonds. She contributed to the anthology *Des Imagistes* (1914) and began to edit volumes of Imagist poetry and criticism, one of which was the anthology *Some Imagist Poets* (1915–1917). When she clashed with Pound, who was usually credited as the movement's founder, over definitions of the style, he renamed the movement Amygism. A celebrity known for her massive bearing and eccentric lifestyle (she smoked cigarillos and maintained a long-term romantic and collaborative relationship with Ada Dwyer Russell), she continued to write, lecture, review, and champion the cause of poetry until her death by cerebral hemorrhage at fifty-one. Her posthumously published volume of poems include *What's O'Clock*, which received the 1926 Pulitzer Prize, *East Wing* (1926), *Ballads for Sale* (1927), and *The Complete Poetical Works* (1955).

WALTER LOWENFELS (1897–1976) was born in New York City. An heir to his father's successful butter business, later known as the Hotel Bar Butter Co., he worked there from 1914 to 1926, when he left for Paris. After World War I he began writing poetry, publishing his first collection, *Episodes and Epistles*, in 1925. During the 1920s and 1930s he became part of the Paris avant-garde. Friends with the writers Henry Miller and Anaïs Nin, he supported himself by selling real estate to clients Tristan Tzara, Marc Chagall, and Archibald MacLeish. He later established Carrefour Press, which printed anonymous works. Other poetry volumes include *Finale of Seem* (1929), a long poem, *Apollinaire an Elegy* (1930), and *Elegy in the Manner of a Requiem in Memory of D. H. Lawrence* (1932). He returned to the United States in the late 1930s, where he worked full-time as an organizer for the Communist Party and as an editor at their newspaper, *The Daily Worker*. In 1953 he was jailed under the Smith Act on charges of conspiring to overthrow the United States government, but was acquitted because the only basis of the charges was his membership in the Communist Party. Besides writing more than twelve books of poetry, he expressed his political and artistic radicalism in the prose works *To an Imaginary Daughter* (1964) and *The Revolution Is to Be Human* (1973), and by editing anthologies made up of an avant-garde group that included African-American poets and poetry from "America's Third World." Among them are *Where Is Vietnam?* (Anchor Books, 1967), which features 87 poets who express their opposition to the Vietnam War; *Found Poems* (1972); *In the Time of Revolution* (1969), a volume of protest poetry; *From the Belly of the Shark* (1973); and *For Neruda, for Chile* (1975). Lowenfels died in Tarrytown, New York. His poetry was published posthumously in *Reality Prime: Selected Poems*.

HAKI R. MADHUBUTI (b. 1942) was born Don L. Lee in Little Rock, Arkansas, and his early writing appears under this name. Raised in Detroit and a long-time resident of Chicago, he is a community activist. He furthers educational reforms and the teaching of poetry as cofounder and director of the Institute of Positive Education (1969); he is also a professor of English at Chicago State University, and the founder and director emeritus of the Gwendolyn Brooks Center, which is housed at the university. In 1967 he founded Third World Press, and he was awarded the 1991 Editor/Publisher Award by the Before Columbus Foundation for his numerous publications of nonfiction, fiction, poetry, and plays by African, African-diaspora, and African-American writers. He sold his first poetry on single sheets, distributing them in the African-American community at local gathering spots like beauty parlors and barbershops. His early volumes of poetry include *Think Black* (1967), *Black Pride* (1968), *Don't Cry, SCREAM* (1969, 1992), and the collection *Directionscore: Selected and New Poems* (1971). His essays include Dynamite Voices I: Black Poets of the 1960s (1971) and Tough Notes: A Healing Call for Creating Exceptional Black Men (2002). Anthologies he editied include *Say that the River Turns: The Impact of Gwendolyn Brooks* and *Confusion by Any Other Name: Essays Exploring the Negative Impact of "The Blackman's Guide to Understanding the Black Woman."*

SUSAN MARSHALL has worked as a writer, teacher, editor, interviewer, and filmmaker. She made her first films at the University of Iowa, and she has also studied at the Michener Center for Writers at the University of Texas. Marshall participated in a writing workshop at the Atlantic Center for the Arts in New Smyrna Beach, Florida, where she was an associate artist during Ishmael Reed's summer 2002 residency.

ANGELA MARTIN participated in Ishmael Reed's fall 1999 poetry workshop at the University of California at Berkeley.

COLLEEN J. McELROY (b. 1936) is a poet, essayist, and short-story writer who was born in St. Louis. Her poetry collections are *The Mules Done Long Since Gone* (1976); *Queen of the Ebony Isles* (Wesleyan University Press, 1984), for which she received the1985 American Book Award; *Bone Flames* (1987); and *What Madness Brought Me Here: New and Selected Poems, 1968–1988* (1990). She collaborated with Ishmael Reed on the libretto to the opera *The Wild Gardens of the Loup Garou*, which premiered in 1982 with music composed by Carman Moore. Her short-story collections are *Jesus and Fat Tuesday* (1987) and *Driving under the Cardboard Pines* (1990). She is a professor of English at the University of Washington in Seattle.

CLAUDE McKAY (1889–1948) was the youngest of eleven children of a peasant farmer in Jamaica, West Indies. His first poetry books, *Songs of Jamaica* and *Constab Ballads*, were awarded prizes after they were published in 1912 in Jamaica, the same year he immigrated to the United States to attend Tuskegee Institute. After a few months, he left to study at the Agricultural College of Kansas, intending to return to Jamaica with skills in scientific farming. But literature proved to be a greater draw, so he moved to New York City, where he lived from 1914 to 1919. He then traveled to Europe, where he remained until 1934, living for some time in the Soviet Union. His sonnet "If We Must Die" was first published in 1919 in Max Eastman's magazine, *The Liberator*. Written in response to the tide of race riots and anti-Communist demonstrations known as the Red Summer, it became a "symbol of the New Negro and the Harlem Renaissance," according to M. B. Tolson. Although McKay was considered a political radical, his sonnet was used as a call to arms during World War II after Winston Churchill read it in the House of Commons. Other poetry collections published during his lifetime are *Spring in New Hampshire* (1920) and *Harlem Shadows* (1922). McKay also worked to assemble the posthumously published *Selected Poems of Claude McKay* (Harcourt, Brace & World, 1953). *The Passion of Claude McKay* (1973) includes selected poetry and prose from 1912 to 1948. He also wrote an autobiography, published in 1937; a short-story collection; and three novels, including the 1928 best-seller *Home to Harlem*.

SANDRA McPHERSON, a native Californian, makes her home in the northern part of the state, teaching in the English Department of the University of California at Davis. Widely published in literary journals and magazines, she has published nine poetry chapbooks, and poetry collections including *The Year of Our Birth* (1978), which received a National Book Award nomination, *The God of Indeterminacy* (1993), *The Spaces Between Birds* (1996), and *The Edge Effect* (1996). McPherson has also published three books on outsider art, and for her most recent collection, *A Visit to Civilization* (Wesleyan University Press, 2002), she researched nineteenth- and twentieth-century "extinct objects," such as postcards, quilts, utilitarian wooden objects, and unpublished diaries of "unfamous" people.

NANCY MERCADO (b. 1959), born of Puerto Rican parents in Atlantic City, New Jersey, came into prominence in 1980 after reading at the Nuyorican Poets Cafe in New York City. She is the author of *It Concerns the Madness* (Long Shot Productions, 2000). Her work has been anthologized in *Poetry After 9/11: An Anthology of New York Poets* (Melville House Publishers, 2002); *Role Call: A Generational Anthology of Social and Political Black Literature and Art* (Third World Press, 2001); *Bum Rush the Page: A Def Poetry Jam* (Crown Publishing, 2001); *Identity Lessons: Contemporary Writing About Learning to Be American* (Viking Penguin, 1999); *Changer L'Amérique Anthologie de la Poésie Protestataire des USA* (Maison De La Poésie); *In Defense of Mumia* (Writers and Readers Press, 1996); and *ALOUD: Voices from the Nuyorican Poets Cafe* (Henry Holt, 1994). An editor for *Long Shot*, a literary and arts publication, she is currently pursuing a doctoral degree.

JOSEPHINE MILES (1911–1985) was born in Chicago and grew up in Southern California. She began writing as a child and was first published in *St. Nicholas*, a children's magazine. During her youth she became severely disabled by rheumatoid arthritis, and she learned to navigate her way around by wheelchair. A member of the English department at the University of California, Berkeley from 1938 to 1978, she, for many years, was the only tenured woman in the English department. After her retirement as professor emerita, *The Berkeley Poetry Review* dedicated a special issue to her and her work. Her first book of poetry, *Trial Balances* (1935), was followed by nine other volumes, among them *Lines at Intersection* (1939), *Civil Poems* (1966), *Coming to Terms* (1979), and *Collected Poems 1930–1983* (1983), which won the Lenore Marshall *Nation* Poetry Prize. She also published many works of literary criticism, including *The*

Continuity of Poetic Language: Studies in English Poetry from the 1540s to the 1940s (1951) and *Style and Proportion: The Language of Prose and Poetry* (1967). She received a Lifetime Achievement Award in 1984 from the Before Columbus Foundation.

MARIANNE MOORE (1887–1972) was born near St. Louis, in Kirkwood, Missouri. Her mother took her and her brother to live in Carlisle, Pennsylvania, in 1894 after they were abandoned by her father. She visited England in 1911 and returned to teach at the U.S. Industrial Indian School in Carlisle for three years. Around 1915 she moved to Greenwich Village, and then later to Brooklyn to be near her brother, who became a Presbyterian minister. She lived quietly with her mother for most of her life, often earning her living with part-time jobs as a secretary or librarian, and later teaching at Vassar College. During this time she managed to connect with major figures in the artistic avant-garde, and became in her later years one of the country's most recognized and read writers, an eccentric who wore her signature three-cornered hat even to her beloved baseball games. In 1915 Monroe published five poems in Poetry. Her first volume of poetry, Poems (1921), was followed by Observations (1924), which won a Dial award, given by an influential literary magazine of the same name, where she served as editor from 1925 to 1929. Other volumes include Selected Poems (1935), Pangolin and Other Verse (1936), What Are Years? (1941), O to Be a Dragon (1959), and Tell Me, Tell Me (1966). She received a 1951 Pulitzer Prize for her Collected Poems and also received a 1953 Bollingen Prize. In 1954 she translated *The Fables of La Fontaine,* soon followed by Predilections (1955), a collection of her critical essays on such writers and artists as poet Ezra Pound, who admired her work; the dancer Anna Pavlova, and the poet Louise Bogan.

MURSALATA MUHAMMAD is a native of Detroit, Michigan. She is currently a faculty member at Grand Rapids Community College in Michigan. Her writing is influenced by the impromptu jazz jam sessions she remembers from her childhood and the necessary flow of rhymes made in the neighborhoods she lived in. Muhammad was an associate artist in Ishmael Reed's summer 2002 writing workshop at the Atlantic Center for the Arts in New Smyrna Beach, Florida.

WILLIAM OANDASAN (b. 1984) A member of the Ukomno'm, known more popularly as the Yuki, from the Round Valley Reservation on the northern California coast, Oandasan is one of less than eighty remaining descendants of the tribe that arrived in California ten thousand years ago. That same tribe may well have been the first people in California, according to Oandasan and Wendy Rose, who wrote the introduction to his poetry collection *Round Valley Songs* (West End Press, 1984). He is also a tribal historian, author of *A Branch of California Redwood, Sermon & Three Waves,* and *Moving Inland.* He taught at various colleges and universities in California, New Orleans, and Chicago, and was senior editor of the *American Indian Culture and Research Journal* and editor of his own publication, *A, a journal of contemporary literature,* which featured many Native American writers.

HILTON OBENZINGER (b. 1947) who was born in Brooklyn and raised in Queens, currently teaches writing and American literature at Stanford University and San Francisco State University. His poetry collections are *This Passover or the Next I Will Never Be in Jerusalem* (Momo's Press, 1980), winner of the 1982 American Book Award; *New York on Fire* (Real Comet Press, 1989); *Cannibal Eliot and the Lost Histories of San Francisco* (Mercury House, 1993), a novel; and a nonfiction study of two "infidel texts": *American Palestine: Melville, Twain, and the Holy Land Mania* (Princeton University Press, 1999).

CHARLES OLSON (1910–1970) was born to a Swedish father and Irish-American mother and grew up in the fishing town of Gloucester, Massachusetts. After the death of Franklin D. Roosevelt in 1945, he ended his career in politically appointed jobs and turned to writing full-time, first publishing *Call Me Ishmael* (1947), a study of Melville's novel, *Moby Dick.* In the late 1940s he started writing poetry, publishing a series of volumes called *The Maximus Poems* (1950–75), and two other collections, *In Cold Hell, in Thicket* (1953) and *The Distances* (1960). Considered a major theoretician of American writing for his essays "Projective Verse" and "Human Universe" Olson worked as an instructor between 1951 and 1956, and he later succeeded painter Josef Albers as rector of Black Mountain College in North Carolina, a school known for incubating many post–World War II developments in the arts. He also taught at the State University of New York, Buffalo, before returning to Gloucester to concentrate on *The Maximus Poems.* George Butterick edited the complete edition in 1983, and he later edited *The Collected Poems of Charles Olson* (Berkeley, 1987), which received the 1988 American Book Award.

ALICIA SUSKIN OSTRIKER (b. 1937) is a poet and critic who was born in New York City. She was educated at Brandeis University and the University of Wisconsin, where she received her Ph.D. in 1964. Ostriker is the author of several books of poetry, beginning with *Songs* (1969) and including *Imaginary Lover* (1986), the winner of the William Carlos Williams Award of the Poetry Society of America, and *The Crack in Everything* (1996), a National Book Award finalist and winner of the Paterson Poetry Award and the San Francisco State Poetry Center Award. Her most recent volume is *The Volcano Sequence* (Pitt Poetry Series, 2002). Besides *Stealing the Language: The Emergence of Women's Poetry in America* (1986), her books of literary criticism include *Feminist Revision and the Bible* (Blackwell, 1993), *The Nakedness of the Fathers: Biblical Visions and Revisions* (Rutgers, 1994), and *Dancing at the Devil's Party: Essays on Poetry, Politics and the Erotic*. She lives in Princeton, New Jersey, with her husband Jeremiah, an astrophysicist, and teaches English and creative writing at Rutgers University.

J. CODY PETERSON participated in a poetry workshop taught by Ishmael Reed at the University of California at Berkeley in the 1990s.

SYLVIA PLATH (1932–1963) was born in Boston. In her junior year at Smith College, she succumbed to depression, suffering a nervous breakdown, and attempting suicide. After six months of intensive therapy, she recovered and graduated summa cum laude. She married the British poet Ted Hughes, whom she met while studying at Cambridge University on a Fulbright scholarship from 1955 to 1957. Her book of poems *The Colossus and Other Poems* (Alfred Knopf, 1960) was the first and only collection published before her suicide at the age of thirty in 1963. Her posthumously published collections are *Ariel* (1965), *Crossing the Water* (1971), *Winter Trees* (1972), and *Selected Poems* (1985), which Hughes edited. *The Collected Poems* (1981) was awarded the 1982 Pulitzer Prize.

N. H. PRITCHARD (NORMAN) (b. 1939), who was born in New York City, was a poet, art history scholar, and teacher. He was a member of the Umbra Poetry Workshop on the Lower East Side in the early 1960s, and some of his earliest work appeared in *Umbra* magazine, the *East Village Other*, *Liberator*, *Poetry Northwest*, and *Eye Magazine*. He was an early practitioner of styles that later were called concrete poetry and performance poetry. His first volume of poetry was *The Matrix, Poems: 1960–1970* (Doubleday, 1970); the second *Eecchhooeess* (1971). He can be heard reading his poems on the record albums *Destinations: Four Contemporary*

American Poets and New Jazz Poets. He taught at the New School for Social Research and Friends Seminary.

NAOMI QUIÑONEZ was born and raised in Los Angeles. Her first book of poetry was *Hummingbird Dream* (West End Press) and she is widely published in anthologies and literary journals. She coedited *Invocation L.A.: Urban Multicultural Poetry* (West End Press), winner of a 1990 American Book Award. Quinonez teaches Chicano Studies at the California State University in Fullerton.

SPECKLED RED (RUFUS PERRYMAN) (1892–1973) was born in Monroe, Louisiana, and as a child lived in Detroit, Hampton, and Atlanta. Part of the second generation of bluesmen who migrated to urban areas in the late 1920s, he first made his name in Memphis and St. Louis, where he scraped together a living as a singer and pianist in jook (or juke) joints, black dance halls, after-hours clubs, blues bars, and rib shacks. It was in such venues that black musicians developed classic music styles such as boogie-woogie, barrelhouse blues, fast blues, slows blues, and jazz that moved from regional recording studios to musical centers like New Orleans, Chicago, and Memphis. In 1929 he had his first recording session and when one song, "The Dirty Dozens," became a jukebox hit that year, he recorded a sequel in 1930, "The Dirty Dozens, No. 2," which did not repeat the success of the first release. He traveled around the country during the 1930s and returned to St. Louis around 1941, playing off and on in local bars and clubs and working as a shipping clerk. He was rediscovered in 1954, and in 1956 he toured the United States and Europe. He also recorded new versions of his first hit on the Tone and Folkways labels, along with his other early hits, "Right String Baby but the Wrong Yo-Yo" and "If You've Ever Been Down." He continued to perform throughout the rest of the 1960s.

EUGENE B. REDMOND (b. 1937) is a poet, playwright, teacher, editor, journalist, and community activist who was born and raised in St. Louis. In 1968 he published his first book of poetry, *A Tale of Two Toms, or Tom-Tom (Uncle Toms of East St. Louis and St. Louis)*. Other poetry volumes include *Sentry of the Four Golden Pillars* (1970) and *The Eye on the Ceiling* (Harlem River Press, 1991), which won a 1991 American Book Award. He is a cofounder of the Black Writers Press with Henry Dumas and Sherman Fowler. In 1976 he was appointed poet laureate of East St. Louis, becoming the first poet to receive that honor from a municipality. He has continued to play an active role in the community, advancing literacy by bringing writers into public schools and organizing events that encourage reading, writing, and awareness of how the media reports on current events. He is also editor of the multicultural literary journal *Drumvoices Review*, which features the work of young writers, and is a professor at Southern Illinois University. In 1993 he won a Pyramid Award from the Pan-African Movement USA for his lifetime contributions to Pan-Africanism through poetry.

JOHN REED (1887–1920) was born in Portland, Oregon. After graduating from Harvard University, he moved to New York City, where within the next year he became editor of *The Masses*, a radical magazine covering art, politics, and culture. Also a journalist and poet, he published his poetry in the chapbooks *Sangar* (1912) and *The Day in Bohemia* (1913). He became legendary, especially through his exploits as a foreign correspondent. Reed accompanied Pancho Villa and his troops in Mexico (*Insurgent Mexico*, 1914), experienced World War I firsthand in Greece, Serbia, Romania, and Russia (*The War in Eastern Europe*, 1916), and in 1917 traveled to Russia, where he was witness to the Bolshevik Revolution (*Ten Days That Shook the World*, 1919). He cofounded the Communist Labor Party, the American wing of the Communist Party, and was editor of their journal, *Voice of Labor*. After traveling to Russia to attend the Second Congress of the Communist International, he contracted typhus and died in Moscow, and was later buried in the Kremlin.

TENNESSEE REED (b. 1977) was born and raised in Oakland. She started writing poetry at the age of five, and published her first poetry collection, *Circus in the Sky* (I. Reed Books, 1988), at the age of eleven. Her next two collections, *Electric Chocolate* (1990) and *Airborne* (1996), were published by Ravens Bone Press. She has read her work on the East and West coasts of the United States, as well as in Alaska, Hawaii, Germany, the Netherlands, and Japan. All three of her collections have been used to help inspire children to read and write poetry. In 2003 her *New and Collected Poems* (Creative Arts Press) will appear. The composer Meredith Monk set one of her poems, "Three Heavens and Hells," to music. It premiered in Oakland at the 1992 Bay Area Dance Series as a performance work by the Children's Troupe of Roberts and Blank. It was later recorded on *Volcano Songs* (ECM, 1997). Composer Carman Moore set her poem "Old Parents Blues" to music for the same event.

ALBERTO ALVARO RIOS (b. 1952) was born in Nogales, Arizona, to a

Mexican father and an English mother. A writer of poetry, essays, and short stories, he received the 1982 Walt Whitman Prize in Poetry for his first poetry collection, *Whispering to Fool the Wind* (1982). Sheep Meadow Press has also published his other poetry collections, which include *Five Indiscretions* (1985), *The Lime Orchard Woman* (1988), and *Teodora Luna's Two Kisses* (1992). *Capirotada: A Nogales Memoir* was published by University of New Mexico Press in 1999. A founder and currently director of the creative writing program at Arizona State University, he has taught there since 1980. Other honors include four Pushcart Prizes and the Western States Book Award for Fiction.

LUIS J. RODRÌGUEZ (b. 1954) was born in El Paso, Texas. He grew up in the Los Angeles neighborhoods of Watts and East L.A., where he joined a gang when he was eleven. By the time he was eighteen, he had lost twenty-five of his friends to gang violence, a story he recounts in his memoir, *Always Running: La Vida Loca—Gang Life in L.A.* (Curbstone Press, 1993). Now an author of journalism, criticism, short stories, and children's books, Rodriguez has also published several poetry collections, including *Poems Across the Pavement* (Tia Chucha Press, 1989), which won the 1989 Poetry Center Book Award; *The Concrete River* (Curbstone Press, 1991), which won the 1991 PEN West/Josephine Miles Literary Award; *Trochemoche* (Curbstone Press, 1998); and *My Name's Not Rodriguez*, a CD of original music and poetry (Dos Manos/Rock A Mole Music, 2002). An activist who works within many communities—among them the homeless, prisoners, and street gangs—he now works as a peacemaker with gangs in Los Angeles and Chicago, his present home. He also serves as publisher and editor of Tia Chucha Press, which publishes young socially conscious poets.

WENDY ROSE (b. 1948) was born in Oakland of mixed lineage. Her mother's family lines trace from both the Miwok and English and Irish miners and ranchers in California, and her father was Hopi. She grew up in Indian communities in the Bay Area, dropped out of high school, and joined the world of San Francisco's bohemia. In 1958 she became involved in "Indian Movement" events, including the occupation of Alcatraz Island. She is author of more than a dozen books of poetry, including *Hopi Roadrunner Dancing* (Greenfield Review Press, 1973), *Academic Squaw: Reports to the World from the Ivory Tower* (1977), *Lost Copper* (Malki Museum Press, 1980), *What Happened When the Hopi Hit New York* (1982), *The Halfbreed Chronicles & Other Poems* (West End Press, 1985), *Going to War with All My Relations* (1993), and *Bone Dance, New and Selected Poems, 1965–1993* (University of Arizona, 1994). She has been nominated for two Pulitzer

Prizes and been appointed to the Women's Literature Project of Oxford University Press, the Smithsonian Native Writers' Series, and the Modern Language Association Commission on Languages and Literature of the Americas. An anthropologist who has served as a facilitator for the Association of Non-Federally Recognized California Tribes, Rose has been a coordinator and instructor for the American Indian studies program at Fresno City College in Fresno, California, since 1984.

CORY ROSEN was a student in the spring 2001 poetry class taught by Ishmael Reed at the University of California, Berkeley.

MURIEL RUKEYSER (1913–1980) was born into a wealthy Jewish family and lived in New York City for most of her life. A translator and a writer of poetry, biographies, a novel, a play, and children's books, she began publishing her verse while still in college. While attending Vassar College with fellow students Elizabeth Bishop and Mary McCarthy, she founded a literary magazine as an alternative to the entrenched *Vassar Review*. Her first of nineteen collections of poetry, *Theory of Flight* (Yale Series of Younger Poets, 1935) was followed by *Mediterranean* (1938), *The Soul and Body of John Brown* (1940), *Wake Island* (1942), *Beast in View* (1944), and *The Green Wave* (1948). A break in her books coincides with the birth of her son and her responsibilities as a single mother. Her writing resumed with *Body of Waking* (1958), *The Outer Banks* (1967), *The Speed of Darkness* (1968), *Breaking Open* (1973), and *The Gates* (1976). In 1978 she published her last book, *Collected Poems of Muriel Rukeyser*. She filled her poetry with her experiences as a witness and participant in important radical causes, saying that "themes and the use I have made of them have depended on my life as a poet, a woman, as an American, and as a Jew." She left college in 1933 to report on the Scottsboro case in Alabama, and the next year went to Spain as a journalist and in support of the Spanish Republic's attempt to overthrow the fascist government of General Franco. In the 1960s she traveled to Hanoi to protest United States. military involvement, and to South Korea to support the cause of a political prisoner. She was a dedicated professor of literature, teaching for many years at Sarah Lawrence College, and she helped develop display concepts that encouraged collaborations between artists and scientists, making San Francisco's Exploratorium a model for science museums across the country.

BRYNN NOELLE SAITO was a student in the 43B poetry class taught by Ishmael Reed at the University of California, Berkeley.

CARL SANDBURG (1878–1967) was born in Galesburg, Illinois, into a family of Swedish descent. Sandburg's first poetry, *Reckless Ecstasy* (1904), was published in a pamphlet. Around 1912, he moved to Chicago, where Harriet Monroe published his poetry in her new and influential journal, *Poetry: A Magazine of Verse*. This linked him to the Imagists' free verse style that the magazine was promoting and brought him into the folds of the Chicago literary renaissance, along with Sherwood Anderson, Theodore Dreiser, Ben Hecht, and Edgar Lee Master. He received his second Pulitzer Prize for his collection of more than 800 pieces in *Complete Poems* (1950), which was revised and expanded in 1969. It included his first published collection, *Chicago Poems* (1916) in addition to *Cornhuskers* (1918), *Smoke and Steel* (1920), *Slabs of the Sunburnt West* (1922), *Good Morning, America* (1928), *The People, Yes* (1936), and other poems that had never been published in book form. The last poetry volumes published during his lifetime were *Harvest Poems, 1910–1960* (1960) and *Honey and Salt* (1963).

EDWARD SANDERS (b. 1939) was born in Kansas City, Missouri, and hitchhiked to New York City's Greenwich Village in 1958. He first became known through reading Beat poetry and his own poetry at antiwar gatherings in the 1960s, and through his publication in 1962 of an avant-garde journal, *Fuck You: A Magazine of the Arts*. A militant peace-and-love activist, he opened the Peace Eye Bookstore in a storefront on the Lower East Side in 1964, and in 1965 he formed the Fugs, a satirical folk-rock band that sang about sex, drugs, and politics, participating in anti–Vietnam War demonstrations across the country. His poetry publications include *Poem from Jail* (1963), *Investigative Poetry (1975), 20,000 A.D.* (North Atlantic Books, 1976), *Chechov* (1995), and *1968: A History in Verse* (1997). His book *Thirsting for Peace in a Raging Century: Selected Poems 1961–1985* (Coffee House Press, 1987) won a 1998 American Book Award. Sanders has also written song lyrics, a three-volume novel, *Tales of Beatnik Glory, Volumes 1 & 2* (1990, with a third volume recently completed), short stories, and a nonfiction profile of the Manson family, *The Family* (1971).

LESLIE SCALAPINO, a poet, essayist, playwright and novelist, has numerous credits to her name. North Point Press published three of her poetry volumes: *Considering how exaggerated music is* (1982), *that they were at the beach—aeolotropic series* (1985), and *Way* (1988), winner of both a 1989 American Book Award from the Before Columbus Foundation and the San Francisco Poetry Center Award. Wesleyan published two other poetry collections: *The Front Matter, Dead Souls* (1996), *New Time* (1999), and *The Public World / Syntactically Impermanence* (1999), a collection of essays, poetry, and a play. She lives in the East Bay of the Bay Area, in Oakland.

DELMORE SCHWARTZ (1913–1966) was born in Brooklyn, New York, of parents who had emigrated from Romania. A promising career in philosophy at Harvard was cut short when he was denied a graduate fellowship, and he then turned to a literary career. His first published poems appeared in 1937 in the pages of *Partisan Review* (where he was poetry editor from 1943–47) and *The New Republic* (where he was poetry editor from 1955–57) and were published in a collection with his fiction and drama, *In Dreams Begin Responsibilities* (1937). He translated Rimbaud's *A Season in Hell*, published a verse play, *Shenandoah* (1941), and a long poem, *Genesis: Book One* (1943). Among his ten poetry collections are *Vaudeville for a Princess* (1950) and *Summer Knowledge: New and Selected Poems, 1938–1958* (1959), with later poems appearing in a posthumously published collection, *The Last and Lost Poems of Delmore Schwartz* (1979). In 1960 he was awarded the Bollingen Prize in Poetry. He was a visiting lecturer at various distinguished American universities between 1946 and 1966, when he left his post at Syracuse University because of his worsening mental and emotional state, evidenced by insomnia, paranoia, and withdrawal. He lived alternately in mental hospitals and hotels until his death from a heart attack in a hotel elevator.

JOAN SELF was a member of Ishmael Reed's poetry writing class at the University of California, Berkeley in fall 1998.

ANNE SEXTON (1928–1974) was born in Newton, Massachusetts, into an upper-middle-class family whose abuse marked the rest of her life. Sexton's first collection of poetry, *To Bedlam and Part Way Back* (1960), was rapidly followed by *All My Pretty Ones* (1962), which was nominated for a National Book Award; *Live or Die* (1966), a 1967 Pulitzer Prize winner; *Love Poems* (1969); *Transformations* (1971); *The Book of Folly* (1972); and *The Death Notebooks* (1974). *The Awful Rowing Toward God* (1975) and *Complete Poems* (1981) were published by her daughter after Sexton committed suicide by carbon monoxide poisoning in 1974.

CHARLES SIMIC (b. 1938), a poet, essayist, translator, and teacher who was born in Belgrade, Yugoslavia, came in 1953 along his mother and brother to join his father in the United States. Until 1958 his family lived in the Chicago area. He published his first poem at the age of twenty-one, in 1959. In 1961 he was drafted into the army. His first collection of poems, *What the Grass Says*, was published in 1966, a year after he graduated from New York University, and he has produced more than sixty books since that time. They include *Unending Blues* (1986); *The World Doesn't End: Prose Poems* (1990), which was awarded the Pulitzer Prize for Poetry; *Walking the Black Cat* (Harcourt Brace, 1966), a finalist for the National Book Award in Poetry; and *Jackstraws* (Harcourt Brace, 1999), which the *New York Times* named Notable Book of the Year. Elected as a chancellor of the Academy of American Poets in 2000, he is also the recipient of Guggenheim and MacArthur Foundation fellowships. He teaches American literature and creative writing at the University of New Hampshire in Durham, where he has lived since 1973.

SUSIE SILOOK is a St. Lawrence Island Yupik and Inupiaq native from Gambell, Alaska, a town of 650 people. Her mother was an Inupiaq-Irish orphan sent to St. Lawrence Island with other orphans during a diphtheria epidemic in the late 1930s, and her father, who has written stories about his life and work, was mayor of Gambol and the first chairman of the Alaska Eskimo Whaling Commission. Besides writing poetry, most of which appeared in the journal *Alaska Native Writers, Storytellers and Orators*, Silook carves sculptures from wood and walrus ivory and bone, a reflection of Gambel's hunting and gathering, subsistence-based economy. A recipient of the 2000 Governor's Award, Silook lives in Anchorage, where she is a grant writer for Gambel's tribal government.

BESSIE SMITH (1894?-1937) was born in Chattanooga, Tennessee. As one of seven children in an impoverished family, she began performing on street corners a year before she was orphaned, at nine years of age. As a teenager she became a singer and dancer in Will Rainey's Rabbit Foot Minstrels, a traveling vaudeville show where Gertrude "Ma" Rainey (known as Mother of the Blues) became her mentor. She continued performing and touring in tent shows and honky-tonks, and as part of the Theater Owners Booking Association circuit. It was not until 1923, when she was already in her thirties, that she was invited to record her first song, "Down Hearted Blues," for Columbia Records in their New York City studios. The record was an instant hit and sold almost 800,000 copies in the first six months after its release. It established her as a star of the black recording market and rescued the record company from bankruptcy. In 1924, she sang "Mistreatin' Papa" and "Chicago Bound" on her first radio broadcast, and in 1929 she made her only film appearance in a black-and-white short, *St. Louis Blues.* She performed standards and popular songs in addition to blues classics such as "Taint Nobody's Bizness If I Do," "Gin House Blues," and "Nobody Knows You when You're Down and Out." In the 1920s she hit her peak, becoming the highest paid black performer of her day. She received $2,000 to $3,000 a week, although she was only paid a flat fee for recording sessions and received no royalties. Smith wrote thirty-three of her own blues lyrics and compositions, including "Cake Walking Babies from Home," "Reckless Blues," "Dixie Flyer Blues," "Standin' in the Rain Blues," "Baby Doll," "Lonesome Desert Blues," "Poor Man's Blues," "Preachin' the Blues," "Long Old Road," "Young Woman Blues," and "Back Water Blues." She made a total of 160 recordings, accompanied by major jazz musicians, including Louis Armstrong, Sidney Bechet, Fletcher Henderson, Clarence Williams, Benny Goodman, and her favorite musicians, Joe Smith (trumpet) and Charlie Green (trombone). The Great Depression proved a hard time for both her career and the blues. Her last recording session was in 1933, for John Hammond on Okeh Records. She died from severe injuries received in an automobile accident near Clarksdale, Mississippi, where she had been performing. A continuing influence on succeeding generations of vocalists, Smith was inducted into the Rock and Roll Hall of Fame in 1989.

CATHY SONG (b. 1955) was born in Honolulu. Her mother's ancestry is Chinese and her father's is Korean. She is widely anthologized and has published four collections of poetry: *Picture Bride* (1983), winner of the 1982 Yale's Series of Younger Poets Award; *Frameless Windows, Squares of Light* (1988); *School Figures* (1994); and *The Land of Bliss* (2001). She has taught creative writing at various universities on the mainland and maintains a home in Honolulu with her husband and three children.

FRANK STANFORD (1948–1978) was born in southeast Mississippi. At the age of one he was adopted by Dorothy Alter, a single woman who was Firestone's first female manager. In 1952 she married A. F. Stanford, and because of his contracting work, the family moved around Tennessee and Arkansas, where Stanford lived most of his life, except for a spell in New York City. He also traveled with his publisher, Irving Broughton, making documentary films of poets and a short film on his own life. He began writing poetry as a child, and his first published poetry collection, *The*

Singing Knives (1971, Mill Mountain Press; 1979 Lost Roads, 1979) included poems written from 1964. He published nine collections of poetry, including the ten-thousand line poem *The Battlefield where the Moon Says I Love You* (Mill Mountain/Lost Roads,1977; Lost Roads, 2000). He founded Lost Roads Publishers in Fayetteville, Arkansas, where he shot himself to death in 1978. The inscription on his tombstone reads "It Wasn't a Dream It Was a Flood."

GERTRUDE STEIN (1874–1946) was the youngest of five surviving children born in Allegheny, Pennsylvania. Her parents were of German Jewish ancestry and moved the family to Vienna and Paris for a few years when she was young, later settling in Oakland in 1880. In 1904 she dropped out of medical school (she had been planning a career in psychology) and emigrated to Paris, where her brother Leo was living. They became patrons of modernist painters, gathering an amazing collection of art by Cezanne, Matisse, Picasso, and Braque, among others, and established a Saturday salon that was attended by expatriate Americans and the international avant-garde. Her first published stories, *Three Lives* (1909), was followed by other experiments in poetry, fiction, and dramatic forms. Her most famous works were *Autobiography of Alice B. Toklas* (1933) and the opera *Four Saints in Three Acts* (1927), a collaboration with composer Virgil Thomson, which toured the United States and England. Stein remained in France during World War II with her lifelong companion Alice B. Toklas, leaving Paris for a summer home in a small village, where they lived without harassment by either the Germans or the Vichy French government. They returned to Paris after the war, opening their apartment to American GIs. In 1946 she completed her last opera, *The Mother of Us All.*

MIKE STOLLER (b. 1933) Born the same year as his longtime songwriting partner and friend, Jerry Leiber, Stoller was a jazz pianist based in Los Angeles when the two met in 1950, at the age of seventeen. Together they created some of the most enduring great rock and roll hits, which were recorded by rhythm and blues stars including Jimmy Witherspoon, Little Esther, Charles Brown, Linda Hopkins, Ray Charles, and Willie Mae "Big Mama" Thornton. Their songs include "Kansas City" by Wilbert Harrison, "Black Denim Trousers and Motorcycle Boots" by the Cheers, and more than twenty songs recorded by Elvis Presley. (Please see the entry on Jerry Leiber for more information.)

PHILLINA SUN was a student in the spring 1997 poetry class taught by Ishmael Reed at the University of California, Berkeley.

MAY SWENSON (1919–1989), who was born in Logan, Utah, was the daughter of Swedish immigrants. She held various jobs, such as newspaper reporter, ghostwriter, editor, secretary, manuscript reader for New Directions, and writer-in-residence at universities, all the while steadily writing poetry. She published eleven volumes of poetry during her life. *Another Animal* (1954) was her first; others include *A Cage of Spines* (1958), *Poems to Solve* (1966), *Half Sun, Half Sleep* (1967), *The Guess and Spell Coloring Book* (1976), and *In Other Words* (1987). She was recipient of many awards, including Guggenheim, Rockefeller, and MacArthur fellowships and a Bollingen Prize for Poetry. She was appointed a member of the American Academy and Institute of Arts and Letters, and chancellor of the Academy of American Poets. *Nature, Poems Old and New* (Houghton Mifflin, 1993) was published posthumously.

ARTHUR SZE (b. 1950) was born in New York City, a second-generation Chinese-American. His poetry collections include *The Willow Wing Rainbow* (Zenith Press, 1972; revised edition, Tooth of Time Books, 1981); *Archipelago*, which won a 1996 American Book Award; and *The Red-shifting Web: Poems 1970–1988* (Copper Canyon Press, 1998), which was a 1999 Lenore Marshall Poetry Prize finalist. He is currently director of the creative writing program at the Institute for American Indian Art in Santa Fe, New Mexico.

KATHRYN WADDELL TAKARA was born and raised in Tuskegee, Alabama, where her father taught veterinary medicine. She is a performance poet whose travels in Africa, Europe, Central America, Tahiti, and China are reflected in her work. Her poetry and essays have been published in various journals and anthologies, and her *New and Collected Poems* will be published by Ishmael Reed Publishing in 2002. She currently lives on the north shore of Oahu and is an assistant professor at the University of Hawaii at Manoa in the ethnic studies department, where she has developed courses in African-American politics, history, and culture since 1972.

MARY TALLMOUNTAIN, a Koyukon Athabaskan, was born in Nulato, Alaska, a village on the Yukon River close to the Arctic Circle in 1918, and was taken from her village when she was adopted by a non-Native couple after her mother became terminally ill. Although she lived for many years in San Francisco's Tenderloin district and did not return to her village for fifty years, she connected with her native ancestry and homeland through her writing, becoming an active voice in the Native

American literary renaissance, and her work is widely taught in Native American studies programs at U.S. universities and colleges. An activist, she gave readings and taught poetry and journal writing in prisons and community-based arts programs to children and elders in the villages of Alaska and the Bay Area, including reporting to Californians what the new state of Alaska was really like. She also spoke out on various issues, especially native rights and the rights of animals, the homeless, and women. She published nine poetry and short story collections, including *Light on the Tent Wall* (UCLA Press, 1990), *A Quick Brush of Wings* (Freedom Voices, 1991), *There Is No Word For Goodbye*, and the posthumously published collection *Listen to the Night* (Freedom Voices, 1995).

LORENZO THOMAS (b. 1944) was born in the Republic of Panama and attended public schools and universities in the New York City area. During the 1960s he was a member of the Umbra Workshop, a creative hub of young writers in Manhattan's Lower East Side. He is a veteran of the Vietnam War. Working as a poet, essayist, critic, and editor, he has had his writing widely published in journals, anthologies, encyclopedias, and other reference texts. His poetry collections include *A Visible Island* (1967), *Fit Music: California Songs* (1972), *Chances Are Few* (1979), *The Bathers* (I. Reed Books, 1981), *Sound Science* (1992), *Es Gibt Zeugen* (Germany, 1997), and *Magnetic Charms* (Walt Whitman Cultural Arts Center, 2002). He also edited *Extraordinary Measures: Afrocentric Modernism and 20th-Century American Poetry* (University of Alabama, 2000). Currently a resident of Houston, Texas, he is a professor of English at the University of Houston–Downtown and director of the university's Cultural Enrichment Center.

YUMI THOMAS was a student in Ishmael Reed's fall 1998 poetry class at the University of California, Berkeley.

ASKIA M. TOURÉ (b. 1938) was born Rolland Snellings in Raleigh, North Carolina. He actively participated in various artists' communities, moving across the country to further the development of a Black Aesthetics movement. A member of the Umbra Workshop, the group of poets that gathered on the New York City's Lower East Side in the early 1960s and counted Calvin Hernton, Tom Dent, David Henderson, Lorenzo Thomas, and Ishmael Reed among its ranks, he joined Amiri Baraka after he founded the Black Arts Repertory Theater School in 1965, becoming a teacher there. In 1965 and 1966, he served on the editorial boards of *Liberator* and *Black*

Dialogue magazines. In 1967 and 1968, at the request of Sonia Sanchez, he joined her, program chair Nathan Hare, and Amiri Baraka to help create African-American history courses for the nation's first black studies program, located at San Francisco State University. He returned to New York City, becoming a member of John Oliver Killens' writers' workshop at Columbia University from 1971 to 1973. He moved to Atlanta in the 1980s, and was one of the founding organizers of the Nile Valley Conference at Morehouse College, which demonstrated that Kemet (Ancient Egypt) was the beginning of Western civilization and that Egyptian priests, scholars, and artists influenced the leaders of the Greco-Roman world. His first publication, co-authored with Tom Feelings and Matthew Meade in 1963, was *Samory Touré,* a biography of the nineteenth century West African freedom fighter against French colonialism who was the grandfather of Ahmed Sekou Touré, the first president of modern Guinea, it was followed by *JuJu* (Third World Press, 1970) *Songhai* (1973); *From the Pyramids to the Projects: Poems of Genocide and Resistance* (1990), which received a 1989 American Book Award, and *Dawnsong!* (Third World Press, 2000).

JANNIFER TRAIG was a student in 43B, the poetry class taught by Ishmael Reed at the University of California, Berkeley.

ERNESTO TREJO (1950–1991) was born in Fresnillo, Mexico, and raised in Mexicali. He attended universities in California and Iowa and also studied poetry writing in Mexico. Like many contemporary writers, he taught creative writing at various colleges, including California State University, Fullerton. He published many chapbooks, writing in both Spanish and English. *Entering a Life* (Arte Publico Press, 1990) was his first published poetry collection. He also coedited *The Selected Poems of Jaime Sabines*. He died of cancer at the age of forty-one.

QUINCY TROUPE (b. 1943) was born in New York City and raised in St. Louis. He is the son of Quincy Troupe Sr., a great catcher who played in the Negro Baseball League. One of the original members of the Watts Writers Workshop, Troupe published his first poetry collection, *Embryo Poems*, in 1971. Subsequent poetry collections include *Snake-Back Solos: Selected Poems, 1969–1997* (I. Reed Books, 1979), which received an 1980 American Book Award; *Skulls along the River* (I. Reed Books, 1984), *Weather Reports* (1991); and *Choruses* (Coffee House Press, 1999). Widely anthologized, he is winner of the World Heavyweight Champion Poet title, a Peabody Award winner, and a featured poet on the Bill Moyers' PBS series *The Power of the World*. He also served as editor of *Confrontation: A Journal of Third World Literature* and edited three anthologies: *Watts Poets: A Book of New Poetry and Essays* (1968), *Giant Talk: An Anthology of Third World Writing* (1975 with Rainer Schulte), and *James Baldwin: The Legacy* (Simon & Schuster, 1989). *Miles, the Autobiography* (Simon & Schuster, 1989) was written in collaboration with Miles Davis and received a 1990 American Book Award. He currently teaches literature at the University of California, San Diego.

NICK VAN BRUNT was a student in 43B, the poetry class taught by Ishmael Reed at the University of California, Berkeley.

SAMIRA VIJGHEN was a student in 43B, the poetry class taught by Ishmael Reed at the University of California, Berkeley.

JULIA VINOGRAD, an alumna of the graduate writing program at the University of Iowa, is a Berkeley street poet famous for her soap bubble displays and her nearly fifty books of poetry. A permanent resident of Berkeley since 1967, she says she has been "trying to write the autobiography of the street, which keeps changing." Her first book, *Revolution and Other Poems* (Oyez Press, 1969) "cost five dollars, and didn't sell." Her second book, *The Berkeley Bead Game* (Cody's, 1971) "was priced at a dollar. . . . [and] sold 3,500 copies and could have sold 4,000 but my feet gave out." Other titles include *Street Pieces* (Thorp Springs, 1974); *Time and Trouble* (Thorp Springs, May, 1976); *Berkeley Street Cannibals: Selections* (Oyez, Summer 1976); *The Book of Jerusalem* (Bench Press), which won the 1985 American Book Award; and three collections from Zeitgeist Press: *Cannibal Carnival, Poems 1986–1996* (1996), *The Cutting Edge* (1998), and *Ask a Mask* (1999).

MARGARET WALKER (b. 1915) was born in Birmingham, Alabama. While working for the WPA Federal Writers' Project, she began a friendship and collaboration with Richard Wright that she documents in *Richard Wright: A Daemonic Genius* (1988). She earned a Ph.D. from the University of Iowa in 1940. Her first poetry volume, *For My People* (1942), won the 1942 Yale University Younger Poet's Award. It was, according to the *Norton Anthology of African American Literature*, "only the second volume of American poetry published by a black woman for more than two decades." Although it was successful, Walker worked for the next two decades as a social worker, newspaper reporter, and teacher before she published her next volume, *Prophets for a New Day* (1970). It was followed by *October Journey* (1973) and the poetry collection *This Is My Century: New and Collected Poems* (1988). Her other published writing includes the novel *Jubilee* (1966), *How I Wrote "Jubilee,"* (1972) and *A Poetic Equation: Conversations Between Nikki Giovanni and Margaret Walker* (1974).

RONALD WALLACE is a writer of poetry, short stories, and essays who has been teaching poetry and English at the University of Wisconsin-Madison since 1972. He has been a professor, founder, and codirector of the Program in Creative Writing since 1975, and the founder and editor of the University of Wisconsin Press Poetry Series since 1985. Over 600 of his poems have appeared in magazines and anthologies such as *The New Yorker*, *The Paris Review*, *The Nation*, *American Poetry Review*, *Yale Review*, and *Poetry*. His first volume of poetry, *Plums, Stones, Kisses & Hooks* (University of Missouri Press, 1981), was followed by *Tunes for Bears to Dance To* (University of Pittsburgh Press, 1983), *People and Dog in the Sun* (University of Pittsburgh Press, 1987), *The Uses of Adversity* (University of Pittsburgh Press, 1998), and *Long for This World: New & Selected Poems* (University of Pittsburgh Press, forthcoming 2003), among others.

DIANE WAKOSKI (b. 1937) was born in Whittier, California, and has published over fifty collections of poetry, starting with *Coins and Coffins* in 1962. Other works include *The Motorcycle Betrayal Poems* (1971), *Dancing on the Grave of a Son of a Bitch* (1973), *The Fable of the Lion and the Scorpion* (1973), and *Why My Mother Likes Liberace: A Musical Selection* (1985). A four-volume series ("The Archaeology of Movies and Books") was published by Black Sparrow Press as *Argonaut Rose* (1998), *The Emerald City of Las Vegas* (1995), *Jason the Sailor* (1993), and *Medea the Sorceress* (1991). *Emerald Ice: Selected Poems 1962–1987* (1988) won the Poetry Society of America's William Carlos Williams Award. Since 1976, she has resided in East Lansing, Michigan, where she teaches at Michigan State University.

WHITNEY WARD was a student in the fall 1999 poetry class taught by Ishmael Reed at the University of California, Berkeley.

WILLIAM CARLOS WILLIAMS (1883–1963) was born and raised in Rutherford, New Jersey. Spanish was the primary language spoken in his childhood home. His father grew up in the West Indies, emigrating to the

United States from Birmingham, England. His mother was Puerto Rican and of Dutch-Spanish and Basque-Jewish descent. Williams started writing poetry in high school. He managed to maintain two professional careers throughout his adult life, practicing as a medical doctor with a specialty in pediatrics and writing poetry, novels, essays, plays, and an autobiography. He published ten collections of poetry, starting with *Poems* (1909), and including *The Tempers* (1913), *An Early Martyr* (1935), *The Complete Collected Poems* (1938), *Pictures from Brueghel* (1962), and *Paterson* (published in a series between 1946 and 1962), which received the 1950 National Book Award Gold Medal for Poetry. After his death, his other poems were republished as *Collected Poems, Volume I: 1909–1939* (1986) and *The Collected Poems, Volume II, 1939–1962* (1988).

TERENCE WINCH is a poet, short-story writer, and musician. His first poetry collection, *Irish Musicians /American Friends* (Coffee House Press, 1986), received a 1986 American Book Award. His second collection, *The Great Indoors* (1995), won the 1996 Columbia Book Award. *The Light of Other Days*, one of three albums he recorded with Celtic Thunder, won the INDIE Award for Best Celtic Album. He has also published a collection of short stories, *Contenders* (1989).

NELLIE WONG was born and raised in Oakland during the 1940s. The daughter of Chinese immigrants from Taishon, in Guanzhou, China, she was the first child in her family to be born in the United States. Wong recently retired after working as a secretary and administrator for most of her working life, including serving as union delegate to the San Francisco Labor Council. She continues her work as a human rights activist and feminist who works within community-based and international organizations. She has published three volumes of poetry, among them *The Death of Long Steam Lady* (West End Press, 1986) and *Stolen Moments* (1997), and is coeditor of an anthology of political essays, *Voices of Color* (1999). She lives in San Francisco.

SHAWN WONG is author of the novels *Homebase* (Reed & Cannon, 1979; reprinted by Plume/New American Library, 1990), and *American Knees* (Simon & Schuster, 1995; Scribner paperback, 1996). Wong also cowrote the screenplay *American Knees* for Celestial Pictures. He has coedited and edited several anthologies of Asian-American literature, including *Aiiieeeee! An Anthology of Asian American Writers* (Howard University Press, 1974). Wong also coedited *The Big Aiiieeeee! An Anthology of Chinese*

American and Japanese American Literature (Meridian/NAL, 1991) and *Literary Mosaic: Asian American Literature* (HarperCollins, 1995). He is coeditor of the *Before Columbus Foundation Fiction/Poetry Anthology: Selections from the American Book Awards, 1980–1990* (W.W. Norton, 1992), two volumes of contemporary American multicultural poetry and fiction. Wong is currently head of the English department at the University of Washington in Seattle. He is a former president and member of the board of directors of the Before Columbus Foundation.

RICHARD WRIGHT (1908–1960) was born the son of impoverished Mississippi sharecroppers, and he described the hardships of his life growing up in his autobiography, *Black Boy* (1945). After leaving the care of relatives at the age of nineteen and moving to Chicago, he worked at menial jobs and started writing poetry, articles, and reviews for radical publications. He joined the John Reed Club in 1933 and became a member of the Communist Party in 1934 until he broke away in the 1940s. He published a short story collection, *Uncle Tom's Children*, in 1937. He wrote his most acclaimed novel, the best-seller *Native Son* (1945), while on a Guggenheim fellowship in 1940. Wright visited Paris in 1946 and took up permanent residency there with his wife and daughter in 1947 before settling in London in 1959. Other published works include *Twelve Million Black Voices* (1941), a text with photographs; the novels *Savage Holiday* (1954), *The Outsiders* (1953), *The Long Dream* (1958); an essay collection, *White Man Listen* (1957); and travel books. In his later years, he wrote almost four thousand haiku.

GREG YOUMANS was a student in the 1996-97 poetry class taught by Ishmael Reed at the University of California, Berkeley.

AL YOUNG (b. 1939) was born on Mississippi's Gulf Coast, in Ocean Springs, and was raised in Detroit. The Bay Area has remained his permanent home for most of his adult life, although he frequently travels to conduct lectures, readings, and teaching residencies, both nationally and internationally. He began writing as a child, and local newspapers and small press publications were accepting his work by the time he was a teenager. His volumes of poetry are *Dancing* (1969), *Song Turning Back on Itself* (1971), *Geography of the Near Past* (1976), *The Blues Don't Change* (1982), and *Heaven: Collected Poems (1956–1990)* (Creative Arts Book, 1992). Widely published in journals and anthologies, he has also written short stories, five novels, essays, journalism, and screenplays for Sidney

Poitier, Bill Cosby, and Richard Pryor. He has edited literary journals and anthologies, including *African American Literature, a Brief Introduction and Anthology* (HarperCollins Literary Mosaic Series, 1996) and was cofounder, with Ishmael Reed, of *Yardbird Reader* (1972–76) and *Quilt* (1981). Young has received many honors, including Wallace Stegner, Guggenheim, Fulbright, and National Endowment for the Arts writing fellowships, a 1982 American Book Award (for a book of musical memoirs, *Bodies and Soul*), and a PEN/Library of Congress Award for short fiction.

TUPAC SHAKUR (1971–1996) was born in Brooklyn, New York. His parents were members of the Black Panther Party, and his mother was incarcerated in a New York prison while pregnant with him. His first hip-hop recording appearance was with Digital Underground. In 1991 he made his solo debut album, *2Pacalype Now*, and became a crossover success with his 1993 album, *I Get Around*. He was arrested on various charges starting in 1992. Shakur parlayed his success as a rapper into a Hollywood acting career. He appeared in Ernest Dickerson's *Juice*; starred opposite Janet Jackson in John Singleton's film *Poetic Justice*; and was in a basketball movie, *Above the Rim*. His final film appearance was in *Gang Related*. An East Coast–West Coast gansta rapper rivalry surfaced in 1994, when Shakur was shot five times and robbed of $40,000 in jewelry in the lobby of Quad Studios in New York City's Times Square. He accused Biggie Smalls (the Notorious B.I.G./Christopher Wallace), Andre Harrell, and Sean "Puffy" Combs of being involved in the shooting. Shakur later served eight months of a four-year sentence for a rape conviction. While he was incarcerated, his album *Me Against the World* was released, rising to the number one spot on the charts. After Suge Knight at Death Row Records arranged his parole pending conviction with a $1.4 million bail, Shakur released *All Eyez in Me* in 1996, which again reached number one in a Billboard ranking. In September 1996 Shakur was murdered in Las Vegas after a Mike Tyson fight. Notorious B.I.G. was killed in a drive-by shooting six months later. Although theories and accusations abound over who is responsible for the murders, they remain unsolved. Shakur's fans remain devoted, and many rappers contributed to a tribute album, *The Rose that Grew from Concrete*. In 1997 his mother released a collection of his material from 1992 to 1994 titled *R U Still Down? (Remember Me)*.

DEAD PREZ (short for "dead presidents") are the rappers known as M-1 and stic.man (aka stickman), whose logo is based on a symbol from the I-Ching, the Chinese oracle system. The two met in Florida, where stic.man was born, after M-1 fled there from a hazardous drug situation. They decided to make their living together by creating and performing politically conscious music that, according to their Web site, is inspired by such revolutionary heroes of self-defense parties as Huey Newton, a founder of the Black Panthers, Mao Tse-tung, and Malcolm X. They debuted on the LOUD '97 Set Up Tape titled "Food, Clothes, and Shelter", and their own album, *Let's Get Free*, making their main points regarding the evils of money and power, the "common issues of the most endangered members of the human society."

Acknowledgments

Acknowledgments to Will Balliett, the brilliant young editor at Thunder's Mouth Press who accepted my unorthodox view of American poetry. To Carla Blank and Shawneric Hachey, whose assistance was invaluable. To Tennessee Reed, who helped to organize this book.

PERMISSIONS

ABOUT THE EDITOR

ISHMAEL REED (b. 1938) was born in Chattanooga, Tennessee, and moved with his family to Buffalo, New York, around the age of four. He grew up in working-class neighborhoods until leaving for New York City to become a writer in 1960. The author of nineteen books, he is a novelist, poet, playwright, essayist, publisher, and editor of various anthologies and literary journals, including *Konch*, online at www.ishmaelreedpub.com. He was a member of the original Umbra Writers Workshop, a Lower East Side meeting of African-American writers. His first published poem was in an anthology of anti–Vietnam War poetry edited by Walter Lowenfels. His first poetry collection was *catechism of d neoamerican hoodoo church* (Paul Breman, 1969), followed by *Conjure: Selected Poems, 1963–1970* (University of Massachusetts Press, 1972), *Chattanooga* (Random House, 1973), *A Secretary to the Spirits* (NOK Publishers, 1978), and *New & Collected Poems* (Atheneum, 1989). He has also written a libretto in verse for the gospera *Gethsemane Park*, with music composed by Carman Moore. It premiered in 1998 at the Black Repertory Theater in Berkeley, California, with subsequent productions at San Francisco's Lorraine Hansberry Theatre and the Nuyorican Poets Cafe. Rounder Records has reissued two CDs of music by various composers using songs by Ishmael Reed, titled *Conjure I* and *Conjure II*. His songs have been recorded and performed by Taj Mahal, Eddie Harris, Bobby Womack, Mary Wilson, and Little Jimmy Scott. He was nominated for a National Book Award for Poetry and received the Poetry in Public Places Award for his poem "From the Files of Agent 22." "Beware Do Not Read This Poem" has been cited by Gale Research Company as one of the twenty poems most frequently studied in literature classes. Recent awards include the Lila Wallace–Reader's Digest Award and a John D. and Catherine T. MacArthur Foundation Fellowship. In 2001, he received a Chancellor's Award for Community Service from the University of California, Berkeley, where he has been a member of the English Department since 1969. In 2002, he received the Integrity Award from the Women's Chamber of Commerce in Oakland, where he makes his home.